# PRAISE

Marlene Crouch has made a huge investment of time and energy in her research, and it shows. I cannot remember in the thirty years of my own ministry reading a more well-researched and passionate comparison of the King James Bible and the *Catechism of the Catholic Church*. All one has to do is read her work, and the truth speaks for itself. If we are truly the sheep of his pasture, we will hear his voice and follow him, not the traditions of man.

—W. Mike Adams, Pastor Emeritus, Sparta Road Baptist Church, Sebring, Florida

*Whose Voice Are You Listening To?* is a clear, cogent, and concise critique of Catholicism. Why did the reformers ultimately break from the Catholic Church? Marlene Crouch does an amazing job of addressing the huge differences between Catholic doctrine and God's holy Word. I especially love that she does this in a spirit of love and concern for our Catholic brothers and sisters, many of whom are not even aware of the teachings of their church. The book is chock full of Scripture, side by side with some of the problematic views of Roman Catholicism. It will be an excellent tool in both the pastor's and layman's library.

—Eric Meyer, senior pastor, Tampa Covenant Church, Tampa, Florida

Marlene Crouch's book is a must read for those seeking the liberating truth of God in Christ. It can be a powerful tool to give to friends and family trapped in religions tradition and superstition. Let Christ's freedom capture your heart.

—Rev. Michael Harris, Calvary
Baptist Church, Fort Wayne, Indiana

# WHOSE VOICE ARE YOU LISTENING TO?

# WHOSE VOICE ARE YOU LISTENING TO?

*A Comparison of the Catholic Catechism to the Bible*

## MARLENE C. CROUCH

TATE PUBLISHING & *Enterprises*

Published by Tate Publishing & Enterprises, LLC
127 E. Trade Center Terrace | Mustang, Oklahoma 73064 USA
1.888.361.9473 | www.tatepublishing.com

Tate Publishing is committed to excellence in the publishing industry. The company reflects the philosophy established by the founders, based on Psalm 68:11,
*"The Lord gave the word and great was the company of those who published it."*

Published in the United States of America
ISBN: 978-1-61566-261-6
1. Religion, Biblical Commentary, General
2. Religion, Biblical Studies, Exegesis & Hermeneutics
09.10.08

# DEDICATION

Lovingly dedicated for the glory and praise of God, to my daughters, Debbie and Jessie, and their families; to my sister, Mildred, and her family; to my other Roman Catholic brothers and sisters in Christ Jesus; and to Lou, my wonderful and beloved husband, whose love, prayers, and encouragement have played a most important part in my endeavor to write this book.

# ACKNOWLEDGMENT

Mike and Linda Smith, my faithful and beloved friends, whose prayers sustained me throughout this past year of struggling to accomplish my goal of sharing the truth of the inerrant Word of God within the pages of this book. I love you both.

# TABLE OF CONTENTS

Introduction . . . . . . . . . . . . . . . . . . . . . . . . . . . . . . . . . . . . . . . .13

Mary's Consent . . . . . . . . . . . . . . . . . . . . . . . . . . . . . . . . . . . .15

Marian Apparitions . . . . . . . . . . . . . . . . . . . . . . . . . . . . . . . .39

Mary's Immaculate Conception? . . . . . . . . . . . . . . . . . . . . .69

Mary, Ever Virgin. . . . . . . . . . . . . . . . . . . . . . . . . . . . . . . . . .79

The Rosary. . . . . . . . . . . . . . . . . . . . . . . . . . . . . . . . . . . . . . . .95

Pray Only to God. . . . . . . . . . . . . . . . . . . . . . . . . . . . . . . . . .109

Keys to the Kingdom and Power of God . . . . . . . . . . . . . . . .115

Peter, the Rock. . . . . . . . . . . . . . . . . . . . . . . . . . . . . . . . . . . .137

Peter's Brethren . . . . . . . . . . . . . . . . . . . . . . . . . . . . . . . . . . .153

Peter, Son of Jonas . . . . . . . . . . . . . . . . . . . . . . . . . . . . . . . . .161

The Church . . . . . . . . . . . . . . . . . . . . . . . . . . . . . . . . . . . . . .173

Grace . . . . . . . . . . . . . . . . . . . . . . . . . . . . . . . . . . . . . . . . . . .203

Transubstantiation . . . . . . . . . . . . . . . . . . . . . . . . . . . . . . . .215

Endnotes . . . . . . . . . . . . . . . . . . . . . . . . . . . . . . . . . . . . . . . .269

# INTRODUCTION

In contemplating the possibility of joining the Roman Catholic Church twenty-nine years ago, I seemed to develop an insatiable desire for truth. Since that time I have been what some may call *obsessed* with the quest for truth, devouring the King James Bible, *Catechism of the Catholic Church*, and *Abingdon's Strong's Hebrew and Greek Concordance*. My conclusions and/or opinions presented in this book are based solely on my personal study and research of the inspired written Word of God and the *Catechism of the Catholic Church* and are totally void of any sectarian influence. Twenty-nine years of Bible study and research have been motivated out of a love for truth and not a quest just to prove someone else wrong.

As I got deeper into the study of the Scriptures, it became more and more clear to me that, contrary to the many good and wonderful things associated with the Roman Catholic Church, there are many definite and even crucial discrepancies between the doctrines and dogmas of Roman Catholicism and the concise harmonious teaching of the inspired Word of God. Finding self-contradictions within the *Catechism of the Catholic Church* added even more intensity to the war that was raging inside of me, which was either to share or not to share my findings with my Roman Catholic family.

The three meager attempts I made during the past twenty-nine years to share some of my findings were unfruitful. The fear of alienating myself from my family was more than I could bear, which has kept me from any further attempts. It was a huge nagging and constant hurt. I knew deep inside that this thing was much bigger than just my family and me. The more I studied, the more I cried. The more I cried, the harder I prayed. It was not until this past year, through intense prayer and deliberation, that I came to the conclusion that I really didn't have a choice. Family or no family, I must follow my heart and trust God totally.

I agree wholeheartedly with what St. Jerome wrote: "If an offense comes out of the truth, it is better that the offense come than the truth be concealed." I began rummaging through and sorting out old manuscripts I had written over the years with a sense of urgency to share the truth of God's Word concerning the erroneous doctrines of Catholicism, not with just my family but with the world.

As you read my objections to certain Roman Catholic doctrines, please know that all of my efforts in compiling these manuscripts were born out of love and compassion for my Roman Catholic brothers and sisters in Christ—brothers and sisters in Christ who love the Lord and who believe the gospel's basic message of salvation through faith in Jesus Christ but who are deceived and held in bondage under false doctrines derived from the traditions of man and who are thereby deprived of the freedom and joy of fully experiencing the magnitude of God's love.

I earnestly pray that the Holy Spirit will quicken the readers' hearts and minds with the truth of God's Word and render void any *personal* opinion of mine, or anyone else's, that is not *truth*.

# MARY'S CONSENT

*Her obedience and submission to God's will*

967 In a wholly singular way she cooperated by her obedience, faith, hope, and burning charity in the Savior's work of restoring supernatural life to souls. For this reason she is a mother to us in the order of grace. This motherhood of Mary in the order of grace continues uninterruptedly from the consent which she loyally gave at the Annunciation.

*Catechism of the Catholic Church*, p. 252

Immediately after Gabriel announced to Mary that she was chosen by God to be the mother of the Christ child, and that Elisabeth had conceived a son in her old age, and that "with God nothing shall be impossible," Mary responded, saying, "Be it unto me according to thy word" (Luke 1:38).

The Roman Catholic Church's teaching that Mary gave her consent to be the mother of the Christ child is based entirely upon this single verse of scripture. Mary was not giving her consent in Luke 1:38. She was affirming her belief in all of what Gabriel had just told her. The erroneous doctrine of Mary's submission, her bowing her will and cooperating with God by consenting to be the mother of the Christ child, is the foundation from which all erroneous Marian doctrines have developed through the centuries, via the living tradition of the Roman Catholic Church.

On page sixteen of the book *The Thunder of Justice*, the Catholic author wrote:

"Although Marian theology has developed over the centuries, the underlying concepts are seen in many writings of the church Fathers that date from the Second Century, according to the famous Nineteenth Century theologian, John Cardinal Newman."

On page forty-two, John Cardinal Newman is quoted again as saying:

> Though I hold, as you know, a process of development in Apostolic truth as time goes on, such development does not supersede the Fathers, but explains and completes them...And, in particular, as regards our teaching concerning the Blessed Virgin, with the Fathers I am content...The Fathers are enough for me.

Cardinal Newman is quoted again on page forty-three as saying, "I fully grant that devotion towards the Blessed Virgin has increased among Catholics with the progress of centuries..." This so-called *ongoing process of development in Apostolic truth* is precisely what the Apostle Paul warned the *earliest* church fathers against, in 63 AD. He told them that even of themselves men would arise, speaking perverse things, to draw away disciples after them.

## *The Apostle Paul's warning to the earliest church fathers of the first century*

> Take heed therefore unto yourselves, and to all the flock, over the which the Holy Ghost hath made you overseers, to feed the church of God, which he hath purchased with his own blood. For I know this, that after my departing shall grievous wolves enter in among you, not sparing the flock. Also of your own selves shall men arise, speaking perverse things, to draw away disciples after them. Therefore watch,

and remember, that by the space of three years I ceased not to warn everyone night and day with tears.

Acts 20:28–31

Contrary to the following excerpt from the *Catechism of the Catholic Church*, it was not *Mary's faith*, but *God's predetermined will* that enabled Mary to become the mother of the Savior. Zacharia's doubting Gabriel, when he was told that he would have a son, did not prevent his becoming the father of John the Baptist. Zacharias temporarily lost his ability to speak because of his unbelief, but nevertheless, God's predetermined will was accomplished.

506 Mary is a virgin because her virginity is the sign of her faith unadulterated by any doubt, and of her undivided gift of her self to God's will. It is her faith that enables her to become the mother of the Savior. Mary is more blessed because she embraces faith in Christ than because she conceives the flesh of Christ.

*Catechism of the Catholic Church*, p. 127

But the angel said unto him, Fear not, Zacharias: for thy prayer is heard; and thy wife Elisabeth shall bear thee a son, and thou shalt call his name John. And Zacharias said unto the angel, whereby shall I know this? for I am an old man, and my wife well stricken in years. And the angel answering said unto him, I am Gabriel, that stand in the presence of God; and am sent to speak unto thee, and to shew thee these glad tidings. And, behold, thou shalt be dumb, and not able to speak, until the day that these things shall be performed, because thou believest not my words, which shall be fulfilled in their season.

Luke 1:13, 18–20

On page eighty-eight of *The Thunder of Justice*, it is stated that "Mary has a decisive role in the salvation of mankind, through her obedience to God." In the Knights of Columbus booklet *The Rosary* (volume eighty-four), it is stated that "Mary bows her will in loving submission to all that God may 'ask' of her. She offers herself with Jesus for the world's salvation."

The salvation of the world did not come through Mary's *alleged* obedience to God but "by the determinate counsel and foreknowledge of God" (Acts 2:23; 4:27–28). Mary, at the annunciation, did not "bow her will in loving submission;" she did not *cooperate* with what God had *asked* of her. God's message to Mary was not a *request* but a proclamation of *glad tidings*. She did not assent to a request but affirmed her belief in those things which Gabriel had told her.

It was God who worked in her "both to will and to do of His good pleasure" (Philippians 2:13; Hebrews 13:21); "according to the purpose of Him who worketh all things after the counsel of His own will"(Ephesians 1:5,11; Isaiah 46:9–13). Man was created with a free will, but only insofar as it does not interfere with God's predetermined purpose, as is evident in the following scriptures.

> Therefore the Lord himself shall give you a sign; behold, a virgin *shall* conceive, and bear a son, and *shall* call his name Immanuel.
>
> Isaiah 7:14, emphasis added

> Remember the former things of old: for I am God, and there is none else; I am God, and there is none like me, declaring the end from the beginning, and from ancient times the things that are not yet done, saying, My counsel shall stand, and I will do all my pleasure: calling a ravenous bird from the east, the man that executeth my counsel from a far country: yea, I have spoken it, I will also bring it to pass; I have purposed it, I will also do it.
>
> Isaiah 46:9–11

Him [Jesus], being delivered by the determinate counsel and foreknowledge of God, ye have taken, and by wicked hands have crucified and slain ...

Acts 2:23

For of a truth against thy holy child Jesus, whom thou hast anointed, both Herod, and Pontius Pilate, with the Gentiles, and the people of Israel, were gathered together, For to do whatsoever thy hand and thy counsel determined before to be done.

Acts 4:27–28

For God hath put in their hearts to fulfill his will, and to agree, and give their kingdom unto the beast, until the words of God shall be fulfilled.

Revelation 17:17

Thou wilt say then unto me, Why doth he yet find fault? For who hath resisted his will? Nay but, O man, who art thou that repliest against God? Shall the thing formed say to him that formed it, Why hast thou made me thus? Hath not the potter power over the clay, of the same lump to make one vessel unto honour, and another unto dishonour?

Romans 9:19–21

With regard to his predetermined will and purpose, God puts in the hearts and minds of all people to do his will, including truly blessed and beloved Mary. He not only moved Herod, Pontius Pilate, the gentiles, and the people of Israel to gather together against Jesus to crucify him (Acts 2:23, 4:27–28), but throughout history (since the fall of Adam), God has moved men and women to do his will in order to accomplish his eternal purpose, even to the most minute details. On occasion, even the very words men spoke were the result of God's sovereign control (cf. John. 11:50–52). Nowhere in the entire Bible is it stated that God has ever given anyone a choice in the matter of his predetermined will and purposes.

Gabriel gave the message of God's predetermined plan to Zacharias and then to Mary. Zacharias doubted and Mary believed. However, God's predetermined will was accomplished in both cases. Given the fact that God inspired these two incidents to be recorded within the same passage of scripture (Luke 1:18, 26), could God not have moved Zacharias to doubt in order to show the immutableness of his Word? God's sovereignty over man's will is seen throughout the scriptures.

> The preparations of the heart in man, and the answer of the tongue, is from the Lord.
>
> Proverbs 16:1

> O Lord, I know that the way of man is not in himself: it is not in man that walketh to direct his steps.
>
> Jeremiah 10:23

> Man's goings are of the Lord; how can a man then understand his own way?
>
> Proverbs 20:24

> The king's heart is in the hand of the Lord, as the rivers of water: he turneth it whithersoever he will.
>
> Proverbs 21:1

> This is the purpose that is purposed upon the whole earth: and this is the hand that is stretched out upon all the nations. For the Lord of hosts hath purposed, and who shall disannul it? and his hand is stretched out, and who shall turn it back?
>
> Isaiah 14:26–27

> Being predestinated according to the purpose of Him who worketh all things after the counsel of His own will.
>
> Ephesians 1:11

And, behold, thou shalt conceive in thy womb, and bring forth a son, and shalt call his name Jesus.

Luke 1:31

For that that is determined shall be done.

Daniel 11:36

God's awesome sovereignty and the immutableness of his Word are seen in the following scriptures, wherein it is stated that certain events occurred "that the Scripture should be fulfilled."

| | | |
|---|---|---|
| Matthew 1:20–23 | Matthew 21:2–5 | Luke 24:44–47 |
| Matthew 2:14–15 | Matthew 26:52–54 | John 13:18 |
| Matthew 2:16–18 | Matthew 26:55–56 | John 15:24–25 |
| Matthew 2:23 | Matthew 27:9 | John 17:12 |
| Matthew 4:14–16 | Matthew 27:35 | John 18:8–9 |
| Matthew 8:16–17 | Mark 14:48–49 | John 19:24 |
| Matthew 12:15–17 | Mark 15:27–28 | John 19:28 |
| Matthew 13:34–35 | Luke 4:17–21 | John 19:33–37 |

Matthew 13:14–15 (with Romans11:8, 25 and John 12:39)

Acts 13:27–29

In that same hour said Jesus to the multitudes, Are ye come out as against a thief with swords and staves for to take me? I sat daily with you teaching in the temple, and ye laid no hold on me. But all this was done, that the scriptures of the prophets might be fulfilled. Then all the disciples forsook him, and fled.

Matthew 26:55–56
cf. Zechariah 13:7; John 16:32; Mark 14:27

They said therefore among themselves, Let us not rend it, but cast lots for it, whose it shall be: that the scripture might be fulfilled, which saith, They parted my raiment among them, and for my vesture they did cast lots. These things therefore the soldiers did.

John 19:24
cf. Psalm 22:18

After this, Jesus knowing that all things were now accomplished, that the scripture might be fulfilled, saith, I thirst.

John 19:28<br>cf. Psalm 69:21

For these things were done, that the scripture should be fulfilled, A bone of him shall not be broken. And again another scripture saith, They shall look on him whom they pierced.

John 19:36–37<br>cf. Psalm 34:20; Exodus 12:46;<br>Zechariah 12:10; Psalm 22:16

And the scripture was fulfilled, which saith, And he was numbered with the transgressors.

Mark 15:28<br>cf. Isaiah 53:12

The Apostle Paul said, "All scripture is given by inspiration of God, and is profitable for doctrine, for reproof, for correction ..." (2 Timothy 3:16). The magisterium, the teaching office of the Roman Catholic Church, obviously does not follow Paul's criteria. The many scripture references that refute each of the erroneous Marian doctrines that are based upon tradition serve to show that the very few verses of Scripture presented by the teaching office of the Roman Catholic Church in support of these doctrines are fallaciously misconstrued in order to accommodate man's living tradition. In the following pages, notice the many statements about Mary in acclaimed Catholic writings, including the Catechism, that contradict the inspired Word of God.

## The Thunder of Justice

Tenets of Marian theology have often excited controversy throughout Church history, yet they have passed the tests of discernment of the Church as a whole many times. A deep Marian perspective enriches rather than obscures our understanding of God's wisdom … Mary never appears on earth to glorify herself; her mission is to lead us by the shortest possible route to her Son. She is sent to us as a gift and should be perceived as such.

p. 16

"A deep Marian perspective" does, in fact, obscure our understanding of God's wisdom. God's wisdom is revealed in his Word, and many statements about Mary that are found in approved Roman Catholic writings, including the Catechism, contradict the Word of God, and thereby obscure the understanding of God's wisdom. As seen in the following, such statements as "Mary's mission is to lead us to her son" and "Mary's Immaculate Heart will be your refuge and the way that will lead you to God" (*Thunder of Justice*, pp. 135, 136; Fatima, June 13, 1917) definitely contradict the Word of God.

According to the Holy Scriptures, it is not Mary's mission to lead us to her son. It was with reference to the Scriptures that Jesus made it perfectly clear that no one can come to him unless that person is drawn to him *by God.* He said:

> No man can come to me, except the Father which hath sent me draw him: and I will raise him up at the last day. It is written in the prophets, And they shall be all taught of God. Every man therefore that hath heard, and hath learned of the Father, cometh unto me.
>
> John 6:44–45

In order to preclude any misunderstanding of the fact, Jesus iterated, saying, "…Therefore said I unto you, no man can come unto me, except it were given unto him of my Father" (John 6:65).

According to *Abingdon's Strong's Exhaustive Greek and Hebrew Concordance*, the phrase *no man* is translated from the

Greek word *oudeis* and includes the Virgin Mary. Therefore it is not Mary's mission to lead us to her son.

*Abingdon's Strong's Concordance*

"no man" #3762-Grk. 'oudeis' including feminine 'oudemia' and neuter 'ouden'

As seen in the following, the perfect harmony of God's holy Word also negates any possibility that Mary's *alleged* Immaculate Heart is the way that leads us to God.

> Blessed is the man whom thou choosest, and causest to approach unto thee, that he may dwell in thy courts: we shall be satisfied with the goodness of thy house, even of thy holy temple.
>
> Psalm 65:4

> And their nobles shall be of themselves, and their governor shall proceed from the midst of them; and I will cause him to draw near, and he shall approach unto me: for who is this that engaged his heart to approach unto me? Saith the Lord.
>
> Jeremiah 30:21

> All things are delivered to me of my Father: and *no man* knoweth who the Son is, but the Father; and who the Father is, but the Son, and he to whom *the Son will reveal him*.
>
> Luke 10:22, emphasis added

> For Christ also hath once suffered for sins, the just for the unjust, *that he might bring us to God*, being put to death in the flesh, but quickened by the Spirit:
>
> 1 Peter 3:18, emphasis added

Jesus saith unto him, I am the way, the truth, and the life: no man cometh unto the Father, *but by me*.

John 14:6, emphasis added

Verily, verily, I say unto you, He that entereth not by the door into the sheepfold, but climbeth up *some other way*, the same is a thief and a robber... *I am the door: by me* if any man enter in, he shall be saved, and shall go in and out, and find pasture.

John 10:1, 9, emphasis added

Enter ye in at *the strait gate*: for wide is the gate, and broad is the way, that leadeth to destruction, and many there be which go in thereat: Because strait is the gate, and narrow is the way, which leadeth unto life, and few there be that find it. Beware of false prophets, which come to you in sheep's clothing, but inwardly they are *ravening wolves*.

Matthew 7:13–15, emphasis added

According to Acts 20:17, 28–32, "false prophets in sheep's clothing" are some of the elders of the church; the first-century church fathers (AD 63) who "the Holy Ghost made overseers, to feed the church of God" and to whom the Apostle Paul was speaking when he said, "For I know this, that after my departing shall *grievous wolves* enter in among you, not sparing the flock. Also of your own selves shall men arise, speaking perverse things to draw away disciples after them" (Acts 20:30). The early church used the terms *bishop*, *elders*, and *presbyters* interchangeably. With this in mind, compare the following statements of the *Catechism of the Catholic Church* regarding bishops.

77 In order that the full and living Gospel might always be preserved in the Church the apostles left bishops as their successors. They gave them their own position of teaching authority.

p. 25

82 As a result the Church, to whom the transmission and interpretation of Revelation is entrusted, "does not derive her certainty about all revealed truths from the holy Scriptures alone. Both Scripture and Tradition must be accepted and honored with equal sentiments of devotion and reverence"

p. 26

On page twenty-nine, paragraph ninety-five, of the Catechism, it is stated that "Sacred Tradition, Sacred Scripture, and the Magisterium of the Church are so connected and associated that one of them cannot stand without the others." In other words, regardless of the fact that Marian doctrines contradict Scripture, they must be accepted as *truth* because they are backed up by the others; namely, *tradition* and the *magisterium*. Truth cannot contradict truth! The magisterium's practice of picking and choosing just one or two verses from the entire Bible as the foundation of a particular doctrine or dogma in support of man's *living tradition* certainly lends credence to the statement commonly made by skeptics: "You can make the Bible say what you want it to say."

*Sacred living tradition*, for the most part, is based upon the teaching and/or writings of church fathers, and every erroneous Marian doctrine and dogma taught in the Roman Catholic Church stems from *living tradition*. Those of the church fathers whom the Apostle Paul said would *"arise speaking perverse things"* started a living tradition of false doctrines. The Bible is totally void of any mention of the many erroneous Marian doctrines and dogmas. In fact, there is very little written in the inspired Scriptures about the Virgin Mary. Even though erroneous Marian doctrines passed down by *some of* the early church fathers actually contradict the Scriptures, leading theologians of the Roman Catholic Church such as John Cardinal Henry Newman hold fast to the teaching of these church fathers. Compare the following excerpt.

## The Thunder of Justice
## Mary as the New Eve

The idea of Mary as "the New Eve" was expressed beautifully in the writings of the famous Nineteenth Century convert from Anglicanism, John Cardinal Henry Newman...On the ancient teaching of Mary as the Second Eve, Newman quoted from three sources: Saint Justin Martyr (AD 120–165), Saint Irenaeus (AD 120–200), and Tertullian (AD 160–240)...Cardinal Newman showed how the widespread territories represented by the three distinct witnesses indicated that this teaching on Mary as "the Second Eve" was firmly established before the year 200. From the earliest written records of the Church, there was general acceptance of Mary's role.

pp. 42–43

According to the Holy Scriptures, and contrary to the *living tradition*, Mary did not *merit* a *role* of power and authority by giving her consent and submitting to God's will at the annunciation; it was God who worked in Mary "both to will and to do of His good pleasure" (Philippians 2:13). Nor did Mary have the power or authority to "consent to" the sacrifice of Jesus and to "offer him for us," as stated in the Catechism and in the encyclical of Pope Pius XII. Compare the following excerpts.

964...There she stood, in keeping with the divine plan, enduring with her only begotten Son the intensity of his suffering, joining herself with his sacrifice in her mother's heart, and lovingly consenting to the immolation of the victim, born of her.

*Catechism of the Catholic Church*, p. 251

## Encyclical of Pope Pius XII
### On proclaiming the *queenship* of Mary-October 11, 1954

For just as Christ, because He redeemed us, is our Lord and king by a special title, so the Blessed Virgin also is our queen, on account of the unique manner in which she assisted in our redemption, by giving of her own substance, by freely offering Him for us by her singular desire and petition for, and active interest in, our salvation.

p. 7, 37

It can likewise be stated that this glorious Lady had been chosen Mother of Christ in order that she might become a partner in the redemption of the human race...It was she who, free of the stain of actual and original sin, and ever most closely bound to her Son, on Golgotha offered that Son to the Eternal Father together with the complete sacrifice of her maternal rights and maternal love.

p. 7, 38

Titles that have been given to Mary over the centuries are indicative of power and authority. Such titles as: Mary, the queen of heaven; the queen of saints and angels; the ark of the covenant; advocate; helper; intercessor; the new Eve; Mediatrix; co-Redemptrix; mother of the church; etc. The following excerpts quoted from the Catechism make it perfectly clear that these titles of power and authority are the direct result of the erroneous teaching that Mary gave her *consent* to be the mother of Christ.

967 By her complete adherence to the Father's will, to his Son's redemptive work, and to every prompting of the Holy Spirit, the Virgin Mary is the Church's model of faith and charity.

968 In a wholly singular way she cooperated by her obedience, faith, hope, and burning charity in the Savior's

28

work of restoring supernatural life to souls. For this reason she is a mother to us in the order of grace.

969 This motherhood of Mary in the order of grace continues uninterruptedly from the consent which she loyally gave at the Annunciation…Taken up to heaven she did not lay aside this saving office but by her manifold intercession continues to bring us the gifts of eternal salvation…Therefore the Blessed Virgin is invoked in the Church under the titles of Advocate, Helper, Benefactress, and Mediatrix.

971 The Church's devotion to the Blessed Virgin is intrinsic to Christian worship. The Church rightly honors the Blessed Virgin with special devotion. From the most ancient time the Blessed Virgin has been honored with the title of "Mother of God," to whose protection the faithful fly in all their dangers and needs.

973 By pronouncing her "fiat" at the Annunciation and giving her consent to the Incarnation, Mary was already collaborating with the whole work her Son was to accomplish. She is mother wherever he is Savior and head of the Mystical Body.
*Catechism of the Catholic Church* pp.252–254

Contrary to the *Catechism's* statement in Paragraph #967, in the above, Mary is not the church's model of faith and love by reason of her *alleged* adherence to the Father's will. The church's model of faith and love is Jesus Christ himself. Mary's faith cannot be compared to the faith Jesus had to have to endure the things he suffered (Luke 22:42–44, Hebrews 5:7–8). Nor could Mary's love be a better example for the church to follow than the love of Jesus Christ, which he displayed when he suffered and died to pay the penalty for the sins of the world. The following scriptures plainly state that Jesus Christ is the model and/or example of faith and love that the church is to follow. There's not a single mention of Mary on either subject.

> But he was wounded for our transgressions, he was bruised for our iniquities: the chastisement of our peace was upon him; and with his stripes we are healed. All we like sheep have gone astray; we have turned every one to his own way; and the Lord hath laid on him the iniquity of us all. He was oppressed, and he was afflicted, yet he opened not his mouth: he is brought as a lamb to the slaughter, and as a sheep before her shearers is dumb, so he openeth not his mouth. He was taken from prison and from judgment: and who shall declare his generation? for he was cut off out of the land of the living: for the transgression of my people was he stricken.
>
> Isaiah 53:5–8

> This is my commandment, That ye love one another, as I have loved you. Greater love hath no man than this, that a man lay down his life for his friends.
>
> John 15:12–13

> I am the good shepherd: the good shepherd giveth his life for the sheep.
>
> John 10:11

> As the Father knoweth me, even so know I the Father: and I lay down my life for the sheep.
>
> John 10:15

> Therefore doth my Father love me, because I lay down my life, that I might take it again.
>
> John 10:17

> For the love of Christ constraineth us; because we thus judge, that if one died for all, then were all dead ...
>
> 2 Corinthians 5:14

But God commendeth his love toward us, in that, while we were yet sinners, Christ died for us.

Romans 5:8

Who is he that condemneth? It is Christ that died, yea rather, that is risen again, who is even at the right hand of God, who also maketh intercession for us. Who shall separate us from the love of Christ? shall tribulation, or distress, or persecution, or famine, or nakedness, or peril, or sword?

Romans 8:34–35

Nor height, nor depth, nor any other creature, shall be able to separate us from the love of God, which is in Christ Jesus our Lord.

Romans 8:39

Behold, I will make them of the synagogue of Satan, which say they are Jews, and are not, but do lie; behold, I will make them to come and worship before thy feet, and to know that I have loved thee.

Revelation 3:9
cf. Romans 2:28–29

But as touching brotherly love ye need not that I write unto you: for ye yourselves are taught of God to love one another.

1 Thessalonians 4:9

And the Lord direct your hearts into the love of God, and into the patient waiting for Christ.

2 Thessalonians 3:5

That Christ may dwell in your hearts by faith; that ye, being rooted and grounded in love, May be able to comprehend with all saints what is the breadth, and length, and depth, and height; And to know the love of Christ, which passeth knowledge, that ye might be filled with all the fulness of God.

Ephesians 3:17–19

Jesus Christ is the church's example.

For I have given you an example, that ye should do as I have done to you. Verily, verily, I say unto you, The servant is not greater than his lord; neither he that is sent greater than he that sent him.

John 13:15–16

For this is thankworthy, if a man for conscience toward God endure grief, suffering wrongfully. For what glory is it, if, when ye be buffeted for your faults, ye shall take it patiently? but if, when ye do well, and suffer for it, ye take it patiently, this is acceptable with God. For even hereunto were ye called: because Christ also suffered for us, leaving us an example, that ye should follow his steps: Who did no sin, neither was guile found in his mouth: Who, when he was reviled, reviled not again; when he suffered, he threatened not; but committed himself to him that judgeth righteously: Who his own self bare our sins in his own body on the tree, that we, being dead to sins, should live unto righteousness: by whose stripes ye were healed.

1 Peter 2:19–24

Forasmuch then as Christ hath suffered for us in the flesh, arm yourselves likewise with the same mind: for he that hath suffered in the flesh hath ceased from sin.

1 Peter 4:1

And walk in love, as Christ also hath loved us, and hath given himself for us an offering and a sacrifice to God for a sweet smelling savour.

Ephesians 5:2

Husbands, love your wives, even as Christ also loved the church, and gave himself for it;

Ephesians 5:25

A new commandment I give unto you, That ye love one another; as I have loved you, that ye also love one another.

John 13:34

As the Father hath loved me, so have I loved you: continue ye in my love. If ye keep my commandments, ye shall abide in my love; even as I have kept my Father's commandments, and abide in his love.

John 15:9–10

But whoso keepeth his word, in him verily is the love of God perfected: hereby know we that we are in him. He that saith he abideth in him ought himself also to walk, even as he walked.

1 John 2:5–6

Forbearing one another, and forgiving one another, if any man have a quarrel against any: even as Christ forgave you, so also do ye.

Colossians 3:13

Take my yoke upon you, and learn of me; for I am meek and lowly in heart: and ye shall find rest unto your souls.

Matthew 11:29

Looking unto Jesus the author and finisher of our faith; who for the joy that was set before him endured the cross, despising the shame, and is set down at the right hand of the throne of God.

Hebrews 12:2

The Catechism takes these statements a step further by referring to the mother of our Lord as "the all holy Virgin Mary": and "the source" of the church's holiness.

2030 It is in the Church, in communion with all the baptized, that the Christian fulfills his vocation … From the Church he receives the grace of the sacraments that sustains him on the "way." From the Church he learns the example of holiness and recognizes its model and source in the all-holy Virgin Mary.

*Catechism of the Catholic Church* p. 490

According to the divinely inspired Scriptures, the Virgin Mary is not *all holy*, and therefore cannot possibly be the *source* of holiness. As prophesied in the Old Testament and fulfilled in the New, the spirit of Jesus Christ, God almighty himself, is the *source* of the Christian's holiness.[1] "God hath said, I will dwell in them, and walk in them; and I will be their God, and they shall be my people" (2 Corinthians 6:16). "I will put my spirit within you, and cause you to walk in my statutes, and ye shall keep my judgments, and do them" (Ezekiel 36:27).

If so be that *the Spirit of God dwell in you.* Now if any man have not *the Spirit of Christ*, he is none of his … For if ye live after the flesh, ye shall die: but if ye through the Spirit do mortify the deeds of the body, ye shall live.

Romans 8:9, 13, emphasis added

I am the vine, ye are the branches. He that abideth in me and *I in him*, the same bringeth forth *much fruit*: for without me you can do nothing.

John 15:5, emphasis added

Being confident of this very thing, that He which hath begun a good work in you will perform it until the day of Jesus Christ … Being *filled with the fruits of righteousness*, which are *by Jesus Christ*, unto the glory and praise of God.

Philippians 1:6, 11, emphasis added

But *we all,* with open face beholding as in a glass the glory of the Lord, are changed into the same image from glory to glory, even as *by the Spirit of the Lord.*

2 Corinthians 3:18, emphasis added

But we have this treasure in earthen vessels, that the excellency of *the power may be of God,* and not of us.

2 Corinthians4:7, emphasis added

For *it is God which worketh in you* both to will and to do of his good pleasure.

Philippians 2:13, emphasis added

Now the God of peace, that brought again from the dead our Lord Jesus, that great shepherd of the sheep, *through the blood of the everlasting covenant,* Make you perfect in every good work to do his will, *working in you* that which is well pleasing in his sight, *through Jesus Christ;* to whom be glory for ever and ever. Amen.

Hebrews 13:20–21, emphasis added

The Holy Spirit indwells everyone who is born again through faith in Jesus Christ's once and for all bloody sacrifice for the remission of their sins (John 7:38–39; John 3:6, 8; 1 John 5:1,4–5; Ephesians 1:13). Jesus said: "Greater love hath no man than this, that a man lay down his life for his friends ... For God so loved the world, that he gave his only begotten Son, that whosoever believeth in him should not perish, but have everlasting life" (John 15:13; John 3:16). It is in knowing the love of Christ that we are filled with all the fulness of God (1 John 3:16; 1 John 4:9–10; 1 John 4:13–16; Ephesians 3:17–19).

In this was manifested the love of God toward us, because that God sent his only begotten Son into the world, that we might live through him. Herein is love, not that we loved God, but that he loved us, and sent his Son to be the propitiation for our sins.

1 John 4:9–10

Hereby perceive we the love of God, because he laid down his life for us: and we ought to lay down our lives for the brethren.

1 John 3:16

Hereby know we that we dwell in him, and he in us, because he hath given us of his Spirit. And we have seen and do testify that the Father sent the Son to be the Saviour of the world. Whosoever shall confess that Jesus is the Son of God, God dwelleth in him, and he in God. And we have known and believed the love that God hath to us. God is love; and he that dwelleth in love dwelleth in God, and God in him.

1 John 4:13–16

That Christ may dwell in your hearts by faith; that ye, being rooted and grounded in love, May be able to comprehend with all saints what is the breadth, and length, and depth, and height; And *to know the love of Christ*, which passeth knowledge, *that ye might be filled with all the fulness of God.* Now unto him that is able to do exceeding abundantly above all that we ask or think, according to *the power that worketh in us*, Unto him be glory in the church by Christ Jesus throughout all ages, world without end. Amen.

Ephesians 3:17–21, emphasis added

Now the God of hope fill you with all joy and peace *in believing*, that ye may abound in hope, through *the power of the Holy Ghost.*

Romans 15:13, emphasis added

That the God of our Lord Jesus Christ, the Father of glory, may give unto you the spirit of wisdom and revelation in *the knowledge of him*: The eyes of your understanding being enlightened; that ye may know what is the hope of his calling, and what the riches of the glory of his inheritance in the saints, And what is *the exceeding greatness of his power to us-ward who believe*, according to the working of his mighty power, Which he wrought in Christ, when he raised him from the dead, and set him at his own right hand in the heavenly places.

Ephesians 1:17–20, emphasis added

In light of the truth of God's Word, it is utterly undeniable that the church's source of holiness is the power of the Holy Spirit of Jesus Christ indwelling born-again believers and not the Virgin Mary. Attributing the church's source of holiness to the Virgin Mary is relevant with what the Apostle Paul was talking about in his epistles to Timothy. He wrote about the perilous times of the last days and "men having a form of godliness, but denying the power thereof ... ever learning, and never able to come to the knowledge of the truth" (2 Timothy 3:1–7). Paul told Timothy to:

Preach the word; be instant in season, out of season; reprove, rebuke, exhort with all longsuffering and doctrine. For the time will come when they will not endure sound doctrine; but after their own lusts shall they heap to themselves teachers, having itching ears; And they shall turn away their ears *from the truth*, and shall be turned *unto fables*.

2 Timothy 4:2–4, emphasis added

Now the Spirit speaketh expressly, that in the latter times some shall depart from the faith, giving heed to seducing spirits, and doctrines of devils ... *Forbidding to marry*, and *commanding to abstain from meats*, which God hath created to be received with thanksgiving of them which believe and know the truth.

1 Timothy 4:1, 3, emphasis added

Satan counterfeits everything that is of God, including the Blessed Virgin Mary, in order to blind our minds to the truth of God's love, his omnipotence, his omnipresence, his omniscience, his grace, and his salvation. He gets his foot in the door of our minds if he, in the smallest degree, succeeds in diverting our attention from God's

Word and our faith and trust in these attributes that belong solely to God onto something or someone else. According to the Roman Catholic faith, and contrary to the Holy Scriptures, most of the attributes that belong solely to God are also attributed to the Virgin Mary, by reason of her role as *mother of the church*, the title which Mary is said to have acquired because she supposedly cooperated by giving her consent to be the mother of the Christ child (cf. Catechism p.252, 968).

The following excerpt is just one of many examples wherein the attributes belonging solely to God are attributed to Mary, thus robbing God of his glory.

### *Knights of Columbus*

We ask Mary also to visit us with her Divine Son, especially in Holy Communion, and to make us so Christlike that we may in turn bring Him to others.

Volume 84, p. 14

# MARIAN APPARITIONS

The hundreds of alleged apparitions of Mary and Jesus, as recorded in books such as *Thunder of Justice*, by Ted & Maureen Flynn, and *The Final Hour*, by Michael H. Brown, have played no small part in the propagation of erroneous Marian doctrines. The messages given by the apparitions are rooted in the Roman Catholic Church's teaching about Mary's role as *mother of the church*. See *The Catholic Encyclopedia*, p.forty-eight, for the Church's stand on these apparitions. Roman Catholics are instructed not to accept the apparitions as articles of faith, but at the same time are *urged to be open and attentive to them.*[1] This directive of the Roman Catholic Church to its followers, "to be open and attentive to these apparitions," most certainly leaves those of the Roman Catholic faith even more vulnerable to Satan's deceptions.

When asked, "What shall be the sign of thy coming, and of the end of the world?" Jesus said, "Take heed that no man deceive you. For many shall come in my name, saying, I am Christ; and shall deceive many" (Matthew 24:4–5). He said, "...there shall arise false Christs, and false prophets, and shall shew *great signs and wonders*; insomuch that, if it were possible, they shall deceive the very elect. Behold, I have told you before" (Matthew 24–25).

These same *great signs* are described in Luke's gospel as coming down from heaven: "...fearful sights and great signs shall there be from heaven" (Luke 21:11). The book of Revelation talks about the same great signs and wonders, "spirits of devils, working miracles" (16:13–14), "…the false prophet that wrought miracles…with which he deceived them that had received the mark of the beast…" (Revelation 19:20).

The Apostle John's vision, as recorded in Revelation 13:13–14, is most certainly comparable to the famous miracle of the sun that was wrought by the sixth Marian apparition at Fatima. It is reported that seventy to one hundred thousand pilgrims came to the Cova da Iria and witnessed the miracle. The apparition had previously told the three children, "I will perform a miracle so that all may believe."

> And he doeth *great wonders*, so that *he maketh fire come down from heaven on the earth in the sight of men*, And *deceiveth them that dwell on the earth by the means of those miracles* which he had power to do in the sight of the beast.
> Revelation 13:13–14, emphasis added

## Sixth Apparition at Fatima of the Virgin Mary

> *The sun* looked like a disc of dull silver, and began dancing wildly. The people shouted out: "Miracle!" It seems that the majority of the people saw the sun trembling and dancing, whirling around like a Catherine wheel; it descended almost low enough *to burn the earth* with its rays
> (emphasis added, http://www.fatimaconference.org/ sixthapparitionoctober131917.htm)

Many of the reported apparitions are undoubtedly very real. However, the Virgin Mary of the apparitions is not the same Virgin Mary of Bible. These entities are ministers of Satan that are transformed to appear as the Blessed Virgin Mary and are sent to deceive. The Blessed Virgin Mary would never contradict the Word of God or appear with baby Jesus in arms, or glorify herself as do the apparitions, on many occasions.

The Apostle Paul said, "And no marvel; for Satan himself is transformed into an angel of light. Therefore it is no great thing if his ministers also be transformed as the ministers of righteousness; whose end shall be according to their works" (2 Corinthians 11:14). According to the many varying descriptions of the apparitions given by eyewitnesses, the entities' actual appearances, whether Caucasian, black, Chinese, etc., and also the apparel, depends on to what part of the world they are sent. The alleged Virgin Mary's huge, unusual, beautiful wardrobe can be seen on many apparition Web sites.[2]

In the following excerpts from *The Thunder of Justice*, compare the contradictory statements of the (alleged Marian) apparitions with those of the Bible; especially the blasphemous statements of the apparitions at Fatima, which the Roman Catholic Church has approved and honors with feasts or celebrations.

The Blessed Mother said to Father Gobbi-February 22, 1992

> In all the land, two thirds of them will be cut off and perish; and one third shall be left. I [*Mary*] will pass this third through fire; I will refine it as silver is refined, test it as gold is tested., emphasis added
>
> *The Thunder of Justice*, p. 342

> And it shall come to pass, that in all the land, saith the Lord, two parts therein shall be cut off and die; but the third shall be left therein. And I will bring the third part through the fire, and will refine them as silver is refined, and will try them as gold is tried: they shall call on my name, and I will hear them: I will say, It is my people: and they shall say, The Lord is my God.
>
> Zechariah 13:8–9:

Marian apparition to three children at Fatima—6/13/1917

> But the Lady said to Lucia, "You, however, are to stay here a longer time. Jesus wants to use you to make me known and loved. He wants to establish the devotion to my Immaculate Heart in the world. I promise salvation to those who embrace it and their soul will be loved by God as flowers placed by myself to adorn His throne."
>
> *The Thunder of Justice*, p. 135

According to the infallible Word of God, we are loved by God because we love his son, Jesus Christ. Being loved by God has absolutely nothing whatsoever to do with loving the Virgin Mary or devotion to her *alleged* immaculate heart. The apparition's self-aggrandizement and utterly blatant and blasphemous statements are exposed in the light of Holy Scriptures

> He that speaketh of himself seeketh his own glory: but he that seeketh his glory that sent him, the same is true, and no unrighteousness is in him.
>
> John 7:18

> He that hath my commandments, and keepeth them, he it is that loveth me: and he that loveth me shall be loved of my Father, and I will love him, and will manifest myself to him.
>
> John 14:21

> For the Father himself loveth you, because ye have loved me, and have believed that I came out from God.
>
> John 16:27

> For I am persuaded, that neither death, nor life, nor angels, nor principalities, nor powers, nor things present, nor things to come, Nor height, nor depth, nor any other creature, shall be able to separate us from the love of God, which is in Christ Jesus our Lord.
>
> Romans 8:38–39

And we have seen and do testify that the Father sent the Son to be the Saviour of the world. Whosoever shall confess that Jesus is the Son of God, God dwelleth in him, and he in God. And we have known and believed the love that God hath to us. God is love; and he that dwelleth in love dwelleth in God, and God in him.

1 John 4:14,16

I in them, and thou in me, that they may be made perfect in one; and that the world may know that thou hast sent me, and hast loved them, as thou hast loved me.

John 17:23

Behold, I will make them of the synagogue of Satan, which say they are Jews, and are not, but do lie; behold, I will make them to come and worship before thy feet, and to know that I have loved thee.

Revelation 3:9

For he is not a Jew, which is one outwardly; neither is that circumcision, which is outward in the flesh: But he is a Jew, which is one inwardly; and circumcision is that of the heart, in the spirit, and not in the letter; whose praise is not of men, but of God.

Romans 2:28, 29

According to *Abingdon's Strong's Exhaustive Greek and Hebrew Concordance* #444, the word *men* in the above as in "whose praise is not of *men*, but of God," includes the Virgin Mary. The word is translated from the Greek word *anthropos*, which means "a human being, whether male or female, generically, to include all human individuals." As seen in the following excerpt, the Marian apparition at Fatima was certainly not giving praise and honor to God but to herself. The real Virgin Mary would never have commanded the three children to pray the rosary daily in honor of her. Nor would she have said that "she alone can help."

[Third Apparition at Fatima] "I want you to come here on the thirteenth of next month and to continue to pray the rosary every day in honor of Our Lady of the Rosary, in order to obtain peace for the world and the end of the war, for she alone can help."

P. 136

Mary was holding the Immaculate Heart in her hand and told Sister Lucia: "The moment has come in which God asks the Holy Father in union with all the bishops of the world to make the consecration of Russia to my Immaculate Heart, promising to save it by this means"

p. .138

During these years, the Church and all of humanity will be left stupefied before the great events of grace and salvation which the Immaculate Heart of your heavenly Mother will bring to you.

*To Father Gobbi*, p.57
cf. 1 Timothy 4:10

Mary revealed to Father Gobbi why she chooses the little ones: "I, the Mother of the Church, am personally intervening and initiating my work of salvation. I am initiating it thus: with simplicity, with hiddenness, and in such a humble manner that most people will not even be aware of it. But this, my son, has always been the way your Mother has acted.

p. 17

Gladys received more than 1,800 messages from October 13, 1983, to February 11, 1990. Father Rene Laurentin, a leading Marian scholar, in his book *An appeal from Mary in Argentina* writes that the message is a simple one: "God wants to renew the covenant with His people through Mary, His Ark of the Covenant"

p. 56

Our Blessed Mother spoke through Gladys of Argentina on February 6, 1987, about her role as the Ark of the New Covenant. "My daughter, in this time, I am the Ark, for all your brethren! I am the Ark of peace, the Ark of Salvation, the Ark where my children must enter, if they wish to live in the Kingdom of God."

p. 56

"Pray very much the prayers of the rosary. I alone am able to save you from the calamities that approach. Those who place their confidence in me [Mary] will be saved...The only arms that will remain for you will be the rosary and Sign left by My Son. The rosary is your weapon"

pp. 188, 189

Compare the above with the following Holy Scriptures.

It is *better to trust in the Lord* than to put *confidence in man.* It is better to trust in the Lord than to put confidence in princes.

Psalm 118:8–9, emphasis added

For *the Lord shall be thy confidence*, and shall keep thy foot from being taken.

Proverbs 3:26, emphasis added

For we are made *partakers of Christ*, if *we hold the beginning of our confidence steadfast unto the end.*

Hebrews 3:14, emphasis added

And this is *the confidence that we have in him*, that, if we ask any thing according to his will, *he heareth us.*

1 John 5:14, emphasis added

By terrible things in righteousness wilt *thou* answer us, O *God of our salvation; who art the confidence of all* the ends of the earth, *and of them* that are *afar off* upon the sea ...

Psalm 65:5, emphasis added

The sun shall be turned into darkness, and the moon into blood, before *that great and notable day of the Lord* come: And it shall come to pass, that *whosoever* shall call on *the name of the Lord* shall be *saved.*

Acts 2:20–21, emphasis added

Thou hast a little strength, and hast *kept my word*, and *hast not denied my name* ... Because thou hast kept the word of my patience, *I also will keep thee from the hour of temptation, which shall come upon all the world*, to try them that dwell upon the earth.

Revelation 3:8, 10, emphasis added

Say to them that are of a fearful heart, Be strong, *fear not*: behold, your *God* will come with vengeance, *even God* with a recompense; *He will* come and *save you.*

Isaiah 35:4, emphasis added
cf. 2 Thessalonians 1:7–10 and 2 Thessalonians 2:1–5, 8–14

The contradictory statements that are made by and about the apparitions are endless gibberish. On p 28 of *The Thunder of Justice,* the author quotes Father Rene Laurentin, a leading Marian scholar, as saying, "God wants to renew the covenant with his people through Mary, his Ark of the Covenant." If the Virgin Mary *is* God's Ark of the New Covenant, it is inconceivable that Mary could build herself, the Ark of the New Covenant, in her *alleged* Immaculate Heart, as stated in the following excerpt.

On July 30, 1986, Our Blessed Mother explained *another of her roles* through Father Gobbi:

This is the moment for all to take refuge in me, because I am the Ark of the New Covenant. At the time of Noah, immediately before the flood, those whom the Lord had destined to survive His terrible chastisement entered into the ark. In these your times, I am inviting all my beloved children to enter into the Ark of the New Covenant which I have built in my Immaculate Heart for you, that they may be assisted by me to carry the bloody burden of the great trial, which precedes the coming of the day of the Lord. Do not look anywhere else. There is happening today what happened in the days of the flood.

pp. 56–58

The Old Testament is replete with scriptures that tell us that God only is our *refuge*. Those who are unable to see the blasphemous statements of the apparitions are either ignorant of God's Word, or they are so rooted in the tradition of man that their eyes are blinded to the truth of God's Word. The alleged Marian apparition says to take refuge in her and "do not look anywhere else." The Bible says we are to look unto God and that there is no other savior.

Compare the following statements of Scripture with those of the apparitions.

Assemble yourselves and come; draw near together, ye that are escaped of the nations: they have no knowledge that set up the wood of their graven image, and *pray unto a god that cannot save.* Tell ye, and bring them near; yea, let them take counsel together: who hath declared this from ancient time? who hath told it from that time? have not I the Lord? and *there is no God else beside me*; a just God and *a Saviour; there is none beside me. Look unto me*, and *be ye saved*, all the ends of the earth: for *I am God*, and *there is none else.* I have sworn by myself, *the word is gone out of my mouth in* righteousness, and shall not return, *That unto me every knee shall bow*, every tongue shall swear. Surely, shall one say, in the Lord have I righteousness and strength: even *to Him* shall men come; and all that are incensed against Him shall be ashamed.

Isaiah 45:20–24, emphasis added
cf. Isaiah 45:20–24 and Philippians 2:9–11 with Pope Pius XII encyclical 48

Wherefore God also hath highly exalted him, *and given him a name* which is *above every name*: That *at the name of Jesus every knee should bow*, of things in heaven, and things in earth, and things under the earth; And that every tongue should confess that *Jesus Christ is Lord, to the glory of God the Father.*

Philippians 2:9–11, emphasis added

And whatsoever ye shall *ask in my name*, that will *I do, that the Father may be glorified in the Son.* If ye shall *ask* any thing in my name, I will do it.

John 14:13–14, emphasis added

Be it known unto you all, and to all the people of Israel, that by the name of *Jesus Christ* of Nazareth, whom ye crucified, whom God raised from the dead, even by him doth this man stand here before you whole ... *Neither is there salvation in any other*: for there is *none other name* under heaven given among men, *whereby we must be saved.*

Acts 4:10, 12, emphasis added

I, even I, am the LORD; and *beside me there is no saviour.*

Isaiah 43:11, emphasis added

For therefore we both labour and suffer reproach, *because we trust in the living God*, who is *the Saviour of all men, specially* of those that *believe.*

1 Timothy 4:10, emphasis added

Therefore I endure all things for the elect's sakes that they may also obtain the *salvation* which is in Christ Jesus with eternal glory.

2 Timothy 2:10, emphasis added

For whosoever shall call upon *the name of the Lord shall be saved.*

Romans 10:13, emphasis added

And it shall come to pass, that whosoever shall call on *the name of the Lord shall be saved.*

Acts 2:21, emphasis added

At that day ye shall *ask in my name*: and *I say not unto you, that I will pray the Father for you*: For the Father himself loveth you, because ye have loved me, and have *believed* that I came out from God.

John 16:26–27, emphasis added

## Mary, *"mother of the church in the order of grace"*?

968–969 ... In a wholly singular way she cooperated by her obedience, faith, hope, and burning charity in the Savior's work of restoring supernatural life to souls. For this reason she is a mother to us in the order of grace ... This motherhood of Mary in the order of grace continues uninterruptedly from the consent which she loyally gave at the Annunciation and which she sustained without wavering beneath the cross, until the eternal fulfillment of all the elect. Taken up to heaven she did not lay aside this saving office but by her manifold intercession continues to bring us the gifts of eternal salvation.... Therefore the Blessed Virgin is invoked in the Church under the titles of Advocate, Helper, Benefactress, and Mediatrix.

*Catechism of the Catholic Church*, p. 252

Regarding the ambiguity of the phrase *order of grace*, the Catechism is void of any mention of Mary's throne of grace. However, according to Pope Pius XII, and contrary to God's holy Word, we are to approach Mary's throne of grace with greater trust.

*Encyclical of Pope Pius XII*
October 11, 1954, on proclaiming the "Queenship" of Mary

Let all, therefore, try to approach with greater trust the throne of grace and mercy of our Queen and Mother, and beg for strength in adversity, light in darkness, consolation in sorrow.

p. 48
http://www.newadvent.org/library/docs_pi12ac.htm

Seeing then that *we have a great high priest*, that is passed into the heavens, *Jesus the Son of God*, let us hold fast our profession. For we have not an high priest [Jesus] which cannot be touched with the feeling of our infirmities; but was in all points tempted like as we are, yet without sin. Let us *therefore come boldly* unto the *throne of grace*, that we may obtain mercy, and *find grace* to help *in time of need*.
Hebrews 4:14–16, emphasis added

Therefore being justified by faith, we have peace with God *through* our Lord *Jesus Christ: By whom* also *we have access by faith* into this *grace* wherein we stand, and rejoice in hope of the glory of God.
Romans 5:1–2, emphasis added

According to the eternal purpose which he purposed in *Christ Jesus* our Lord: In *whom* we have *boldness and access* with confidence *by the faith of Him*.
Ephesians 3:11–12, emphasis added

For *through* Him we both have *access by one Spirit* unto the *Father*.
Ephesians 2:18, emphasis added

And because ye are sons, God hath sent forth *the Spirit of his Son into your hearts*, crying, Abba, Father.

*Galatians 4:6, emphasis added*

Having therefore, brethren, *boldness to enter into the holiest by the blood of Jesus*, By a new and living way, which *he* hath consecrated for us, through the veil, that is to say, *his flesh*. And over the house of God; Let us draw near with a true heart *in full assurance of faith*, having our hearts *having an high priest* sprinkled from an evil conscience, and our bodies washed with pure water. Let us hold fast the profession of our faith without wavering; for *he is faithful that promised*.

*Hebrews 10:19–23, emphasis added*

Mary does not bring us the gifts of eternal salvation by *her intercession*

969 Taken up to heaven she did not lay aside this saving office but by her manifold intercession continues to bring us the gifts of eternal salvation…Therefore the Blessed Virgin is invoked in the Church under the titles of Advocate, Helper, Benefactress, and *Mediatrix.*,emphasis added

*Catechism of the Catholic Church*, p. 252

~~~~~~~~~~~~~~~~~

For *there is one God, and one mediator between God and men*, the man *Christ Jesus*; Who gave himself a ransom for all, to be testified in due time.

*1 Timothy 2:5–6, emphasis added*

He that spared not his own Son, but delivered him up for us all, how shall he not *with him also freely give us all things?* Who is he that condemneth? It is *Christ that died*, yea rather, that is risen again, who is even at the right hand of God, *who also maketh intercession for us*.

*Romans 8:32, 34, emphasis added*

Likewise the Spirit also helpeth our infirmities: for we know not what we should pray for as we ought: but *the Spirit itself maketh intercession for us* with groanings which cannot be uttered. And he that searcheth the hearts knoweth what is the mind of the Spirit, because *He maketh intercession for the saints* according to the will of God.

Romans 8:26–27, emphasis added

Wherefore He [Jesus] *is able also to save them to the uttermost* that come unto God *by Him*, seeing *He* ever liveth to make *intercession* for them.

Hebrews 7:25, emphasis added

Mary does not bring us the *gifts of eternal salvation* by her intercession (Catechism, 969 p. 252).

And being made perfect, *He* became *the author of eternal salvation* unto all them that *obey* Him.[3]

Hebrews 5:9, emphasis added

Neither by the blood of goats and calves, but *by His own blood* He entered in once into the holy place, *having obtained eternal redemption for us*.

Hebrews 9:12, emphasis added

And *for this cause* He is the mediator of the new testament, *that by means of death*, for the redemption of the transgressions that were under the first testament, they which are called might *receive* the *promise of eternal inheritance*.

Hebrews 9:15, emphasis added

If God be for us who can be against us? He that spared not His own Son, but delivered Him up for us all, how shall He not *with Him* also *freely give us all things?*

Romans 8:31–32, emphasis added

For the wages of sin is death; but *the gift* of God is *eternal life* through *Jesus Christ our Lord.*

Romans 6:23, emphasis added

And he said unto me, *It is done.* I am Alpha and Omega, the beginning and the end. *I will give* unto him that is athirst of the fountain of *the water of life freely.* He that *overcometh shall inherit all things*; and I will be his God, and he shall be my son.[4]

Revelation 21:6–7, emphasis added

Now we have received, not the spirit of the world, but the spirit which is of God: *that* we might *know* the *things* that are *freely given* to us *of God.*

1 Corinthians 2:12, emphasis added

For *by grace are ye saved* through faith; and that not of yourselves: it is the *gift* of *God*: Not of works, lest any man should boast.

Ephesians 2:8–9, emphasis added

Forasmuch then as *God gave* them the like *gift* as he did unto us, who *believed* on *the Lord Jesus Christ*; what was I, that I could withstand God?

Acts 11:17, emphasis added

Being justified *freely* by *His grace* through the redemption that is in Christ Jesus: Whom God hath set forth to be a propitiation *through faith in his blood*, to declare his righteousness for the remission of sins that are past, through the forbearance of God; To declare, I say, at this time his righteousness: that he might be just, and the justifier of *him which believeth in Jesus.*

Romans 3:24–26, emphasis added

As every man hath *received* the *gift*, even so minister the same one to another, as good stewards of the manifold *grace of God.* If any man speak, let him speak as the oracles of God; if any man minister, let him do it as of *the ability* which *God giveth*: that *God* in *all things* may be *glorified through Jesus Christ*, to whom be praise and dominion for ever and ever. Amen.

1 Peter 4:10–11, emphasis added

*Every* good *gift* and *every* perfect *gift* is from above, and cometh down *from the Father* of lights, with whom is no variableness, neither shadow of turning.

James 1:17, emphasis added

Grace and peace be multiplied unto you through the knowledge of God, and of Jesus our Lord, According as *His* divine power hath *given* unto us *all things* that pertain unto life and godliness, through the knowledge of Him that hath called us to glory and virtue.

2 Peter 1:2–3, emphasis added

Fear not, little flock; for it is your Father's good pleasure to *give* you the kingdom.

Luke 12:32, emphasis added

According to the (alleged Marian) apparition we *must* enter Mary, the Ark of the New Covenant, to live in the kingdom of God.

Refutation of the Catechism's paragraph number 971

It is stated in the *Catechism of the Catholic Church*, paragraph 971, p.253: "The Church's devotion to the Blessed Virgin is intrinsic to Christian worship." Roman Catholics insist that devotion and prayers to Mary is not *worship*. However, as seen in the following, their denial of worshipping Mary is discredited by comparing the Scriptures with *Abingdon's Strong's* Greek and Hebrew definitions of the word *worship*, and *Webster's Dictionary*.

WORSHIP:

Greek:#4352 proskuneo {pros-koo-neh'-o}

1    to kiss the hand to (towards) one, in token of reverence
2    among the Orientals, esp. the Persians, to fall upon the knees and touch the ground with the forehead as an expression of profound reverence
3    in the NT by kneeling or prostration to do homage (to one) or make obeisance, whether in order to express respect or to make supplication
3a   used of homage shown to men and beings of superior rank
3a1  to the Jewish high priests - 3a2) to God - 3a3) to Christ - 3a4) to heavenly beings - 3a5) to demons

Hebrew # 07812 shachah {shaw-khaw'} -a primitive root; TWOT - 2360; v AV - worship 99, bow 31, bow down 18, obeisance 9, reverence 5, fall down 3, themselves 2, stoop 1, crouch 1, misc 3; 172

1)   to bow down - 1a) (Qal) to bow down - 1b) (Hiphil) to depress (fig) - 1c) (Hithpael) - 1c1) to bow down, prostrate oneself - 1c1a) before superior in homage - 1c1b) before God in worship - 1c1c) before false gods - 1c1d) before angel

*#4352 Abingdon's Strong's Exhaustive Concordance*
And saith unto him, All these things will I give thee, if thou wilt fall down and worship ,<#4352> me. Then saith Jesus unto him, Get thee hence, Satan: for it is written, Thou shalt worship <#4352> the Lord thy God, and him only shalt thou serve.

Matthew 4:9–10

For thou shalt worship <# 07812> no other god < 'el -# 0410> : for the Lord, whose name is Jealous, is a jealous God:

Exodus 34:14

And I John saw these things, and heard them. And when I had heard and seen, I fell down to worship <#4352> before the feet of the angel which shewed me these things. Then saith he unto me, See thou do it not: for I am thy fellow servant, and of thy brethren the prophets, and of them which keep the sayings of this book: worship God.

Revelation 22:8–9

Note:

Also: - Deuteronomy5:8–9; Judges 2:19; Matthew 6:24 w/- Luke 14:26 *"hate"* <*#3404*>}; Acts 10:25–26; Romans 1:25; Ephesians 3:14–16; Philippians 2:10–11; Revelations 4:10–11.

OBEISANCE:

1.  a gesture of respect or reverence, as a bow or curtsy. 2. homage; deference.

WORSHIP:

1.  A prayer, church service, or other rite showing reverence for a deity.
2.  Intense love or admiration of any kind. 3. something worshipped. 4. [chiefly Brit.], a title of honor, used in addressing magistrates, etc. *v.t.*[-SHIPED or SHIPPED, SHIPING OR SHIPPING] 1. to show religious reverence for. 2. to have intense love or admiration for.

*Webster's Dictionary*

It is also stated in paragraph number 971; p.253, that Mary is "honored with the title of Mother of God, to whose protection the faithful fly in all their dangers and needs." At first glance, I thought this statement had to be saying that the faithful fly to *God's* protection. Not so! According to the encyclical of Pope Pius XII, Catholics have been taught via *the living tradition* to "fly to Mary's powerful protection in all their dangers and needs" for the past forty-plus years.

*Encyclical of Pope Pius XII*
October 11, 1954
{on proclaiming the 'Queenship' of Mary}
*http://www.newadvent.org/library/docs_pi12ac.htm*

No one should think himself a son of Mary, worthy of being received under her powerful protection, unless, like her, he is just, gentle and pure, and shows a sincere desire for true brotherhood, not harming or injuring but rather helping and comforting others.

p. 10, # 49

And in another place he prays to her: "Majestic and Heavenly Maid, Lady, Queen, protect and keep me under your wing lest Satan the sower of destruction glory over me, lest my wicked foe be victorious against me." P. 3, -# 10

*Missionary Oblates of Mary Immaculate*
{National Shrine of Our Lady of the Snows}
*http://www.oblatesusa.org/MissionaryWork.*
*aspx?path=root/momi/MissionaryWork/novenas/ourladynovena*

Remember, O most gracious Virgin Mary, that never was it known that anyone who fled to thy protection, implored thy help, or sought thy intercession was left unaided. Inspired with this confidence, I fly unto thee, O virgin of virgins, my Mother; to thee do I come, before thee I stand, sinful and sorrowful; O Mother of the Word Incarnate, despise not my petitions, but in thy mercy hear and answer me.

Novena Prayers to Our Lady of the Snows

The following scriptures not only show the error of *trusting and flying to Mary's protection* but also serve as an example of those who teach erroneous Marian doctrines consistently using quotes from Scripture that speak of God's attributes: refuge, protection, salvation, mercy, glory, etc., and applying them to Mary. With regard to Mary's *powerful protection*, the same phraseology *under your wing* is used in the encyclical of pope Pius XII that is used in the following scriptures that speak of God's protection.

### *Trusting in God's protection:*

I have called *upon thee*, for thou wilt hear me, *O God*: incline thine ear unto me, and hear my speech. Shew thy marvelous lovingkindness, O *thou that savest* by thy right hand *them which put their trust in thee* from those that rise up against them. Keep me as the apple of the eye, hide me *under the shadow of thy wings*, From the wicked that oppress me, from my deadly enemies, who compass me about.

Psalm 17:6–9, emphasis added

*He shall cover thee with his feathers*, and *under His wings* shalt thou trust: *his truth* shall be thy shield and buckler. Thou shalt not be afraid for the terror by night; nor for the arrow that flieth by day; Nor for the pestilence that walketh in darkness; nor for the destruction that wasteth at noonday. A thousand shall fall at thy side, and ten thousand at thy right hand; but it shall not come nigh thee. Only with thine eyes shalt thou behold and see the reward of the wicked. *Because thou hast made the Lord, which is my refuge, even the most High*, thy habitation.

Psalm 91:4–9, emphasis added

How excellent is *thy* lovingkindness, O *God*! therefore the children of men *put their trust* under the shadow of *thy wings*.

Psalm 36:7, emphasis added

Be merciful unto me, O *God*, be merciful unto me: for my soul *trusteth in thee*: yea, in the shadow of *thy wings* will I make my *refuge*, until these calamities be overpast.

Psalm 57:1, emphasis added

For thou hast been a shelter for me, and a strong tower from the enemy. I will abide in thy tabernacle for ever: *I will trust in* the covert of *thy wings*. Selah.

Psalm 61:3–4, emphasis added

Because *thou* hast been my help, *therefore* in the shadow of *thy wings* will I rejoice. My soul followeth hard after thee: *thy* right hand upholdeth me.

Psalm 63:7–8, emphasis added

*The Lord* recompense thy work, and a full reward be given thee of the Lord God of Israel, *under whose wings* thou art come *to trust.*

Ruth 2:12, emphasis added

For therefore we both labour and suffer reproach, *because we trust in the living God*, who is the Saviour of all men, *specially of those that believe.*

1 Timothy 4:10, emphasis added

[Jesus] Saying, I will declare *thy name* unto my brethren, *in the midst of the church will* I sing *praise unto thee.* And again, *I will put my trust in Him.* And again, *Behold I and the children which God hath given Me.*

Hebrews 2:12–13, emphasis added

I will declare thy name unto my brethren: *in the midst of the congregation* will I *praise thee.* Ye that fear the Lord, *praise* Him; all ye the seed of Jacob, *glorify Him*; and fear him, all ye the seed of Israel. For he hath not despised nor abhorred the affliction of the afflicted; neither hath he hid his face from him; but *when he cried unto Him, he heard. My praise shall be of thee* in the *great congregation*: I will pay my vows before them that fear him.

Psalm 22:22–25, emphasis added

There is not one verse in the inspired Scriptures that refers to the people of God praying to anyone other than God himself, but the Bible is replete with verses that speak of God's hearing and answering the prayers of his people because they trust in his salvation and/or deliverance from adverse circumstances, with the result that God receives all the glory and praise. We are to "show forth the praises of Him who hath called us out of darkness into marvellous light" (1 Peter 2:9). Those who "fly to Mary's protection in all their dangers and needs" are showing forth the praises of Mary and robbing God of his glory and praise.

> I am the Lord: that is my name: and my glory will I not give to another, neither my praise to graven images.
> Isaiah 42:8

> ... A Psalm of David. Truly my soul waiteth upon God: from Him cometh my salvation. He only is my rock and my salvation; He is my defense; I shall not be greatly moved. How long will ye imagine mischief against a man? ye shall be slain all of you: as a bowing wall shall ye be, and as a tottering fence. *They only consult to cast Him down from His excellency*: they delight in lies: they bless with their mouth, but they curse inwardly. Selah. My soul, wait thou *only upon God*; for my expectation is from Him. He only is my rock and my salvation: He is my defense; I shall not be moved. In God is my salvation and my glory: the rock of my strength, and my refuge, is in God. Trust in Him *at all times*; ye people, pour out your heart before Him: God is a refuge for us. Selah. Surely men of low degree are vanity, and men of high degree are a lie: to be laid in the balance, they are altogether lighter than vanity.
> Psalm 62:1–9, emphasis added

In the above, it is *God only* whom we are to trust *at all times*. In the following three excerpts, notice the Catechism's contradiction of the Holy Scriptures and also that the statements within the Catechism are self-contradictory.

In paragraph number 150: "It is right and just to entrust oneself wholly to God" but "futile and false to place such faith in a creature."

In paragraph number 2677: "We give ourselves over to her [Mary] now, in the Today of our lives. And our trust broadens further, already at the present moment, to surrender the hour of our death wholly to her care."

In paragraph number 971: It is "the Blessed Virgin … to whose protection the faithful fly in all their dangers and needs."

*Catechism of the Catholic Church*

150 Faith is first of all a personal adherence of man to God. At the same time, and inseparably, it is a free assent to the whole truth that God has revealed. As personal adherence to God and assent to his truth, Christian faith differs from our faith in any human person. It is right and just to entrust oneself wholly to God and to believe what he says. It would be futile and false to place such faith in a creature.

pp. 40, 41

2677 … Pray for us sinners, now and at the hour of our death: By asking Mary to pray for us, we acknowledge ourselves to be poor sinners and we address ourselves to the "Mother of Mercy," the All-Holy One. We give ourselves over to her now, in the Today of our lives. And our trust broadens further, already at the present moment, to surrender "the hour of our death" wholly to her care. …

p. 644

971 All generations will call me blessed: "The Church's devotion to the Blessed Virgin is intrinsic to Christian worship." The Church rightly honors the blessed Virgin with special devotion. From the most ancient times the Blessed Virgin has been honored with the title of 'Mother of God,' to whose protection the faithful fly in all their dangers and needs.

p. 253

The only statement in the above that is in agreement with sacred Scripture is in paragraph number 150, which says: "It is right and just to entrust oneself wholly to God...It would be futile and false to place such faith in a creature." Paragraph numbers 2677 and number 971 not only contradict the Bible but also contradict paragraph number 150 and are obviously not based upon the holy Scriptures but upon tradition.

Another example of the teaching office of the Catholic Church extracting verses from Scripture that pertain exclusively to Jesus Christ and applying them to the Virgin Mary is seen in a comparison of the passage of Romans 15 with an *Encyclical of Pope Pius XII*. In Romans 15:4 the Apostle Paul said, "whatsoever things were written in the Scriptures were written for our learning, that we through patience and comfort of the scriptures might have hope." From verse 4 through 13, Paul talked about believing what the Scriptures teach about Jesus Christ, about *his rising* from death and *his reigning*, about placing our hope and trust in Christ and praising *him*. In verse 13, he said: "Now the God of hope fill you with all joy and peace in believing, that ye may abound in hope, through the power of the Holy Ghost" (Romans 15:4–13).

There is not one word in all of Scripture that even remotely hints of placing hope and trust in Mary, or of praising her, or of Mary's *reigning*. Nevertheless, this is what is taught in the Roman Catholic Church via living tradition. Compare the following statements in the *Encyclical of Pope Pius XII* with subsequent scriptures.

*Encyclical of Pope Pius XII*
October 11, 1954, on proclaiming the 'Queenship' of Mary
*http://www.newadvent.org/library/docs_pi12ac.htm*

From the earliest ages of the Catholic Church a Christian people, whether in time of triumph or more especially in time of crisis, has addressed prayers of petition and hymns of praise and veneration to the Queen of Heaven. And never has that hope wavered which they placed in the Mother of the Divine King, Jesus Christ; nor has that faith ever failed by which we are taught that Mary, the Virgin Mother of God, reigns with a mother's solicitude over the entire world, just as she is crowned in heavenly blessedness with the glory of a Queen.

> Looking for that blessed *hope*, and the glorious appearing of the great God and our *Saviour Jesus Christ;* Who gave himself for us, that he might redeem us from all iniquity, and purify unto himself a peculiar people, zealous of good works.
>
> Titus 2:13–14, emphasis added

> Multitudes, multitudes in the valley of decision: for *the day of the Lord is near* in the valley of decision. The sun and the moon shall be darkened, and the stars shall withdraw their shining. The Lord also shall roar out of Zion, and utter his voice from Jerusalem; and the heavens and the earth shall shake: but *the Lord will be* the *hope* of his people, and the strength of the children of Israel.
>
> Joel 3:14–16, emphasis added

> Behold, the eye of the Lord is upon them that fear him, upon them that *hope* in *his mercy;* To deliver their soul from death, and to keep them alive in famine. Our soul waiteth for the Lord: *he is our help* and our shield. For our heart shall rejoice in him, because we have trusted in his holy name. Let *thy mercy, O Lord*, be upon us, according as we *hope* in thee.
>
> Psalm 33:18–22, emphasis added

> Blessed be the God and Father of our Lord Jesus Christ, which according to his abundant mercy hath begotten us again unto *a lively hope by the resurrection of Jesus Christ from the dead*, To an inheritance incorruptible, and undefiled, and that fadeth not away, reserved in heaven for you.
>
> 1 Peter 1:3–4, emphasis added

Who by him do believe in *God*, that *raised him up from the dead*, and gave him glory; *that* your *faith* and *hope* might be *in God*.

1 Peter 1:21, emphasis added

If in this life only we have HOPE IN CHRIST, we are of all men most miserable. But *now is Christ risen from the dead*, and become the firstfruits of them that slept.

1 Corinthians 15:19–20, emphasis added

Paul, an apostle of Jesus Christ by the commandment of God our Saviour, and Lord Jesus Christ, which is our *hope*; Unto Timothy, my own son in the faith: Grace, *mercy*, and *peace*, from *God our Father* and *Jesus Christ our Lord*.

1 Timothy. 1:1–2, emphasis added

Remembering without ceasing your work of faith, and labour of love, and patience of *hope* in our Lord *Jesus Christ*, in the sight of God and our Father.

1 Thessalonians 1:3, emphasis added

Now our Lord *Jesus Christ himself*, and God, even our Father, which hath loved us, and *hath given us everlasting* consolation and good *hope* through grace, Comfort your hearts, and stablish you in every good word and work.

2 Thessalonians 2:16–17, emphasis added

Compare the statement Pope Pius made in his Encyclical concerning *Mary, the Queen of Heaven reigning over the entire world* with 1 Timothy 6:14–16 and Abingdon's Strong's Greek definitions of the words *only* and *Potentate*.

That thou keep *this* commandment without spot, unrebukeable, until the appearing of our Lord Jesus Christ: Which in his times he shall shew, *who is* the blessed and *only Potentate* , the King of kings, and Lord of lords; *Who only hath immortality*, dwelling in the light which no man can approach unto; whom no man hath seen, nor can see: to whom *be* honour and power everlasting. Amen.

1 Timothy 6:14–16, emphasis added

Only:     #3441 Greek: monos {mon'-os}; probably from 3306; adj.
AV-only 24, *alone* 21, by (one's) self 2; 47
1) *alone (without a companion)*, forsaken, destitute of help, *alone*, only, merely

Potentate: #1413 Greek: dunastes {doo-nas'-tace}; from #1410; TDNT - 2:284,186; n m
AV-mighty 1, *of great authority* 1, *Potentate* 1; 3
1) a prince, a *potentate*
2) a courtier, high officer, *royal minister of great authority*

Mary? Reigning? Over the entire world? Not according to the Word of God. Jesus Christ is the *only* potentate. "Every word of God is pure: he *is* a shield unto them that put their trust in him. Add thou not unto his words, lest he reprove thee, and thou be found a liar" (Proverbs 30:5–6).

As previously stated, the Roman Catholic Church does not derive its certainty about all revealed truth from the Scriptures alone but also from the living tradition passed down by the church fathers, some of whom Jesus and the Apostle Paul warned would arise and speak perverse things to draw away disciples after themselves. Consequently, those who subsequently spoke perverse things also started a living tradition of false doctrines. Catholics read the Bible in light of the Church's living tradition. Would it not be best to read of the church's living tradition in light of the inspired Word of God, in order to discern a tradition of truth from that of false doctrines?

When the Apostle Paul said, "whatsoever things were written aforetime were written for our learning," and "all Scripture is given by inspiration of God, and is profitable for doctrine, reproof, and for correction," he was referring to the Old Testament, which is not only void of the slightest support of the Catholic teachings about Mary but is also full of reproof of these doctrines. Paul told Timothy to

> preach the word; be instant in season, out of season; reprove, rebuke, exhort with all longsuffering and doctrine. For the time will come when they will not endure sound doctrine; but after their own lusts shall they heap to themselves teachers, having itching ears; and they shall turn away their ears from the truth, and shall be turned unto fables.
> 2 Timothy 4:2–4

In defense of *the living tradition* as a source of truth, the Roman Catholic Church contends that the Bible does not teach *sola Scripture* and/or *the Bible only*. Living tradition does, in fact, contain truth, but it also contains error, as seen in many examples of the church fathers' writings contradicting not only the inspired Word of God but also one another. Relying on the living tradition of the church as a source of truth is a pick-and-choose method of obtaining truth. According to the Apostle Paul, the Bible is the only source whereby man can determine what is truth and what is not truth.

> And Paul, as his manner was, went in unto them, and three sabbath days *reasoned with them out of the scriptures*... These were more noble than those in Thessalonica, in that they received the word with all readiness of mind, and *searched the scriptures daily, whether those things were so.*
> Acts 17:2, 11, emphasis added

> But this I confess unto thee, that after the way which they call heresy, so worship I the God of my fathers, *believing all things which are written in the law and in the prophets*...
> Acts 24:14, emphasis added

Having therefore obtained help of God, I continue unto this day, witnessing both to small and great, *saying none other things than those which the prophets and Moses did say should come:* That Christ should suffer, and that he should be the first that should rise from the dead, and should shew light unto the people, and to the Gentiles.

Acts 26:22–23, emphasis added

And when they had appointed him a day, there came many to him into his lodging; to whom he expounded and testified the kingdom of God, *persuading them concerning Jesus, both out of the law of Moses, and out of the prophets, from morning till evening.*

Acts 28:23, emphasis added

*Search the scriptures;* for in them ye think ye have eternal life: and they are *they which testify of me.* For **had ye believed Moses**, ye would have believed me: for *he wrote of me. But if ye believe not his writings, how shall ye believe my words?*

John 5:39, 46–47, emphasis added

Every word of God is pure: he is a shield unto them that put their trust in him. Add thou not unto his words, lest he reprove thee, and thou be found a *liar.*

Proverbs 30:5–6, emphasis added

Now the Spirit speaketh expressly, that in the latter times some shall depart from the faith, giving heed to seducing spirits, and *doctrines of devils*; Speaking *lies* in hypocrisy; having their conscience seared with a hot iron; *Forbidding to marry*, and commanding to *abstain from meats*, which God hath created to be received with thanksgiving of them which believe and know *the truth.*

1 Timothy 4:1–3, emphasis added

# MARY'S IMMACULATE
# CONCEPTION?

### *Mary, "full of grace"*

Catholic theologian Thomas Aquinas (AD 1225–74), who insisted that revealed truths must be believed even when they cannot be fully understood, and who set himself the task of harmonizing Aristotle's philosophical teachings with Christian doctrine, taught that all original sin was extinguished within Mary before she was born. The Scriptures clearly warn against the wisdom and philosophy of man opposing the truth of the Word of God. Compare *Webster's Dictionary* and *Abingdon's Strong's* definition of *philosophy* with the following Scriptures.[1]

> Beware lest any man spoil you through philosophy and vain deceit, after the tradition of men, after the rudiments of the world, and not after Christ.
>
> Colossians 2:8

> For Christ sent me not to baptize, but to preach the gospel: not with wisdom of words, lest the cross of Christ should be made of none effect. For the preaching of the cross is to them that perish foolishness; but unto us which are saved it is the power of God. For it is written, I will destroy the wisdom of the wise, and will bring to nothing the understanding of the prudent. Where is the wise? where

is the scribe? where is the disputer of this world? hath not God made foolish the wisdom of this world? For after that in the wisdom of God the world by wisdom knew not God, it pleased God by the foolishness of preaching to save them that believe.

1 Corinthians 1:17–21

And I, brethren, when I came to you, came not with excellency of speech or of wisdom, declaring unto you the testimony of God. For I determined not to know any thing among you, save Jesus Christ, and him crucified.

1 Corinthians 2:1–2

And my speech and my preaching was not with enticing words of man's wisdom, but in demonstration of the Spirit and of power: That your faith should not stand in the wisdom of men, but in the power of God.

1 Corinthians 2:4–5

Which things also we speak, not in the words which man's wisdom teacheth, but which the Holy Ghost teacheth; comparing spiritual things with spiritual.

1 Corinthians 2:13

Let no man deceive himself. If any man among you seemeth to be wise in this world, let him become a fool, that he may be wise. For the wisdom of this world is foolishness with God. For it is written, He taketh the wise in their own craftiness. And again, The Lord knoweth the thoughts of the wise, that they are vain.

1 Corinthians 3:18–20

At that time Jesus answered and said, I thank thee, O Father, Lord of heaven and earth, because thou hast hid these things from the wise and prudent, and hast revealed them unto babes. Even so, Father: for so it seemed good in thy sight.

Matthew 11:25–26

The *revealed truth* Thomas Aquinas referred to is derived from the inspired Scriptures and also from living tradition. According to the Catechism, pp.26–27 (#82 and #86), the inspired Scriptures and living tradition are one *single deposit of faith*. Thomas Aquinas's doctrine of the Immaculate Conception was solemnly defined as dogma by Pope Pius IX on December 8, 1854.

According to the Catechism, *Mary was full of grace* at the moment of the annunciation, before she conceived. According to *The Catholic Encyclopedia*, it is from Luke's declaration of Mary as "full of grace" and *other sources* that the Roman Catholic Church declared Mary's Immaculate Conception (Papal bull, *Ineffabilis Deus*, Pius IX, 1854).

490 To become the mother of the Savior, Mary was enriched by God with gifts appropriate to such a role. The angel Gabriel at the moment of the annunciation salutes her as *"full of Grace."* In fact, in order for Mary to be able to give the *free assent* of her faith to the announcement of her vocation, it was necessary that she be wholly borne by God's grace., emphasis added

491 *Through the centuries, the Church has become ever more aware* that Mary, *"full of Grace"* through God, *was redeemed from the moment of her conception*. That is what the dogma of the Immaculate Conception confesses, as Pope Pius IX proclaimed in 1854. , emphasis added

The most Blessed Virgin Mary was, *from the first moment of her conception*, by a singular grace and privilege of almighty God and by virtue of the merits of Jesus Christ, Savior of the human race, *preserved immune from all stain of original sin.*

492 The *splendor of an entirely unique holiness* by which Mary is enriched *from the first instant of her conception* comes wholly from Christ: she is redeemed, in a more

exalted fashion, *more than any other created person in Christ.*
, emphasis added

Catechism of the Catholic Church,* pp. 123–124

In the New Testament, the Gospels of Matthew and Mark narrate events concerning the life of the Blessed Mother, but in the Gospel of St. Luke we find the fullest treatment. He records the annunciation and from his declaration of Mary as *full of grace* and other sources, the Church declared Mary's Immaculate Conception.,emphasis added (Papal bull, Ineffabilis Deus, Pius IX, 1854).

*The Catholic Encyclopedia,* pp. 374–375

The phrase *full of grace* is used only one time throughout the Scriptures, and it is attributed to Jesus Christ and to him only (John 1:14). Gabriel *did not say*: "Hail Mary full of grace," as is stated and expounded upon in the Catechism. He said: "Hail, thou that art highly favoured." The English words *highly favoured* are translated from a single Greek word: *charitoo* (khar-ee-to'-o).

> #5487 charitoo {khar-ee-to'-o} from 5485;
> AV-be *highly favoured* 1, *make accepted* 1; 2 1) to make *graceful* 1a) *charming*, lovely, agreeable 2) to peruse with grace, compass with favour 3) to honour with blessings

This Greek word *charitoo* is used only twice in the New Testament; once with reference to Mary and once with reference to all who are in Christ. If *charitoo* proves that "Mary was, from the first moment of her conception, by virtue of the merits of Jesus Christ, preserved immune from all stain of original sin," it also proves that all who are in Christ were preserved immune from all stain of original sin before the foundation of the world, by virtue of the merits of Jesus Christ.

MARLENE C. CROUCH

According as he hath chosen us *in him before the foundation of the world*, that we should be holy and without blame before him in love: Having predestinated us unto the adoption of children by Jesus Christ to himself, according to the good pleasure of his will, To the praise of the glory of his grace, wherein he hath *made* <#5487 *charitoo*> us *accepted* <#5487*charitoo*> in the beloved.

Ephesians 1:4–6, emphasis added

And the angel came in unto her, and said, Hail, thou that art highly favoured <#5487 *charitoo*>, the Lord is with thee: blessed art thou among women.

Luke 1:28, emphasis added
*cf.* Judges 5:24-"Blessed above women shall Jael the wife of Herber the Kenite be."

As a result of past dealings with the doctrines of the Jehovah Witnesses and Mormons, I'm extremely skeptical of doctrines that are based on only a few isolated verses of Scripture; especially when the Scriptures presented as *proof text* are misquoted with disregard for the original Hebrew and Greek languages. There can be absolutely no doubt that Mary was *greatly* blessed among women. However, the erroneous dogma of the *Immaculate Conception* that stems from *living tradition* and that has *developed through the centuries*, not only lacks scriptural support but grossly contradicts the divinely inspired Scripture's teaching on original sin.

The basic message of the Scriptures, from Genesis to Revelation, is that of salvation from the penalty of sin that passed down from Adam "upon all men" (Romans 5:12). Jesus Christ, God himself, is the only "all-holy one." If the Virgin Mary were, in fact, all holy, born without the stain of sin, that fact would certainly have been recorded at least one time in the Scriptures. The Bible is replete with Scriptures that refute the Catechism's erroneous statement of "all-holy Virgin Mary," of which the following are just a few. It is inconceivable that

Jesus, or the Apostles Paul and John, would not have made it perfectly clear that the Virgin Mary was an exception to their statements, in the following verses.

> Who shall not fear thee, O Lord, and glorify thy name? for thou only art holy: for all nations shall come and worship before thee; for thy judgments are made manifest.
>
> Revelation 15:4

> And he [Jesus] said unto him, Why callest thou me good? there is none good but one, that is, God.
>
> Matthew 19:17

> What then? are we better than they? No, in no wise: for we have before proved both Jews and Gentiles, that they are all under sin; As it is written, There is none righteous, no, not one.
>
> Romans 3:9–10

> For all have sinned, and come short of the glory of God.
>
> Romans 3:23

> Wherefore, as by one man sin entered into the world, and death by sin; and so death passed upon all men, for that all have sinned.
>
> Romans 5:12

> But the scripture hath concluded all under sin, that the promise by faith of Jesus Christ might be given to them that believe.
>
> Galatians 3:22

> For in thy sight shall no man living be justified.
>
> Psalm 143:2

God is not a respecter of persons. [2] He most certainly honored Mary more than any other created person in Christ when he chose her to be the mother of the Messiah but not to the point of exalting her to the position of sinlessness. Jesus Christ is the only one who was ever born sinless. In John 1:1 and 14, we're told that "the Word was God ... And the Word was made flesh, and dwelt among us." Jesus is God in the flesh. In Luke 18:19, Jesus asked a man, "Why callest thou me good? There is none good but one, that is God."

The following definition of the word *none*, is according to *Abingdon's Strong's Exhaustive Greek and Hebrew Concordance.*

> No    *man*-#3762-Greek:    OUDEIS;    includ.    fem. OUDEMIA; and neut. OUDEN; FROM 3761 and 1520; not even one (man, woman, or thing), i.e. none, nobody, nothing:-any (man), aught, man, neither any (thing), never (man), no (man), none (+ of these things), not (any, at all, -thing), nought.

When Jesus said: "There is *none* good but one, that is God," he used the same word (*none -oudeis*) that John used to describe his vision in Revelation chapter five. The subject of the entire chapter is that of God's judgment at the end of the world. The dialogue in this passage precludes the possibility of anyone being sinless other than the lion of the tribe of Judah, the Root of David, the Lamb, Jesus Christ himself.

When an angel, with a loud voice, asked, "Who is worthy to open the book, and to loose the seals thereof?" John said, "No man in heaven, nor in earth, neither under the earth, was able to open the book, neither to look thereon. And I wept much, because no man was found worthy to open and to read the book, neither to look thereon" (Revelation 5:2–4).

According to *Abingdon's Strong's Exhaustive Greek and Hebrew Concordance,* "no man" includes Mary.

The Apostle John continued, saying, "And one of the elders saith unto me, Weep not: behold, the Lion of the tribe of Juda, the Root of David, hath prevailed to open the book, and to loose the seven seals thereof" (Revelation 5:5). Jesus is the only one worthy to open the book and loose the seals of God's judgment because he is the only one who is without sin. The four beasts and the twenty-four elders affirmed the fact that no one but the Lamb was worthy, and so did ten thousand times ten thousand, and thousands of thousands of angels.

"And every creature in heaven, and on the earth, and under the earth and such as are in the sea, and all that are in them, said, Blessing and honour and glory and power be unto him that sitteth upon the throne, and unto the Lamb for ever and ever" (Revelation 5:13).

God said, "I will not give my glory unto another" (Isaiah 48:11). Those who adhere to the false dogma of the Immaculate Conception are giving glory to Mary for attributes that belong solely to God. In the vision of the last seven plagues, John saw those who had gotten victory over the beast standing on a sea of glass. He heard them saying, "Who shall not fear thee, O Lord, and glorify thy name? for thou only art holy: for all nations shall come and worship before thee; for thy judgments are made manifest" (Revelation 15:4).

Between the judgments of the trumpets and vials, John saw

> another angel fly in the midst of heaven, having the everlasting gospel to preach unto them that dwell on the earth, and to every nation, and kindred, and tongue, and people, Saying with a loud voice, Fear God, and give glory to him; for the hour of his judgment is come: and worship him that made heaven, and earth, and the sea, and the fountains of waters.
>
> Revelation 14:6–7

After the fourth angel poured out his vial on the sun and scorched men with fire, there were still those who refused to "give him glory" (Revelation 16:9).

The Apostle John described his vision of the last phase of God's judgment, in Revelation chapter nineteen, saying,

> And I saw heaven opened, and behold a white horse; and he that sat upon him was called Faithful and True, and in righteousness he doth judge and make war. His eyes were as a flame of fire, and on his head were many crowns; and he had a name written, that no man knew, but he himself. And he was clothed with a vesture dipped in blood: and his name is called The Word of God.
>
> Revelation 19:11–13

"No man" in verse 12, is translated from the same Greek word -"OUDEIS" (includ. fem. OUDEMIA; and neut. OUDEN).

If Mary, by virtue of the merits of her son, was "preserved sinless from the moment of her conception," as stated in the Catechism, and exalted above every other child of God to the positions of queen of heaven, queen of saints and angels, the ark of the covenant, mother of the church, mediatrix, co-redemptrix, etc., etc., it would be more than unlikely that she would not also know the hidden name of her son.

If Mary were "free from the stain of original sin," she would have no need of a "savior" and therefore would not have said, "My spirit hath rejoiced in God my Saviour" (Luke 1:47). Nor would she have offered the sacrifice of two turtledoves or pigeons for a "sin" offering.[3]

> And thou, child (John the Baptist), shalt be called the prophet of the Highest: for thou shalt go before the face of the Lord to prepare His ways: To give knowledge of *salvation unto His people by the remission of their sins.*
>
> Luke 1:76–77, emphasis added

> And Jesus said unto him, This day is *salvation* come to this house ... For the Son of man is come *to seek and to save that which was lost.*
>
> Luke 19:9–10, emphasis added

And she shall bring forth a son, and thou shalt call his name Jesus: for he shall save his people from their sins.

Matthew1:21, emphasis added

This is a faithful saying, and worthy of all acceptation, that Christ Jesus came into the world to save sinners; of whom I am chief.

1 Timothy 1:15, emphasis added

The foregoing Scriptures are all talking about salvation from the penalty of sin that passed down from Adam "upon all men, for that all have sinned" (Romans 5:12). The doctrine of Mary's Immaculate Conception not only rejects the clear teaching of the holy Scriptures and confuses the issue of original sin but also deprives Jesus Christ of *his uniqueness as the sinless one*. Had Mary been sinless before she gave birth to Jesus, the *preeminence of sinlessness* would not be attributed to Jesus but to Mary.

"And he is the head of the body, the church: who is the beginning, the firstborn from the dead; that *in all things* he might have the *preeminence*" (Colossians 1:18, emphasis added).

*preeminence*: #4409 proteuo (prote-yoo'-o)-from 4413 have the preeminence, to be first, hold the first place.

# MARY, EVER VIRGIN

498 The meaning of this event [Jesus's virginal conception] is accessible only to faith, which understands in it the "connection of these mysteries with one another" in the totality of Christ's mysteries, from his Incarnation to his Passover. St. Ignatius of Antioch already bears witness to this connection: "Mary's virginity and giving birth, and even the Lord's death escaped the notice of the prince of this world: these three mysteries worthy of proclamation were accomplished in God's silence."

499 The deepening of faith in the virginal motherhood led the church to confess Mary's real and perpetual virginity, even in the act of giving birth to the Son of God made man. In fact, Christ's birth did not diminish his mother's virginal integrity but sanctified it. And so the liturgy of the church celebrates Mary as Aeiparthenos, the "Ever-Virgin."
*Catechism of the Catholic Church* p. 126

There are literally dozens of New Testament Scriptures concerning Jesus that say *it is written* of him, much of which is written in the psalms. Jesus said, "All things that are written in the law, the prophets and in the Psalms, concerning me, must be fulfilled" (Luke 24:44). When Jesus drove the moneychangers out of the temple, "his disciples remembered that it was written, The zeal of thine house hath eaten me up" (John 2:15–17).

The very scriptures that came to the disciples' minds also speak of Jesus's siblings, Mary's other children (Psalm 69:8–9).

> Because for thy sake I have borne reproach; shame hath covered my face. I am become a stranger unto my brethren and an alien unto my mother's children. For the zeal of thine house hath eaten me up; and the reproaches of them that reproached thee are fallen upon me.
>
> Psalm 69:7–9

In Psalm 69:8, the words *brethren* and *children* are translated from two entirely different Hebrew words, thus indicating two entirely different types of relationships. The Hebrew word for *brethren ('ach -#251)*, in Psalm 69:8, is the same word Cain used in Genesis 4:9 in reference to his sibling Abel, saying, "Am I my brother's keeper?"

The Hebrew word for *children (ben -#1121)* is the same word that is used in Genesis 3:16, when God told Eve: "in sorrow thou shalt bring forth children."

When Paul quoted Psalm 69:9 in his epistle to the Romans, and then said, "whatsoever things were written aforetime were written for our learning," he was not oblivious to the fact that Psalm 69:8–9 is prophetic of Jesus and Mary and of Mary's other children. The subject matter of both passages is the same. He was talking about "reproach." He was admonishing his readers to be of the same mind as Christ and to follow his example of not pleasing self but others (Romans 15:1–5). See the following:

> For even Christ pleased not himself; but, as it is written, *The reproaches of them that reproached thee fell on me.* For whatsoever things were written aforetime were written for our learning.
>
> Romans 15:3–4, emphasis added

> Because for thy sake I have borne reproach; shame hath covered my face. I am become a stranger unto my brethren,

and an alien unto my mother's children. For the zeal of thine house hath eaten me up; and *the reproaches of them that reproached thee are fallen upon me.*

Psalm 69:7–9, emphasis added

When the Apostle Paul said, "all Scripture is given by inspiration of God, and is profitable for doctrine, reproof and correction," he was talking about the Old Testament (2 Timothy 3:16). Paul taught "none other things than those which the prophets and Moses did say should come" (Acts 26:22), and he "believed all things that are written therein" (Acts 24:14). If the doctrine of perpetual virginity had in fact been taught in the early church, Paul most certainly would have made it perfectly clear to his readers when he quoted Psalm 69:8 that the context of the verse he quoted only seems to contradict the doctrine of perpetual virginity.

Since all scripture is inspired of God and is profitable for doctrine, reproof, and correction, and is totally silent on the doctrine of Mary's perpetual virginity, the doctrine has to have been born out of the living tradition of the Roman Catholic Church, which is not, in its entirety, inspired of God. The living tradition of the Church should be adhered to in that it may afford us a better understanding of the early church, but only insofar as that it does not contradict the divinely inspired Word of God. Just because the Roman Catholic Church *has always understood* something to be true, doesn't automatically make it true. In the following excerpt from the Catechism, the phrase "The Church has always understood" is, of course, referring to Living Tradidion, the writings of the *early* church fathers.

> 500 Against this doctrine ["ever-virgin"] the objection is sometimes raised that the Bible mentions brothers and sisters of Jesus. The Church has always understood these passages as not referring to other children of the Virgin Mary. In fact James and Joseph, "brothers of Jesus," are

the sons of another Mary, a disciple of Christ, whom St. Matthew significantly calls "the other Mary." They are close relations of Jesus, according to an Old Testament expression.

*Catechism of the Catholic Church*, p. 126,

According to Roman Catholic doctrine, the word *brethren* is to be interpreted as *cousins* when in reference to a relative of Jesus.[1] The word *cousin(s)* is not in the Old Testament. However, in both the Old and New Testaments, where the words *brother* or *brethren* are used, it could mean either *brother* (as in sibling) or *cousin*.

By comparing the following definitions of the Greek words *adelphos* and *suggenes* with the verses in Luke's gospel, wherein these words are used, it is obvious that Luke differentiated between the words *adelphos* and *suggenes* and that he said what he meant.

> *Brother, Bretheren*-Grk. #80-*adelphos*-from #1 (as a connective particle) and delphus (the womb); a brother (lit. or fig.) near or remote (much like 1):-brother. [*Hebrews* #251]
>
> *Cousin, Cousins*-Grk. #4773-*suggenes*, from #4862 and #1085; a relative (by blood); by extens. a fellow countryman;-cousin, kin (-sfolk, -sman).

Then said he also to him that bade him, When thou makest a dinner or a supper, call not thy friends, nor thy *brethren* (*#80-adelphos*), neither thy *kinsmen* (#4773-suggenes), nor thy rich neighbours; lest they also bid thee again, and a recompence be made thee.

Luke 14:12, emphasis added

And ye shall be betrayed both by parents, and brethren (*#80-adelphos*), and kinsfolks (#4773-*suggenes*), and friends; and some of you shall they cause to be put to death.

Luke 21:16, emphasis added

Notice the distinctiveness of these words in the above and compare Luke 1:36 and Luke 1:58 with Luke 8:19–21 in the following. Luke used the word *cousin(s)* (*suggenes*) in Luke 1:36 and 58. Why would he not have used the same word in Luke 8:19–21 if he were referring to Jesus's "cousins" and not to his siblings (*adelphos*)?

> And, behold, thy cousin <#4773> Elizabeth.
> Luke 1:36, emphasis added

> Her neighbours and her cousins <#4773> heard.
> Luke 1:58, emphasis added

> Then came to him his mother and his *brethren* <#80>, and could not come at him for the press. And it was told him by certain which said, Thy mother and thy *brethren* <#80> stand without, desiring to see thee. And he answered and said unto them, My mother and my *brethren* <#80> are these which hear the word of God, and do it.
> Luke 8:19–21, emphasis added

In the following verses, the meaning of the word *"brother"* (*adelphos* <#80>) has never been questioned. Why, then, should there be any doubt as to the meaning of the same word in Luke 8:19–21 (above); especially since all of these verses were written by the same man?

> Luke 3:1, 19-Herod's brother <#80> Philip
> Luke 6:14-Andrew, Peter's brother <#80>
> Luke 12:13-brothers <#80> dividing an inheritance
> Luke 15:27, 32-brother <#80> of the prodigal son
> Luke 16:19–28-rich man's five brothers <#80>
> Luke 20:28–29-seven brothers <#80>

When Gabriel told Mary she would conceive a child, she said,

"How shall this be, seeing I know not a man?" (Luke 1:31, 34). Mary was referring to sexual intercourse. The word *know* was a Jewish idiom for sexual intercourse. Because of the many examples of the use of this word throughout the Scriptures, the virgin birth of Jesus Christ is undeniable.

> Genesis 4:1-Adam "knew" Eve his wife, and she conceived and bare a son.
> Genesis 4:25-Adam "knew" his wife again, and she conceived.
> Genesis 4:17-Cain "knew" his wife, and she conceived.
> Genesis 19:5–8-Lot's two daughters which have not "known" man.
> Genesis 38:18–26-Judah came in unto Tamar-she conceived by him. After he learned she was his daughter-in-law, "he knew her again no more."
> 1 Kings 1:4-And the damsel was very fair, and cherished the king, and ministered to him: but the king "knew" her not.
> Ruth 3:14-And she lay at his feet until the morning: and she rose up before one could "know" another. And he said, "Let it not be known that a woman came into the floor."
> Judges 19:22–25-The men "knew" the concubine and abused her all the night.
> 1 Samuel 1:19, 30-Elkonah "knew" Hanna his wife and she conceived and bare a son.
> Luke1:34-Then said Mary to the angel, how shall this be seeing I know (#1097) not a man.

Matthew was also referring to sexual intercourse in his account of the virgin birth of Christ, saying, "Now the birth of Jesus Christ was on this wise: When as his mother Mary was espoused to Joseph, before they came together, she was found with child of the Holy Ghost" (Matthew 1:18). The Apostle Paul used the same terminology "come together" in his dissertation on the subject of marriage.

84

In the following, compare Paul's use of the phrase *come together* with Matthew 1:18 [2]

> Now concerning the things whereof ye wrote unto me: It is good for a man not to touch a woman. Nevertheless, to avoid fornication, let every man have his own wife, and let every woman have her own husband. Let the husband render unto the wife due benevolence: and likewise also the wife unto the husband. The wife hath not power of her own body, but the husband: and likewise also the husband hath not power of his own body, but the wife. Defraud ye not one the other, except it be with consent for a time, that ye may give yourselves to fasting and prayer; and come together again, that Satan tempt you not for your incontinency.
>
> 1 Corinthians 7:1–5, emphasis added

> Now the birth of Jesus Christ was on this wise: When as his mother Mary was espoused to Joseph, before they came together, she was found with child of the Holy Ghost... And (Joseph) knew (#1097) her not till (#2193) she had brought forth her firstborn (#4416).
>
> Matthew1:18 and 25, emphasis added

Matthew's account of the virgin birth of Christ makes it very clear that Mary and Joseph did have sexual intercourse, but not until after Christ was born. Matthew not only began his account of the virgin birth with reference to sexual intercourse, he also ended it the same way, saying, "And knew her not *till* she had brought forth her firstborn son: and he called his name Jesus" (Matthew 1:25, emphasis added). Paul and Matthew were both referring to sexual intercourse.

> *Till*-#2193-"*heos*" -prep. and adv. of continuance, *until* (of time and place):-even (until, unto), (as) far (as), how long *un (til)*-etc. etc.
>
> *Abingdon's Strong's Concordance*

In the Catholic Reader's Edition of *The Jerusalem Bible*, the word *knew* is translated as *intercourse*, but the word *till* is omitted.³ On the first page of this edition, reference is not made as to who the translators are but, it is stated that "the translators of this edition made full use of the ancient Greek, Aramaic and Hebrew texts to ensure complete conformity with the ancient text and is an entirely faithful version of the ancient texts; faithful in all respects to the original sources."

According to James Strong and Kenneth Wuest, two authoritative Greek scholars, both agree that the word *till* is in the ancient text. Whether this word appears in the original text or not, the doctrine of the Virgin Mary's perpetual virginity is clearly refuted throughout both the Old and New Testament Scriptures wherein the words "firstborn" and "only" are used. ⁴

In the New Testament, according to *Abingdon's Strong's Concordance*, the word *firstborn* -#4416- is translated from the Greek word: *prototokos* and means "firstborn" or "first begotten." The word *only* - #3439 is translated from the Greek word *monogenes* and means; "only born i.e. sole; only begotten, child." The beautiful harmony of God's Word is irrefutable.

*First Begotten Child*

*Firstborn*-#4416, *prototokos*
from #4413 and the alternative of #5088; firstborn. (usually as a noun, lit. or fig.) first begotten.

~~~~~~~~~~~~~~~~~

Jesus, Mary's "firstborn" (#4416).
                                                Matthew 1:25

That he [Jesus] might be the "firstborn" (#4416) [from the dead] *among many brethren.*
                                Romans 8:29, emphasis added

[Jesus] the "firstborn" (#4416) of every creature … the firstborn (#4416) from the dead.

Colossians 1:15, 18, emphasis added

Jesus Christ, who is the faithful witness, and the "first begotten" (#4416) of the dead.

Revelation 1:5, emphasis added

When he [God the Father] bringeth the *first begotten* (#4416) into the world.

Hebrews 1:6, emphasis added

Through faith, he kept the passover and the sprinkling of blood, lest he that destroyed the "firstborn" (#4416) should touch them (see Psalms 78:51 firstborn Hebrews #1060).

Hebrews 11:28, emphasis added

To the general assembly and church of the "firstborn" (#4416) which are written in heaven.

Hebrews 12:23, emphasis added

Mary brought forth her "firstborn" (#4416) and wrapped Him in swaddling clothes.

Luke 2:7, emphasis added

*Only Begotten Child*
*Only* (#3439) *monogenes*-from #3441 and #1096; only born i.e. sole; only begotten, child.

For he is mine "only" (#3439) child.

Luke 9:38, emphasis added

The "only" (#3439) son of his mother died.

Luke 7:12, emphasis added

He had one "only" (#3439) daughter.

Luke 8:42, emphasis added

God's "only" (#3439) begotten son (conceived, begotten of the Holy Ghost- Matthew 1:20).

John 3:16, emphasis added

God sent His "only" (#3439) begotten Son into the world, that we may live through Him.

1 John 4:9, emphasis added

God offered up His "only" (#3439) begotten Son.

Hebrews 11:17, emphasis added

And the Word was made flesh, and dwelt among us, and we beheld His glory, the glory as of the "only" (#3439) begotten of the Father, full of grace and truth.

John 1:14, emphasis added

In much of Catholic literature that I've read, *human reason* is emphasized as one of the essential parts of correct biblical interpretation. Albeit, human reason has also given birth to some very *reasonable* but erroneous doctrines.

*Hypothetically*, consider Luke 20:28, Galatians 1:19, and Matthew 3:55–56 with the following: According to Jewish law, if a married man dies without having fathered a child, the man's brother is to impregnate his deceased brother's wife as to "raise up seed unto his brother." Consider the possibility that Alphaeus was Joseph's brother and that Joseph died without having fathered children of his own, and that James the Less was the son of both Alphaeus and the Virgin Mary. If James was the son of Alphaeus and the Virgin Mary, he would be both brother and cousin to Jesus; which in turn would explain the double usage of the word *brother*. To me, this seems more "reasonable" than to assume, without the slightest evidence in Scripture, that Mary had no other children. In either case, it would be conjectural to state either position as *fact* without sufficient evidence from the Scriptures.

> Moses wrote unto us, If any man's brother die, having a wife, and he die without children, that his brother should take his wife, and raise up seed unto his brother.
> Luke 20:28
> *cf.* Deut. 25:5–10

> James [*the son of Alphaeus?*] the Lord's brother.
> Galatians 1:19, emphasis added

> Is not this the carpenter's son? is not his mother called Mary? and his brethren James, and Joses, and Simon, and Judas? And his sisters are they not all with us? Whence then hath this man all these things?
> Matthew 13:55–56

What sounds more *reasonable?* His father, mother, *cousins,* and sisters? Or his father, mother, *brothers*, and sisters?

To quote a ninth-century Catholic theologian, John Scotus Erigena, "Reason and authority come alike from the one source of Divine Wisdom ... The fathers, great as their authority is, often contradict each other ... In last resort, reason must be called in to decide between them" (*http://plato.stanford. edu/entries/scottus-eriugena/*).

The false doctrine of *perpetual virginity* was born out of the tradition and *reason* of man, perhaps to defend the doctrine of the virgin birth of Christ. However, the Virgin Mary's having had other children can in no way negate the truth of God's Word concerning the virgin birth of Christ. If we receive the witness of men, the witness of God is greater.

According to the *witness* of St. Ignatius of Antioch, "Mary's virginity and giving birth, and even the Lord's death, escaped the notice of the prince of this world" (*Catechism of the Catholic Church*, p.126, paragraphs 498 and 499).

According to the Holy Scriptures, Christ's birth and death did not escape the notice of the prince of this world:

> And the chief priests and scribes sought how they might kill him; for they feared the people. *Then entered Satan into Judas* surnamed Iscariot, being of the number of the twelve. And he went his way, and communed with the chief priests and captains, how he might betray him unto them.
>
> Luke 22:2–4, emphasis added

> When Jesus had thus said, he was troubled in spirit, and testified, and said, Verily, verily, I say unto you, that one of you shall betray me. Then the disciples looked one on another, doubting of whom he spake. Now there was leaning on Jesus' bosom one of his disciples, whom Jesus loved. Simon Peter therefore beckoned to him, that he should ask who it should be of whom he spake. He then lying on Jesus' breast saith unto him, Lord, who is it? Jesus answered, He it is, to whom I shall give a sop, when I have dipped it. And when he had dipped the sop, he gave it to *Judas Iscariot*, the son of Simon. And *after the sop Satan entered into him.* Then said Jesus unto him, That thou doest, do quickly.
>
> John 13:21–27, emphasis added

According to inspired scriptures, Satan played a major role in the circumstances that led to Christ's crucifixion. Thus, Satan was very well aware of Christ's death. Compare John 12:31 with Revelation 12, which speaks not only of Satan, the prince of this world, being "cast out" but also of Satan's awareness of Christ's birth and death (verses 4–5).

> Now is the judgment of this world: now shall *the prince of this world be cast out.*
>
> John 12:31, emphasis added

And there appeared another wonder in heaven; and behold a great red dragon, having seven heads and ten horns, and seven crowns upon his heads. And his tail drew the third part of the stars of heaven, and did cast them to the earth: and *the dragon stood before the woman which was ready to be delivered, for to devour her child as soon as it was born.* And she brought forth a man child, who was to rule all nations with a rod of iron: and *her child was caught up unto God, and to his throne.* And the woman fled into the wilderness, where she hath a place prepared of God, that they should feed her there a thousand two hundred and threescore days. And *there was war in heaven*: Michael and his angels fought against the dragon; and the dragon fought and his angels, And prevailed not; neither was their place found any more in heaven. And *the great dragon was cast out,* that old serpent, called *the Devil, and Satan,* which deceiveth the whole world: *he was cast out into the earth,* and his angels were cast out with him. And I heard a loud voice saying in heaven, Now is come salvation, and strength, and the kingdom of our God, and the power of his Christ: *for the accuser of our brethren is cast down,* which accused them before our God day and night. And they overcame him by the blood of the Lamb, and by the word of their testimony; and they loved not their lives unto the death. Therefore rejoice, ye heavens, and ye that dwell in them. Woe to the inhabiters of the earth and of the sea! for the devil is come down unto you, having great wrath, because he knoweth that he hath but a short time. And when the dragon saw that he was cast unto the earth, he persecuted the woman which brought forth the man child.

Revelation 12:3–13, emphasis added

The Apostle Peter wrote of this same *war in heaven*, and so did the Apostle Paul. Revelation chapter 12 along with the following scriptures all contradict St. Ignatius's statement that the Lord's birth and death "escaped the notice of the prince of this world."

[Jesus Christ] Who is gone into heaven, and is on the right hand of God; *angels and authorities and powers being made subject unto him.*

1 Peter 3:22, emphasis added

Blotting out the handwriting of ordinances that was against us, which was contrary to us, and took it out of the way, nailing it to his cross; And *having spoiled principalities and powers, he made a shew of them openly, triumphing over them in it.*

Colossians 2:14–15, emphasis added

And being found in fashion as a man, he humbled himself, and became obedient unto death, even *the death of the cross.* Wherefore God also hath highly exalted him, and given him a name which is above *every name: That at the name of Jesus every knee should bow, of things in heaven, and things in earth, and things under the earth;* And that every tongue should confess that Jesus Christ is Lord, to the glory of God the Father.

Philippians 2:8–11, emphasis added

Forasmuch then as the children are partakers of flesh and blood, he also himself likewise took part of the same; that through death *he might destroy him that had the power of death, that is, the devil.*

Hebrews 2:14, emphasis added

The dogma of the perpetual virginity of the Virgin Mary is just one of the many Roman Catholic doctrines that cannot be validated in the Holy Scriptures. According to the *Catechism of the Catholic Church*, "In keeping with the Lord's command, the Gospel was handed on in two ways: Orally by the apostles" and "In writing by those apostles and other men associated with the apostles who under the inspiration of the same Holy Spirit, committed the message of salvation to writing…" The apostles left bishops as their successors. They gave them "their own position of teaching authority" (pp. 24–25, #76–77).

Saint Ignatius (35–110), bishop of Antioch, a disciple of the Apostle John, was one of the "other men associated with the apostles" who, contrary to scripture, spuriously declared in writing: "Mary's virginity and giving birth, and even the Lord's death escaped the notice of the prince of this world: these three mysteries worthy of proclamation were accomplished in God's silence" (Catechism: p. 126, #498).

Saint Ignatius may very well have been one of the most holy Christians in all of church history. However, he nevertheless was '*man*' whose declarations are subject to the divinely inspired Word of God, as were the teachings of the apostles (Acts 17:2; 11; 1 Corinthians 15:3–4; 2 Timothy 3:16; Acts 26:22; Acts 28:23; Romans 15:4; Acts 8:35; Acts 18:28; Acts 24:14).

# THE ROSARY

Many defenders of the Roman Catholic faith insist that those who are opposed to Roman Catholic teaching on the Virgin Mary "simply do not know what the church actually teaches about her; that Mary is not prayed to, but with." According to The Catechism, p. 644, #2679, "We can pray with and to her."

According to *The Final Hour*, by Michael H. Brown, p. 4, and several other Roman Catholic publications, "She is not prayed to but prayed with." It is my contention that most Catholics simply do not know what the scriptures actually teach and are therefore duped into believing the many erroneous doctrines of the Roman Catholic Church.

The Catholic Encyclopedia attests to the fact that "devotion is directed to the Blessed Mother" in the prayers of the rosary. It also reveals the rosary's role in propagating the erroneous doctrine of purgatory, which in turn denies and/or rejects Jesus Christ's all-sufficient sacrifice as full payment for the sins of all who receive him as their one and only God and savior.

> 1498 Through indulgences the faithful can obtain the remission of temporal punishment resulting from sin for themselves and also for the souls in Purgatory.
> *Catechism of the Catholic Church*, p. 374

*The Catholic Encyclopedia p. 529*
Rosary

This is the name of both a devotion and the chain of beads used for counting the prayers...The devotion is directed to the Blessed Mother and has been highly indulgenced by the Church...One of the many indulgences attached to the devotion is that the faithful who recite the Rosary together in a family group, besides the partial indulgence of 10 years, are granted a plenary indulgence twice a month, if they perform this recitation daily for a month, go to confession, receive Holy Communion, and visit some church or public oratory.

S.P.M. March 18, 1932 and July 26, 1946

Daily recitation of the rosary for a month is 4,500 "Hail Marys" and 900 "Our Fathers" and "Glory be to the Father."
In Matthew 6:7–9, Jesus said:

But when ye pray, use not vain repetitions, as the heathen do: for they think that they shall be heard for their much speaking. Be not ye therefore like unto them: for your Father knoweth what things ye have need of, before ye ask him. After this manner therefore pray ye: Our Father which art in heaven, Hallowed be thy name.

The rosary is referred to in the Catechism (p. 253, # 971) as "an epitome of the whole gospel." In defense of the rosary, it is often stated that the prayers and *mysteries* of the rosary embrace *all* the Christian truths and completely and beautifully illustrate them. This simply is not true. Certain prayers and *mysteries* of the rosary do, in fact, embrace certain Christian truths. However, the Hail Mary prayer and certain other so-called mysteries do not. If the few scriptures presented herein with regard to the Hail Mary prayer have not yet enlightened your understanding of the *truth* of the written Word of God, I suggest a personal in-depth search of the many other passages of Scripture on the subject of prayer.

Concerning the spurious mysteries of the rosary, number five of "The Luminous Mysteries" is "The Institution of the Eucharist" and refers to "The Real Presence;" which is addressed in another chapter. Numbers four and five of the "Glorious Mysteries" are "The Assumption" and "The Coronation" of the Virgin Mary. These are among the Hail Mary prayers and meditations of the rosary that are nowhere to be found in the Bible.

These so-called *Christian truths* are derived from the tradition of man, which is not necessarily truth.

> For this cause also thank we God without ceasing, because, when ye received *the word of God* which ye heard of us, ye received it *not as the word of men*, but *as it is in truth*, the *word of God*, which effectually worketh also in you that *believe*.
>
> 1 Thessalonians 2:13, emphasis added

> Paul, an apostle, not of men, neither by man, but by Jesus Christ, and God the Father, who raised him from the dead; But I certify you, brethren, that *the gospel which was preached of me is not after man*. For **I neither received it of man, neither was I taught it, but by the revelation of Jesus Christ.**
>
> Galatians 1:1, 11–12, emphasis added

In the following excerpt, notice the phrases *gradual development, began to be, in time*, and again *in time certain religious teachers encouraged the people to greater awareness of…* A greater awareness not only of the saving love of God but also, as evidenced, a greater awareness and devotion to the Virgin Mary.

## THE ROSARY: MY DAILY PRAYER
## KNIGHTS OF COLUMBUS, VOL #84

by Most Reverend Charles H. Helmsing, D.D.
Bishop of Kansas City, St. Joseph
*http://11796.kofc-de.org/Top/first/books/*
*The%20rosary/subpages/mydaily.htm*

There is a popular tradition that the Rosary in its present form was given to St. Dominic in a vision. However this tradition began, it does not seem to have any historical foundation. More likely, the Rosary is the end result of a gradual development in Christian devotion. Familiar with the fact that the monks in their monasteries prayed often during the day, reciting in the course of the week's liturgy the 150 psalms of David, the then unlettered laity wished to have a similar form of ongoing prayer. Since the Our Father (Pater Noster) was the best known prayer, the people began to say this 150 times a day. To make it easy to keep count, a string of 150 knots or beads was fashioned and, for ease in carrying around the neck, made into a closed circle. The act of putting the string of beads around the neck suggested to the popular imagination the image of a garland or wreath of flowers. This gave rise to words like "chaplet" which means garland, and "rosary," a garland of roses.

In the beginning, the beads were called "Paternoster beads" and in old literature we find many references to saying one's Paters. Side by side with development of the Paternoster beads was a similar devotion to the sacred humanity of Christ and, consequently, great attention to his human Mother. The names of Jesus and Mary began to be recited every day along with the Paters. In time, certain religious teachers encouraged the people to greater awareness of the saving love of God in the mystery of Redemption that was at the heart of their prayers to the Father and Jesus and to Mary. In time, some form of meditation on Redemption, as revealed in the life and death of Jesus with Mary in obedience to the Father, came to be a regular feature of reciting one's daily prayers.

These various currents of Catholic devotion came together in the course of time until the Rosary as we have it today took shape in the 16th century ... the prayers and mysteries of the Rosary embrace all the Christian truths and completely and beautifully illustrate them.

The Hail Mary, which is repeated more than one hundred and fifty times in the Rosary, is a message of joy brought by the Archangel Gabriel to the fallen world, continued by our Blessed Mother's cousin, St. Elizabeth, and concluded by the Church ... The Hail Mary is a prayer giving highest praise to the Mother of God, a prayer that abounds in blessings. "For each salutation of Mary," St. Bernard wrote, "you will receive a grace from her."

As the united Rosaries of Christendom obtained a singular triumph for Christianity in the battle of Lepanto, so Our Blessed Mother in the now-famous apparitions which took place at Fatima, Portugal, between May 13 and October 13, 1917, gave a specific remedy against the spread of Communism and the many evils that afflict our times. "Do penance and say the Rosary," she commanded. Acting as God's messenger, Our Blessed Mother gave the assurance that if her request for penance and fervent Rosaries were complied with through the world, "Russia would be converted, many souls would be saved from hell, and peace would be granted to the world."

The prayer "Our Father," that in the beginning was said to God 150 times, has been replaced with a prayer that is said to the Virgin Mary 150 times. The reciting of 150 Hail Marys does not encouraged people to greater awareness of the saving love of God, as stated by the bishop of Kansas City, in the above. It instills a greater awareness and love of Mary with confidence in her (alleged) power and ability to save. Endeavoring to instill an even greater awareness and love of Mary with confidence in her power and ability to save, the Most Reverend Charles H.

Helmsing continues in his discourse on "The Family Rosary," saying:

> With divorce on the increase, and youthful contempt for authority and disregard for property leading to an unprecedented increase in crimes and excesses, there is the greatest need to turn to the Mother of God who is always ready to crush the head of Satan ... every Catholic must go into battle against the princes of the world of evil. But he will go with Rosary in hand. United under Mary's standard, this great Christian army will call upon Mary as their leader, for it is she "who has conquered all heresies." It is she who is "the Victres in all God's battles," as Pius XII called her ... The Family Rosary! May the faithful everywhere seize and hold fast to this anchor of salvation!

First of all, in rebuttal of the above statements, according to the Word of God and contrary to the Catechism's paragraph 410, several Catholic theologians, and the *Douay Rheims Bible*, it is not the Virgin Mary but Jesus Christ who *crushes the head of Satan*. Genesis 3:15 is the only scripture throughout the Douay Rheims Bible that is in disagreement with the King James Version's portrayal of Jesus Christ as the one who crushes the head of Satan. Compare the following:

## DOUAY RHEIMS BIBLE

Genesis 3:15 I will put enmities between thee and the woman, and thy seed and her seed: *she* shall crush thy head, and thou shalt lie in wait for *her* heel. Emphasis added

Douay Rheims Bible note:
"She shall crush" ... Ipsa, the woman; so divers of the fathers read this place, conformably to the Latin: others read it ipsum, viz., the seed. The sense is the same: for it is by her

seed, Jesus Christ, that the woman crushes the serpent's head.

> http://www.google.com/search?hl=en&q=crush%2
> 0head%20of%20satan+site:http://campus.udayton.
> edu/mary&btnG=Google+Search

### KING JAMES VERSION:

I will put enmity between thee and the woman, and between thy seed and her seed; *it* shall bruise thy head, and thou shalt bruise *his* heel. Emphasis added

Genesis 3:15And

And the God of *peace* shall bruise Satan under your feet shortly. The grace of our Lord Jesus Christ be with you. Amen. Emphasis added

Romans 16:20

For unto us a child is born, unto us a son is given: and the government shall be upon his shoulder: and his name shall be called Wonderful, Counsellor, The mighty God, The everlasting Father, The *Prince of Peace*. Emphasis added

Isaiah 9:6

Peace I leave with you, *my peace* I give unto you: not as the world giveth, give I unto you. Let not your heart be troubled, neither let it be afraid. Emphasis added

John 14:27

Second of all: Christians going into battle against the princes of the world of evil with rosary in hand, united under Mary's standard and calling upon her as leader, is a blasphemous contradiction of the scriptures. The Virgin Mary is not "the Victress in all God's battles," and the weapons of Christian warfare is not the rosary but weapons "mighty through God to the pulling down of strong holds" (2 Corinthians 10:4).

Christians are to "be strong in the Lord, and in the power of his might" and "put on the whole armour of God, that ye may be able to stand against the wiles of the devil." The whole armour of God is the breastplate of righteousness, the gospel of peace, the shield of faith, the helmet of salvation, and the sword of the Spirit, which is the word of God (Ephesians 6:10–17). And which says absolutely nothing about the Virgin Mary in relationship to spiritual warfare. The Apostle Paul made it perfectly clear, as did the Old Testament prophets, that Christians are to "be strong in the Lord and in the power of his might

> … Not by might, nor by power, but by my spirit, saith the LORD of hosts.
>
> Zechariah 4:6

> Were not the Ethiopians and the Lubims a huge host, with very many chariots and horsemen? yet, because thou didst rely on the Lord, he delivered them into thine hand. For the eyes of the Lord run to and fro throughout the whole earth, to shew himself strong in the behalf of them whose heart is perfect toward him. Herein thou hast done foolishly: therefore from henceforth thou shalt have wars.
>
> 2 Chronicles 16:8–9

> And lead us not into temptation, but deliver us from evil: For thine is the kingdom, and the power, and the glory, for ever. Amen.
>
> Matthew 6:13

> Who is this King of glory? The Lord strong and mighty, the Lord mighty in battle. Lift up your heads, O ye gates; even lift them up, ye everlasting doors; and the King of glory shall come in. Who is this King of glory? The Lord of hosts, he is the King of glory. Selah.
>
> Psalm 24:8–10

Now unto him that is able to do exceeding abundantly above all that we ask or think, according to the power that worketh in us,

Ephesians 3:20

And I heard a loud voice saying in heaven, Now is come salvation, and strength, and the kingdom of our God, and the power of his Christ: for the accuser of our brethren is cast down, which accused them before our God day and night.

Revelation 12:10

Strengthened with all might, according to his glorious power, unto all patience and longsuffering with joyfulness.

Colossians 1:11

But we have this treasure in earthen vessels, that the excellency of the power may be of God, and not of us.

2 Corinthians 4:7

Now the God of hope fill you with all joy and peace in believing, that ye may abound in hope, through the power of the Holy Ghost.

Romans 15:13

But ye shall receive power, after that the Holy Ghost is come upon you: and ye shall be witnesses unto me both in Jerusalem, and in all Judaea, and in Samaria, and unto the uttermost part of the earth.

Acts 1:8

And what is the exceeding greatness of his power to us-ward who believe, according to the working of his mighty power.

Ephesians 1:19

And Jesus came and spake unto them, saying, All power is given unto me in heaven and in earth. Go ye therefore, and teach all nations, baptizing them in the name of the Father, and of the Son, and of the Holy Ghost: Teaching them to observe all things whatsoever I have commanded you: and, lo, I am with you alway, even unto the end of the world. Amen.

Matthew 28:18–20

Thirdly: the rosary? "Anchor of salvation"? Not according to the inspired Word of God. Jesus Christ is able to save to the uttermost those who come unto God by him. By *him,* not by Mary.

Which hope we have as an anchor of the soul, both sure and steadfast, and which entereth into that within the veil; Whither the forerunner is for us entered, even Jesus, made an high priest for ever after the order of Melchisedec.

Hebrews 6:19–20

Neither is there salvation in any other: for there is none other name under heaven given among men, whereby we must be saved.

Acts 4:12

The sun shall be turned into darkness, and the moon into blood, before that great and notable day of the Lord come: And it shall come to pass, that whosoever shall call on the name of the Lord shall be saved.

Acts 2:20–21

Be not afraid of sudden fear, neither of the desolation of the wicked, when it cometh. For the Lord shall be thy confidence, and shall keep thy foot from being taken.

Proverbs 3:25–26

But the salvation of the righteous is of the Lord: he is their strength in the time of trouble. And the Lord shall help them, and deliver them: he shall deliver them from the wicked, and save them, because they trust in him.

Psalm 37:39–40
(also: Psalm 96:7–9; Psalm 89:1)

The Lord's hand is not shortened, that it cannot save; neither his ear heavy, that it cannot hear.

Isaiah 59:1

The eyes of the Lord run to and fro throughout the whole earth, to shew himself strong in the behalf of them whose heart is perfect toward him.

2 Chronicles 16:9

For the eyes of the Lord are over the righteous, and his ears are open unto their prayers: but the face of the Lord is against them that do evil.

1 Peter 3:12

The Lord is nigh unto all them that call upon him, to all that call upon him in truth.

Psalm 145:18

For therefore we both labour and suffer reproach, because we trust in the living God, who is the Saviour of all men, specially of those that believe.

1 Timothy 4:10

In the following excerpt, notice the self-aggrandizing statements made by the *alleged Marian* apparition and how these statements are topped off, so to speak, with an ever so slight and inconsequential mention of Jesus, saying, "It will help them to love Jesus more." This may or may not be one of the approved apparitions of the Roman Catholic Church, but it is certainly typical of those that are; including the famous apparitions which took place at Fatima. The self-aggrandizing, blasphemous statements of the alleged Marian apparition in the following excerpt are exposed as such in the light of the subsequent scriptures.

## "Daily Rosary"
## Wearing Rosary & Scapular for protection from Satan

Do not worry, my children who are living the sign of my protection. Wear it always. It will help you to do good because it is a sign of my love and *will remind you of me often.* This is the purpose of all sacramentals, to remind you of the person behind them and to help you to imitate their virtues. The scapular and the rosary are the greatest of these and will afford you the most protection. I want all my children to wear one. It will help them to love Jesus more. This is a simple means by which God helps His children. Wear it always., emphasis added

*The Thunder of Justice,* P. 396

*He that speaketh of himself seeketh his own glory:* but he that seeketh His glory that sent him, the same is true, and no unrighteousness is in him.

John 7:18, emphasis added

Howbeit when he, the Spirit of truth, is come, he will guide you into all truth: for he shall not speak of himself… *He shall glorify me.*

John 16:13–14, emphasis added

I am the Lord: that is my name: and *my glory* will I not give to another, *neither my praise to graven images.*

Isaiah 42:8, emphasis added

According to the Most Reverend Charles H. Helmsing, "The Hail Mary is a prayer giving highest praise to the Mother of God" ("The Rosary: My Daily Prayer." *Knights of Columbus,* Vol. 84 by Most Reverend Charles H. Helmsing, D.D.). Praying to the Virgin Mary, or anyone other than God, does not give God the glory and praise. God almighty created and predestined us for the praise of his glory, as stated in the scriptures, of which the following are just a few.

Offer unto God thanksgiving; and pay thy vows unto the most High: and *call upon Me* in the day of trouble: *I* will deliver thee, and thou shalt *glorify Me.*

Psalm 50:14, emphasis added

Give unto the Lord ye kindreds of the people, *give unto the Lord glory and strength.* Give unto the Lord *the glory due unto His name*, bring an offering and come before Him: worship the Lord in the beauty of holiness.

1 Chronicles 16:28- 29, emphasis added

A Psalm of David. Give unto the Lord, O ye mighty, *give unto the Lord glory* and strength. Give unto the Lord the *glory due unto his name*; worship the Lord in the beauty of holiness.

Psalm 29:1–2, emphasis added

Bring my sons from far and my daughters from the ends of the earth, even everyone that is called by my name: for *I have created him for my glory.*

Isaiah 43:6–7, emphasis added<br>cf. James 2:7

But ye are a chosen generation, a royal priesthood, an holy nation, a peculiar people; that ye should shew forth *the praises of him* who hath called you out of darkness into his marvellous light.

1 Peter 2:9, emphasis added

[Jesus Christ] In whom also we have obtained an inheritance, *being predestinated* according to the purpose of him who worketh all things after the counsel of his own will: *That we should be to the praise of his glory*, who first trusted in Christ.

Ephesians 1:11–12, emphasis added

# Pray Only to God

Nowhere in the Scriptures is it recorded that anyone prayed to Abraham, Isaac, Jacob, or any of the many other Old Testament saints. It is unequivocally stated throughout the inspired Word of God that prayer is not to be directed to anyone or anything (angels, saints, etc.) except to God and to him only.

> And [Satan] saith unto him, All these things will I give thee, if thou wilt *fall down and worship me. Then saith Jesus* unto him, Get thee hence, Satan: for *it is written*, Thou shalt worship the Lord thy God, and *him only shalt thou serve.*
>
> Matthew 4:9–10, emphasis added

> And the residue thereof he maketh a god, even his graven image: *he falleth down unto it*, and worshippeth it, and *prayeth unto it*, and *saith, Deliver me*; for *thou art my god.*
>
> Isaiah 44:17, emphasis added

> Thou shalt have *no other gods* before me. Thou shalt not make unto thee any graven image, or any likeness of any thing that is in heaven above, or that is in the earth beneath, or that is in the water under the earth: Thou *shalt not bow down thyself* to them, *nor serve them*: for I the Lord thy God am a jealous God, visiting the iniquity of the fathers upon the children unto the third and fourth generation of them that hate me.
>
> Exodus 20:3–5, emphasis added

Then shall ye *call upon me*, and ye shall go and *pray unto me*, and *I* will hearken unto you.

Jeremiah 29:12, emphasis added

Hearken unto the voice of my cry, my King, and my *God*: for *unto Thee will I pray*. My voice shalt Thou hear in the morning, O Lord; in the morning will I *direct my prayer unto Thee*, and will look up.

Psalm 5:2–3, emphasis added

*Call unto Me, and I will answer thee*, and shew thee great and might things, which thou knowest not.

Jeremiah 33:3, emphasis added

And call upon *me* in the day of trouble: *I* will deliver thee, *and thou shalt glorify me*.

Psalm 50:15, emphasis added

Jesus prayed to God the Father and instructed his followers to do the same; and so did the apostles Paul, Peter, and John. Jesus's instructions and prayers to God the Father:

But thou, when thou prayest, enter into thy closet, and when thou hast shut thy door, *pray to thy Father* which is in secret; and thy Father which seeth in secret shall reward thee openly... After this manner therefore pray ye: *Our Father* which art in heaven, Hallowed be thy name.

Matthew 6:6, 9, emphasis added

And I say unto you, Ask, and it shall be given you; seek, and ye shall find; knock, and it shall be opened unto you. If ye then, being evil, know how to give good gifts unto your children: how much more shall *your heavenly Father give the Holy Spirit to them that ask Him?*

Luke 11:9, 13, emphasis added

How much more shall *your Father which is in heaven* give good things to them that ask Him?

Matthew 7:11, emphasis added

And shall not God avenge His own elect, which cry day and night *unto Him?*

Luke 18:7, emphasis added

At that day ye shall ASK IN MY NAME: and I say not unto you, that I will pray *the Father* for you: For the Father himself loveth you, because ye have loved me, and have believed that I came out from God.

John 16:26–27, emphasis added

Thinkest thou not that I can *pray to my Father* and He will give me more than twelve legions of angels?

Matthew 26:53, emphasis added

Jesus *prayed to the Father* and an angel appeared and strengthened Him.

Luke 22:41–43, emphasis added

And it came to pass in those days, that He went out into a mountain to pray, and continued all night in *prayer to God.*

Luke 6:12, emphasis added

And He went a little farther, and fell on His face, and *prayed*, saying, O *my Father*, if it be possible, let this cup pass from me: nevertheless not as I will, but as thou wilt.

Matthew 26:39, emphasis added

And in that day ye shall ask me nothing. Verily, verily, I say unto you, Whatsoever ye shall *ask the Father in my name*, He will give it you. Hitherto have ye ask nothing in my name: ask, and ye shall receive, that you joy may be full.

John 16:23–24, emphasis added

[Jesus], Who in the days of His flesh, when He had *offered up prayer* and *supplications* with strong crying and tears *unto Him* that was able to save Him from death and was heard in that He feared.

Hebrews 5:7, emphasis added

The apostles' instructions and prayers to God the Father:

I exhort therefore, that, first of all, *supplications, prayers, intercessions,* and *giving of thanks,* be made for all men; For kings, and for all that are in authority; that we may lead a quiet and peaceable life in all godliness and honesty. For this is good and acceptable in the sight of God our Saviour; Who will have all men to be saved, and to come unto the knowledge of the truth. For there is one God, and one mediator between God and men, the man Christ Jesus.

1 Timothy 2:1–5, emphasis added

Rejoice in the Lord always, be careful for nothing but in *everything by prayer* and supplication, with thanksgiving, let *your request* be made known *unto God.*

Philippians 4:1, emphasis added

For it is written, As I live, saith the Lord, every knee shall bow *to me,* and every tongue shall confess *to God.*

Romans 14:11, emphasis added

For this cause *I bow my knees unto the Father* of our Lord Jesus Christ.

Ephesians 3:14, emphasis added

Now I beseech you, brethren, *for the Lord Jesus Christ's sake,* and *for the love of the spirit,* that ye strive together with me in *your prayers to God for me.*

Romans 15:30, emphasis added

Brethren, my [Paul's] heart's desire and *prayer to God* for Israel is, that they might be saved.

Romans 10:1, emphasis added

To *the church of God,* to them that are sanctified in Christ, called to be saints, with *all* that in *every place call upon the name of Jesus Christ* our Lord.

1 Corinthians 1:2, emphasis added

For *the scripture saith* Whosoever believeth on Him shall not be ashamed. For there is no difference between the Jew and the Greek, for the same Lord over all is rich unto *all that call upon Him.* For *whosoever* shall *call upon the name of the Lord* shall be saved.

Romans 10:11–13, emphasis added

*God's ears* are open to *our prayers.*

1 Peter 3:12, emphasis added
cf. 2 Chronicles 16:9

Cornelius *prayed to God always*-an angel came to him.

Acts 10:2–4, 30–31, emphasis added

Unceasing *prayer made to God* for Peter, *by the church.* An angel came and helped Peter to escape prison ... *The Lord hath sent His angel.*

Acts 12:5–7, 11, emphasis added

# KEYS TO THE KINGDOM AND POWER OF GOD

Thy kingdom come. Thy will be done in earth, as it is in heaven … Deliver us from evil: For thine is the kingdom, and the power, and the glory, for ever. Amen.

Matthew 6:10, 13

Contrary to Roman Catholicism's interpretation of Matthew 16:18–19, the keys of the kingdom of heaven were not given exclusively to the Apostle Peter. The keys of the kingdom and power of God are faith in Jesus Christ, serving the Lord with a pure heart, and making requests to God Almighty *according to his will* and thereby experiencing the power, work, peace and joy of the Holy Spirit of Christ; which is available to every born again child of God.[1]

When Jesus said, "The kingdom of God cometh not with observation … The kingdom of God is within you" (Luke 17:20–21), he was referring to the Holy Spirit and power that indwells every born-again child of God. The Apostle Paul wrote about the "exceeding greatness of God's power to us-ward who believe" (Ephesians 1:19–20). He said, "Now unto him that is able to do exceeding abundantly above all that we ask or think, according to the power that worketh *in us, Unto him be glory* in

115

the church *by Christ Jesus* throughout all ages, world without end. Amen" (Ephesians 3:20–21, emphasis added).

Praying to anyone other than our Creator totally disregards what is written in the inspired Scriptures concerning prayer and the glory and praise that is to be given to God alone, by and through Jesus Christ. Jesus said that whatever we ask the Father in his name, he would do, "that the Father may be glorified in the Son" (John 14:13). Just prior to the passion, from John 14:13 to John 16:26, Jesus said six different times that we were to ask the Father in his name.[2] The repetitiveness of Jesus's directive to pray to the Father in his name should leave absolutely no doubt as to whom or in whose name we are to pray.

In another place, Jesus said, "Now is my soul troubled; and what shall I say? Father, save me from this hour: but for this cause came I unto this hour. Father, glorify thy name." Then a voice came from heaven, saying, "I have both glorified it, and will glorify it again."

Jesus told those who were standing by and had heard the voice: "This voice came not because of me, but for your sakes" (John 12:27–30). The voice came for their sakes that they might know that whatsoever they asked the Father in Jesus' name, according to the Father's will, Jesus would do that the Father may be glorified in the Son.

Jesus said: "Whatsoever ye shall ask in my name, that will I do, that the Father may be glorified in the Son. If ye shall ask any thing in my name, I will do it" (John 14:13–14). "He that abideth in me, and I in him, the same bringeth forth much fruit: for without me ye can do nothing (John 15:5). "If ye abide in me, and My words abide in you, ye shall ask what ye will and it shall be done unto you. Herein is my Father glorified, that ye bear much fruit, so shall ye be my disciples (John 15:7–8).

The far-reaching ramifications of praying to the Father in Jesus' name are virtually impossible to address herein without going off onto a trail of several correlative subjects in detail and thus losing the reader's attention to the subject at hand, which is the *keys* of the kingdom and power of God.

Nevertheless, since the subject of *fruit* is mentioned numerous times throughout the Holy Scriptures in relationship to the kingdom of God, it is noteworthy that the *much fruit* Jesus spoke of in John chapter 15 is the same fruit he was referring to when he told the Jewish chief priests and elders of the people: "The kingdom of God shall be taken from you, and given to a nation bringing forth the fruits thereof" (Matthew 21:43). The apostles Peter and Paul both made it unquestionably clear that the *nation* Jesus referred to in Matthew 21:43 is, in fact, the church of Jesus Christ.[3] Born-again children of God, translated into God's kingdom of marvelous light and "filled with the fruits of righteousness, which are by Jesus Christ, unto the glory and praise of God" (Philippians 1:11).

Jesus said: "He that doeth truth cometh to the light, that his deeds, may be made manifest, that they are wrought in God" (John 3:21). "I am the light of the world: he that followeth me shall not walk in darkness, but shall have the light of life" (John 8:12 ). "Let your light so shine before men, that they may see your good works, and glorify your Father which is in heaven. Think not that I [Jesus] am come to destroy the law, or the prophets: I am not come to destroy, but to fulfill" (Matthew 5:16–17).[4]

"We are his workmanship, created in Christ Jesus unto good works (*fruits*) which God hath before ordained that we should walk in them" (Ephesians 2:10). It is only by the exceeding greatness of the power of God working in us that we are enabled, through the indwelling Spirit of Jesus Christ, to do good works (cf. Ephesians 1:17–20). Without him, we can do nothing. If we ask anything in his name, according to the Father's will, he will do it. Anything!

And *I will put my spirit within you*, and cause you to *walk in my statutes*, and ye shall keep my judgments, and do them.

Ezekiel 36:27, emphasis added

For *it is God which worketh in you* both *to will and to do of his* good pleasure.

Philippians 2:13, emphasis added

Having your conversation honest among the Gentiles: that, whereas they speak against you as evildoers, they may *by your good works*, which they shall behold, *glorify God* in the day of visitation.

1 Peter 2:12, emphasis added

*To God only wise, be glory* through *Jesus Christ* for ever. Amen.

Romans 16:27, emphasis added

If any man speak, let him speak as the oracles of God; if any man minister, let him do it as of *the ability which God giveth*: that *God* in all things *may be glorified through Jesus Christ*, to whom be *praise* and dominion for ever and ever. Amen.

1 Peter 4:11, emphasis added

Now the *God* of peace, that brought again from the dead our Lord Jesus, that great shepherd of the sheep, *through the blood* of the *everlasting covenant, Make you perfect* in *every good work to do his will, working in you* that which is wellpleasing in his sight, *through Jesus Christ*; to whom be glory for ever and ever. Amen.

Hebrews 13:20–21, emphasis added

And call upon *me* in the day of trouble: *I* will deliver thee, and *thou shalt glorify me*. But unto the wicked God saith, What hast thou to do to declare my statutes, or that thou shouldest take *my covenant* in thy mouth? Seeing thou hatest instruction, and castest *my words* behind thee. When thou sawest a thief, then thou consentedst with him, and hast been partaker with adulterers. Thou givest thy mouth to evil, and thy *tongue frameth deceit* ... Now consider this, *ye that forget God*, lest I tear you in pieces, and there be none to deliver. *Whoso offereth praise glorifieth me*: and to him that ordereth his conversation aright will I shew the *salvation of God*.

Psalm 50:15–23, emphasis added

The perfect harmony of the written Word of God in its entirety is irrefutable and does not give way to that which is not truth; such as praying to the Virgin Mary and saints. Jesus repeatedly said that we were to pray to the Father in his name. He also repeatedly said that the *words* he spoke were not his words but the Father's[5] (John 12:44, 49, 50; John 14:10, 24; John 3:34—cf. Deuteronomy 18:18; Acts 3:22; John 17:8, 17). Unless one is totally steeped in tradition, it is incomprehensible that the harmony and authority of the Scriptures could be held in disregard. One of many examples of the perfect harmony of God's Word is seen in John chapter 14 and Psalm 91:14–16.

In John chapter 14, Jesus talked about him and the Father making their abode with the person who *loves him*, who *keeps his words* and who prays to the Father in *his name*. Psalm 91:14–16 is talking about the same things and the phraseology is virtually the same.[6]

And whatsoever ye shall *ask in my name, that will I do*, that the Father may be glorified in the Son ... *If a man love me*, he will keep my words: and my Father will love him, and we will come unto him, and *make our abode with him*. He that loveth me not keepeth not my sayings: and the word which ye hear is not mine, but the Father's which sent me.

John 14:13, 23–24, emphasis added

Because *he hath set his love upon me*, therefore will *I* deliver him: *I will set him on high* because he hath known *my name*. He shall *call upon me*, and *I will answer him*: I will be with him in trouble; *I* will deliver him and *honour him*. With long life will I satisfy him, and shew him my *salvation*.

Psalm 91:14–16, emphasis added

In the above, notice the phrase, *I will set him on high*. Everyone who believes in Jesus Christ's all-sufficient sacrificial blood as full payment for their sins and who receives him as their one and only God and Saviour is indwelt by the Holy Spirit of eternal life and is *presently seated on high*, seated in heavenly places in Christ at the right hand of God the Father (Ephesians 2:6).[7] This is what Jesus was talking about when he said, "If any man serve me, let him follow me; and where I am, there shall also my servant be: if any man serve me, him will my Father honour" (John 12:26). "If I go and prepare a place for you, I will come again, and receive you unto myself; that where I am, there ye may be also" (John 14:3). "Father, I will that they also, whom thou hast given me, be with me where I am; that they may behold my glory" (John 17:24, cf. 2 Corinthians 3:18).

Blessed be the God and Father of our Lord Jesus Christ, who hath blessed us with all spiritual blessings *in heavenly places in Christ*... And what is the exceeding greatness of *his power to us-ward who believe*, according to the working of his mighty power, Which he wrought in Christ, when he raised him from the dead, and *set him at his own right hand in the heavenly places*.

Ephesians 1:3, 19–20, emphasis added

But *God*, who is rich in mercy, for his great love wherewith he loved us, Even when we were dead in sins, hath quickened us together with Christ, (by grace ye are saved;)

And *hath raised us up together, and made us sit together in heavenly places in Christ Jesus.*

Ephesians 2:4–6, emphasis added

Thou wilt shew me the path of life: *in thy presence is fulness of joy; at thy right hand* there are pleasures for evermore.

Psalm 16:11, emphasis added

But *let all those that put their trust in thee rejoice*: let them ever shout for *joy*, because thou defendest them: let them also that *love thy name be joyful* in thee.

Psalm 5:11, emphasis added

...The king shall *joy* in thy *strength*, O LORD; and in thy salvation how greatly shall he rejoice! Thou hast given him his heart's desire, and hast not withholden *the request of his lips.* Selah.

Psalm 21:1–2, emphasis added

The Apostle Paul said, "For the kingdom of God is not meat and drink; but righteousness, and peace, and joy in the Holy Ghost" (Romans 14:17). "Now the God of hope fill you with all joy and peace in believing, that ye may abound in hope, through the power of the Holy Ghost" (Romans 15:13). "For the kingdom of God is not in word, but in power" (1 Corinthians 4:20).

Jesus was talking about the kingdom of God when he said, "These things have I spoken unto you, that my joy might remain in you, and that your joy might be full" (John 15:11), and "Hitherto have ye asked nothing in my name: ask, and ye shall receive, that your joy may be full" (John 16:24). He was talking about *faith*, about praying to the Father in his name. He was talking about the *keys of the kingdom of heaven,* which, according to Roman Catholicism, were given exclusively to the Apostle Peter. However, these same keys are, in fact, available to every born-again child of God who, according to the Word of God, has already been *translated into* the kingdom of Jesus

Christ (Colossians1:9–13 [with Acts 26:18 and 1 Peter 2:9]; Revelation 1:6 & 9, 5:10, and 12:10).[8]

> For this cause we also, since the day we heard it, do not cease to pray for you, and to desire that ye might be filled with the knowledge of his will in all wisdom and spiritual understanding; That ye might walk worthy of the Lord unto all pleasing, being *fruitful* in every *good work*, and increasing in the knowledge of God; *Strengthened* with all might, according to *his* glorious *power*, unto all *patience* and *longsuffering* with *joyfulness*; Giving thanks unto the Father, which *hath* made us meet to be partakers of the inheritance of the saints in light: Who hath delivered us from the power of darkness, and hath translated us *into the kingdom of his dear Son.*
>
> Colossians 1:9–13, emphasis added

> I John, who also am your brother, and companion in *tribulation*, and *in* the *kingdom* and *patience* of Jesus Christ, was in the isle that is called Patmos, for the word of God, and for the testimony of Jesus Christ.
>
> Revelation 1:9, emphasis added

> And I heard a loud voice saying in heaven, *Now is come* salvation, and *strength*, and *the kingdom of our God*, and *the power of his Christ*: for the accuser of our brethren is cast down, which accused them before our God day and night. And *they overcame him by the blood of the Lamb*, and by *the word of their testimony*; and *they loved not their lives unto the death.*
>
> Revelation 12:10–11, emphasis added

Paul's epistle to the Ephesians is in view of the kingdom and power of God. He talked about *the hope of God's calling*, the riches of the glory of *his inheritance in the saints*, and the exceeding greatness of *God's power* towards us who *believe*. He talked about Christ's resurrection from the dead and the exceeding riches of his grace in his kindness toward us "in the ages to come ... through Christ Jesus for by grace are ye saved through faith" (Ephesians 1:16–20; 2:7–8). He expounded on the power of God again in Ephesians 3:20–21, saying, "Now unto him that is able to do exceeding abundantly above all that we ask or think, according to the power that worketh in us, *Unto him be glory* in the church *by* Christ Jesus *throughout all ages*, world without end. Amen."

The word *ages*, in the above, is indicative of perpetuity; the here and now, in this world and throughout eternity. God's power and kindness toward us who believe is definitely salvation that can be experienced on a daily basis. Faith in Jesus Christ is not only the key to eternal salvation and life in the hereafter, but also the key to the salvation, power, peace, and joy of the kingdom of God in this life, in this world, in the here and now.

Jesus talked about the *daily* salvation available to us in the kingdom of God, saying:

> If any man will come after me, let him deny himself, and take up his cross *daily*, and follow me ... Whosoever will lose his life for my sake, the same shall save it ... Whosoever shall be ashamed of me and of my words, of him shall the son of man be ashamed, when he shall come in his own glory, and in his Father's and of the holy angels. But I tell you of a truth, *there be some standing here*, which *shall not taste of death*, till they *see* the kingdom of God.
>
> Luke 9:23–27, emphasis added

> For the Son of man shall come in the glory of his Father with his angels; and then he shall reward every man according to his works. Verily I say unto you, There be *some standing here*, which *shall not taste of death*, till they *see* the Son of man coming in his kingdom.
>
> Matthew 16:27–28, emphasis added

Jesus was not referring to his coming from heaven with his mighty angels in flaming fire to judge at the end of the world (2 Thessalonians. 1:7–10), but to his coming in his kingdom with his angels, his coming to indwell all who believe in him. As he said in John 14, "…I go to prepare a place for you…I will come again, and receive you unto myself; that where I am, there ye may be also…I will come to you…At that day ye shall know that I am in my Father, and ye in me, and I in you" (John 14:2–3, 18–20). The Bible has much to say about the part angels play in our *daily* salvation (Acts 12:5–11; Acts 10:2–4, 30–31; Revelation. 3:5, 6 w/- 1 John 5:1–5).

> But to which of the angels said he at any time, Sit on my right hand, until I make thine enemies thy footstool? Are they not all ministering spirits, sent forth to minister for them who shall be heirs of salvation…How shall we escape, if we neglect so great salvation; which at the first began to be spoken by the Lord, and was confirmed unto us by them that heard him.
>
> Hebrews 1:13–14; 13–2:3

> But ye are come unto mount Sion, and unto the city of the living God, the heavenly Jerusalem, and to an innumerable company of angels, To the general assembly and church of the firstborn…
>
> Hebrews 12:22–23

> Take heed that ye despise not one of these little ones; for I say unto you, That in heaven their angels do always behold the face of my Father which is in heaven.
>
> Matthew 18:10 10

> Bless the Lord, ye His angels, that excel in strength, that do His commandments, hearkening unto the voice of His word…Bless ye the Lord, all ye His host; ye ministers of His, that do His pleasure.
>
> Psalm 103:20, 21

The Apostle Paul was very much aware of the angels' participation in our daily salvation. He knew that angels hearken unto the voice of God's Word. He wrote:

> I suffer trouble, as an evil doer, even unto bonds; but the word of God is not bound. Therefore I endure all things for the elect's sakes, that they may also obtain the salvation which is in Christ Jesus with eternal glory.
>
> 2 Timothy 2:9–10

The Apostle Peter also alluded to the angels participation in our daily salvation when he wrote:

> Of which salvation the prophets have enquired and searched diligently, who prophesied of the grace that should come unto you...the sufferings of Christ, and the glory that should follow. Unto whom it was revealed, that not unto themselves, but unto us they did minister the things, which are now reported unto you by them that have preached the gospel unto you with the Holy Ghost sent down from heaven; which things the angels desire to look into.
>
> 1 Peter 1:10–12

Angels desiring to look into things connotes action.

LOOK- #3879 parakupto {par-ak-oop'-to} from 3844 and 2955;AV - stoop down 3, look 2; 5
    1) to stoop to a thing in order to look at it; 2) to look at with head bowed forward; 3) to look into with the body bent; 4) to stoop and look into; 5) metaph. to look carefully into, inspect curiously; 5a) of one who would become acquainted with something

INTO- #1519 eis {ice} a primary preposition;
   AV - into 573, to 281, unto 207, for 140, in 138, on 58,
   toward 29, against 26, misc 321; 1773
   1) into, unto, to, towards, for, among
   Abingdon's Strong's Concordance, #3879 & 1519

The Apostles Peter and Paul were both talking about the same things; faith in the Word of God, the *sufferings of Christ*, and the angels' participation in the *daily* salvation and/or deliverance available to every born again child of God in the kingdom of God, *according to the will of God*. The Apostle Peter said:

> If the righteous scarcely be *saved*, where shall the ungodly and the sinner appear? Wherefore let them that *suffer according to the will of God* commit the keeping of their souls *to him* in well doing, as unto a faithful Creator.
> 1 Peter 4:18–19, emphasis added

God's power and kindness toward us who believe is definitely salvation that can be experienced on a *daily* basis. However, experiencing the peace, joy, and power of the kingdom of God is contingent on the degree of one's faith, patience, and willingness to suffer for Christ's sake.

As James, the brother of our Lord Jesus Christ, said:

> My brethren, count it all *joy* when ye fall into divers temptations; Knowing this, that the trying of your *faith* worketh *patience*. But let patience have her perfect work, that ye may be perfect and entire, *wanting nothing ...* But let him *ask in faith*, nothing wavering. For he that wavereth is like a wave of the sea driven with the wind and tossed. For let not that man think that he shall *receive any thing of the Lord*. A double minded man is unstable in all his ways. *Let the brother of low degree rejoice* in that he is exalted.
> James 1:2–4, 6–9, emphasis added

The brother of low degree is precisely what Jesus was talking about in Luke 9:23–24; denying self and taking up our cross daily. Jesus said, "whosoever will lose his life for my sake, the same shall save it."

The Apostle Paul said, "It is given in the behalf of Christ, not only to believe on him, but also to suffer for his sake" (Philippians 1:29). "Therefore I endure all things for the elect's sakes, that they may also obtain the salvation which is in Christ Jesus with eternal glory" (2 Timothy 2:10). Paul was not talking about the salvation of eternal life but about daily salvation; because the *elect* he referred to had already obtained eternal life through faith in Jesus Christ. Nor was his mention of *eternal glory* referring to eternal life, but to a reward of eternal glory the child of God receives *each time* he or she endures suffering through patience and faith in Christ's promise, power and ability to either sustain or deliver him/her from an adverse circumstances or suffering. Thus, suffering*s* (plural), *weight* of glory, and a *full reward*.

> For our *light affliction*, which is but for a moment, worketh for us a far more exceeding and eternal *weight* of glory; While we look not at the things which are seen, but at the things which are not seen: for the things which are seen are temporal; but the things which are not seen are eternal.
>
> 2 Corinthians 4:17–18, emphasis added

> And if children, then heirs; heirs of God, and *joint-heirs with Christ*; if so be that we *suffer with him*, that we may be also glorified together. For I reckon that the sufferings of this present time are not worthy to be compared with the *glory* which shall be revealed in us.
>
> Romans 8:17–18, emphasis added

> Look to yourselves, that we lose not those things which we have wrought, but that we receive a *full reward*.
>
> 2 John 1:8

In Luke 9:23–27, Jesus talked about our dying to self, taking up a cross daily and *losing our life* for his sake in order to save it. The Apostle Paul was talking about the same thing, when he said, "It is a faithful saying: For *if we be dead with him*, we shall also live with him: If we suffer, we shall also reign with him: if we deny him, he also will deny us: If we believe not, yet he abideth faithful: he cannot deny himself" (2 Timothy 2:11–13). Different degrees of suffering require different levels of faith and not everyone has the same measure of faith. What Paul was saying, in essence, was that if we deny Christ by not trusting him to sustain or deliver us from a particular circumstance or suffering, Christ will deny us that deliverance and we will not receive a full reward (2 John 8). Jesus said, " … Whosoever shall confess me before men, him shall the Son of man also confess before the angels of God: But he that denieth me before men shall be denied before the angels of God" (Luke12:8–9 ).

Nevertheless, even if we were to deny Christ's ability to deliver us from an adverse circumstance, "yet He abideth faithful, He cannot deny Himself" (2 Timothy 2:13). He cannot deny himself because we are one with him (1 Corinthians 6:17; Hebrews 2:11; Ephesians 5:30–32; Matthew 19:5–6; Hosea 2:19–20). [9]

Through lack of faith in Christ's promise, power, and ability to deliver us from a particular circumstances or suffering, we forfeit that deliverance and lose one of our rewards of *eternal glory*. However, according to the Word of God and contrary to Catholicism, we can never lose our eternal salvation and/or eternal life. [10]

When the Apostle Paul said, "For if we be dead with him, we shall also live with him: If we suffer, we shall also reign with him," he was talking about the crucified life in Christ.

> I am crucified with Christ: nevertheless I live; yet not I, but Christ liveth in me: and the life which I now live in the flesh I live by the faith of the Son of God, who loved me, and gave himself for me.
> Galatians 2:20, emphasis added

Now if we be dead with Christ, we believe that we shall also live with him.

Romans 6:8, emphasis added

And I heard a voice from heaven saying unto me, Write, Blessed are the dead which die in the Lord from henceforth: Yea, saith the Spirit, that they may rest from their labours; and their works do follow them.

Revelation 14:13, emphasis added

Precious in the sight of the Lord is the *death of his saints*.

Psalm 116:15, emphasis added

This spake he (Jesus), signifying *by what death* he [Peter] should *glorify God*. And when he had spoken this, he saith unto him, *Follow me*.

John 21:19, emphasis added

I beseech you therefore, brethren, by the mercies of God, that ye present your bodies *a living sacrifice*, holy, *acceptable unto God*, which is your reasonable *service*. And be not conformed to this world: but be ye transformed by the renewing of your mind, that ye may prove what is that good, and acceptable, and *perfect, will of God*.

Romans 12:1–2, emphasis added

The Apostle Peter wrote about the "acceptable, and perfect will of God." He made it very clear that to present our bodies living sacrifices is to follow Jesus Christ's example of love and of suffering. He said:

For this is thankworthy, if a man for conscience toward God endure grief, suffering wrongfully. For what glory is it, if, when ye be buffeted for your faults, ye shall take it patiently? but if, when ye do well, and suffer for it, ye take it patiently, this is *acceptable with God*. For even hereunto were ye called: because Christ also suffered for us, leaving us an example, that ye should follow his steps: Who did no sin, neither was guile found in his mouth: Who, when he was reviled, reviled not again; when he suffered, he threatened not; but committed himself to him that judgeth righteously.

1 Peter 2:19–23, emphasis added

To resist the temptation to retaliate with unkind words, or by any other means, is not only *suffering*, but it is also impossible to do, unless we follow Jesus's example and commit ourselves to God. James, the brother of our Lord, said: "If any man offend not in word, the same is a perfect man, and able also to bridle the whole body...But the tongue can no man tame" (James 3:2, 8).

It is only by the mercies and grace of God that we are enabled, through the power of the Holy Spirit, to present our bodies a living sacrifice. Therefore, it is absolutely essential to come boldly to God's throne of grace, that we may obtain mercy and find grace to help in time of need. We then must patiently wait for the *hope* of righteousness: to be filled with *the fruit* of righteousness which is by faith of Jesus Christ. Jesus said, "He that abideth in me, and I in him, the same bringeth forth much fruit: for without me ye can do nothing."[11]

Man's inability to bridle his tongue was established many years ago by King David.

A Psalm of David. I said, *I* will take heed to my ways, *that I sin not with my tongue: I will keep my mouth with a bridle,* while the wicked is before me. *I was dumb* with silence, *I held my peace,* even from good; and *my sorrow was stirred. My heart was hot within me,* while I was musing the fire burned: *then spake I with my tongue,* Lord, make me to know mine end, and the measure of my days, what it is; that I may know how frail I am. Behold, thou hast made my days as an handbreadth; and mine age is as nothing before thee: verily every man at his best state is altogether vanity. Selah. Surely every man walketh in a vain shew: surely they are disquieted in vain: he heapeth up riches, and knoweth not who shall gather them. And *now*, Lord, *what wait I for? my hope is in thee.* Deliver me from all my transgressions: make me not the reproach of the foolish. *I was dumb*, I opened not my mouth; *because thou didst it.*

Psalm 39:1–9, emphasis added

The Apostle Peter talked about this same hope in his dissertation on the crucified life in Christ (1 Peter 2:19–3:17). He said that we were called to *follow Christ's example* of suffering wrongfully, to *refrain our tongue from evil* and to commit ourselves to God who judges righteously (1 Peter 2:23). He said, "Ye are *thereunto called,* that ye should *inherit a blessing*...be ready always to give an answer to every man a reason of the *hope* that is *in you*" (1 Peter 3:9, 15).

> Finally, be ye all of one mind, having compassion one of another, *love* as brethren, be pitiful, be courteous: Not rendering evil for evil, or railing for railing: but contrariwise blessing; knowing that *ye are thereunto called* that ye should *inherit a blessing.* For he that will love life, and *see good days*, let him *refrain his tongue from evil*...seeks peace, and ensue it. For the eyes of the Lord are over the righteous, and *his ears are open unto their prayers*: but the face of the Lord is against them that do evil. And who is he that will harm you, if ye be followers of that which is good? But and if ye *suffer for righteousness' sake*, happy are ye: and be not afraid of their terror, neither be troubled; But sanctify the Lord God in your hearts: and be ready always to give an answer to every man that asketh you a reason of the hope that is in you ... For it is better, if *the will of God* be so, *that ye suffer for well doing*, than for evil doing.

1 Peter 3:8–17, emphasis added

The Apostle Paul talked about the same hope, the same calling and the same inheritance saying:

The eyes of your understanding being enlightened; that ye may know what is the *hope of his calling*, and what the riches of *the glory* of his *inheritance* in the saints.

Ephesians 1:17–18, emphasis added

For whatsoever things were written aforetime were written for our learning, that we through patience and comfort of the scriptures might have *hope* ... Now the God of *hope* fill you with all *joy and peace in believing*, that ye may *abound in hope, through the power of the Holy Ghost.*

Romans 15:4, 13, emphasis added

It couldn't be more obvious that the Apostles Peter and Paul were both talking about the same *hope* of *daily* salvation that is available to every born-again child of God by living a crucified life in Christ. That is, by *following Jesus Christ's* example of love and suffering. Denying self and suffering wrongfully.

Love is the essence of the kingdom of God. Love never fails (1 Corinthians 13:8). Love is the master key that unlocks the power, peace, and joy of the kingdom of God in heaven and on earth. We are to follow peace with all men and holiness, without which no man shall *"see"* the Lord (Hebrews 12:14). Emphasis added.

Verily I say unto you, There be *some standing here*, which shall not taste of death, till they *see the Son of man coming in* his kingdom.

Matthew16:28 28, emphasis added

Jesus said he would *manifest himself to the person* who keeps his commandment (John 14:21). He said: *"This is my commandment, That ye love one another*, as I have loved you. Greater love hath no man than this, that a man lay down his life for his friends" (John 15:12–13), emphasis added. Love, suffering, and answered prayer go hand in hand. [12]

*Suffering According to the will of God*

The Apostle John said, "Whatsoever we ask, we receive of him because we keep his commandments and do those things that are pleasing in his sight" (1 John 3:22). To keep his commandments and do those things that are pleasing in his sight is to love one another and *suffer according to the will of God* for the sake of Christ and righteousness. This, I believe, is what Jesus meant when he said, "If any man will do his will, he shall know of the doctrine, whether it be of God, or whether I speak of myself"(John 7:17).

> This is the confidence that we have in him, that, if we ask any thing *according to his will*, he heareth us: And if we know that he hear us, whatsoever we ask, we know that we have the petitions that we desired of him.
>
> 1 John 5:14–15, emphasis added

> Who gave himself for our sins, that he might *deliver us from* this present evil world, *according to the will of God* and our Father.
>
> Galatians 1:4, emphasis added

> Wherefore let them that *suffer according to the will of God* commit the keeping of their souls *to him* in well doing, as unto a faithful Creator.
>
> 1 Peter 4:19, emphasis added

> For ye have need of patience, that, *after ye have done the will of God*, ye might *receive the promise*.
>
> Hebrews 10:36, emphasis added

> And not only so, but *we glory in tribulations* also: knowing that *tribulation* worketh *patience*; And patience, experience; and experience, *hope*: And hope maketh not ashamed; because the *love* of *God* is shed abroad *in our hearts* by *the Holy Ghost* which is given unto us.
>
> Romans 5:3–5, emphasis added

Remembering without ceasing your *work of faith*, and labour of *love*, and *patience* of *hope in* our Lord *Jesus Christ*, in the sight of God and our Father.

1 Thessalonians 1:3, emphasis added

My brethren, count it all *joy* when ye fall into divers *temptations*; Knowing this, that the *trying of your faith* worketh *patience*. But let *patience* have her perfect work, that ye may be perfect and entire, *wanting nothing*... But let him *ask in faith*, nothing wavering. For he that wavereth is like a wave of the sea driven with the wind and tossed. For let not that man think that he shall *receive* any thing *of the Lord*.

James 1:2–4, 6–7, emphasis added

Knowing that whatsoever good thing any man doeth, the same *shall he receive of the Lord*, whether he be bond or free.

Ephesians 6:8, emphasis added

And whatsoever ye do, do it heartily, as to the Lord, and not unto men; Knowing that *of the Lord* ye shall *receive the reward of the inheritance*: for ye *serve the Lord*.

Colossians 3:23–24, emphasis added

If any man *serve* me, him will *my* Father honour.

John 12:26, emphasis added

Wherefore also we pray always for you, that our God would count you worthy of *this calling*, and fulfil all the good pleasure of *his* goodness, and the work of faith with power.

2 Thessalonians 1:11, emphasis added

Your faith groweth exceedingly, and the *charity* of every one of you all *toward each other aboundeth*; So that we ourselves glory in you in the churches of God for your *patience* and *faith* in all your *persecutions* and *tribulations* that ye *endure*:

Which is a manifest token of the righteous judgment of God, that ye may be counted worthy of *the kingdom of God*, for which ye also *suffer*: Seeing it is a righteous thing with God to *recompense tribulation to them that trouble you.*

2 Thessalonians 1:3–6, emphasis added

Let *love* be without dissimulation. Abhor that which is evil; cleave to that which is good. Be kindly affectioned one to another with *brotherly love*; in honour preferring one another; Not slothful in business; fervent in spirit; *serving the Lord*; *Rejoicing in hope; patient in tribulation*; continuing instant *in prayer* ... *Bless them which persecute you: bless, and curse not* ... *Recompense to no man evil for evil* ... If it be possible, as much as lieth in you, live peaceably with all men. Dearly beloved, *avenge not yourselves*, but rather give place unto wrath: for *it is written*, Vengeance is mine; *I will repay*, saith the Lord. Therefore if thine enemy hunger, feed him; if he thirst, give him drink: for in so doing thou shalt heap *coals of fire on his head.* Be not overcome of evil, but *overcome evil with good.*

Romans 12:9–21, emphasis added

If thine enemy be hungry, give him bread to eat; and if he be thirsty, give him water to drink: For thou shalt heap *coals of fire upon his head*, and the Lord shall *reward* thee.

Proverbs 25:21–22, emphasis added

And of the angels he saith, Who maketh his angels spirits, and his ministers a *flame of fire* ... Are they not all ministering spirits, sent forth to minister for them who shall be heirs of salvation?

Hebrews1:7, 14, emphasis added

Jesus said: "This gospel of the kingdom shall be preached in all the world for a witness unto all nations; and then shall the end come" (Matthew 24:14).[13] The fullness and consummation of the kingdom of God will not be experienced until the Lord descends from heaven with a shout on the last day; at which time the dead in Christ shall rise with eternal glorified bodies, and the bodies of those who are alive and *in* Christ will likewise be changed[14] (1 Thessalonians 4:16–17; 1 Corinthians15:51–52; Job 14:14–15; Philippians 3:20–21; Matthew 13:43; Daniel 12:2–3).

Meanwhile, the peace, joy and power of the kingdom of God is available to every born again child of God in the here and now. Jesus said, "Except a man be born again, he cannot see the kingdom of God" (John 3:3, 8).

> Sing unto the Lord, all the earth; *shew forth from day to day his salvation.* Declare *his glory* among the heathen; *his marvellous* works among all nations. For *great is the Lord,* and *greatly to be praised*: he also is to be feared above all gods. For all the gods of the people are idols: but the Lord made the heavens. *Glory* and *honour* are *in his presence*; strength and gladness are in his place. *Give unto the Lord,* ye kindreds of the people, *give unto the Lord glory and strength. Give unto the lord the glory due unto his name*: bring an offering, and come before him: worship the Lord in the beauty of holiness.
>
> 1 Chronicles 16:23–29, emphasis added

# PETER, THE ROCK

552 Simon Peter holds the first place in the college of the
Twelve; Jesus entrusted a unique mission to him. Through
a revelation from the Father, Peter had confessed: "You
are the Christ, the Son of the living God." Our Lord then
declared to him: "You are Peter, and on this rock I will build
my Church, and the gates of Hades will not prevail against
it." Christ, the "living stone," thus assures his Church,
built on Peter, of victory over the powers of death. Because
of the faith he confessed Peter will remain the unshakable
rock of the Church. His mission will be to keep this faith
from every lapse and to strengthen his brothers in it.

*Catechism of the Catholic Church*, p. 141

The Evangelical interpretation of Matthew 16:18 is that the
rock upon which Christ is building his church is the rock of
*faith*. One of the arguments presented in support of this view
is that when Jesus said, "Thou are Peter and upon this rock I
will build my church," he used two different words for *Peter*
and *rock*. The word he used for Peter is *Petros*, which is found
in ninety-four verses of Scripture. The word he used for rock
is *petra*, which is found in only fourteen verses of Scripture,
and not one time is the word *petra* used with reference to the
Apostle Peter.

On page seventy-six of *Born Fundamentalist*, in rebuttal of the Evangelical interpretation, Roman Catholic author David B. Currie says,

> The insurmountable problem with the Evangelical analysis of the Greek text is that in Aramaic, the language of Jesus, there was only one word for rock (kepha). The Greek text is itself a translation of the original Aramaic. There was no possibility of the original hearers being confused about Jesus' meaning. The disciples had to have heard Jesus saying, in Aramaic, 'I tell you that you are Rock (Kepha), and on this Rock (Kepha) I will build my church.' There is not the slightest room for any other meaning in the words Jesus originally uttered! The church would be built on Peter as rock, as distinguished from the other apostles there that day with him. The Aramaic word for rock, transliterated into English, can be written Cephas. That this name for Peter is used elsewhere in Scripture lends further support for the Catholic understanding of this passage. See John 1:42; 1 Corinthians 1:12; 3:22; 4:5; 15:5; Galatians 2:9–14

Neither of the foregoing arguments are strong enough to prove their particular interpretation as fact. The scriptures presented in the following pages speak for themselves as to which is the correct interpretation. According to the Roman Catholic understanding, Peter is the rock upon which Christ is building his church because Peter's was the first profession of faith (#442, pp. 111–112). According to the chronological order of the gospel's events, Peter's profession in Matthew 16:16 was not the first profession of faith that Jesus is the Christ, the Son of the living God. Compare the chronological order of the disciples' professions of faith.

27 AD (February)
    *Andrew*-John 1:41–42

*Philip*-John 1:45
*Nathanael*-John 1:49
*Disciples* -John 2:11

29 AD (April)
*Peter* -"We believe and are sure thou art the Son of
God" -John 6:69
(Summer)
*Disciples*-"Of a truth thou art the Son of God"-
Matthew 14:33

*Peter*-"Thou art the Christ, the Son of the living God"-
Matthew 16:16

In AD 27, two years prior to Peter's profession of faith, Andrew,
after having met Jesus, went to find Peter to tell him, "We
have found the Messiah, which is, being interpreted, the
Christ"(John 1:41). The following day, Philip found Nathanael
and said, "We have found him, of whom Moses in the law, and
the prophets, did write" (John 1:45). When Jesus told Nathanael
that he saw him under the fig tree, even before Philip called
him, Nathanael said, "Thou art the Son of God; thou art the
King of Israel" (John 1:43–49). Shortly thereafter, Jesus performed his first miracle at the wedding in Cana; at which time
"His disciples believed on Him" (John 2:1–11).

It is true that in the Old Testament, the title *Son of God* is
given to angels, the chosen people, the children of Israel, and
their kings. However, italicized statements in the following
quotation from the *Catechism of the Catholic Church* (#441, p.
111) undermine the plainly stated facts of the Word of God.

In the Old Testament, "son of God" is a title given to the
angels, the Chosen People, the children of Israel, and their
kings. It signifies an adoptive sonship that establishes a
relationship of particular intimacy between God and his

creature. When the promised Messiah-King is called "son of God," it does not necessarily imply that he was more than human, according to the literal meaning of these texts. Those who called Jesus "son of God," as the Messiah of Israel, *perhaps* meant nothing more than this. *Such is not the case for Simon Peter when he confesses Jesus as "the Christ, the Son of the living God," for Jesus responds solemnly:* "Flesh and blood has not revealed this to you, but my Father who is in heaven."

The above italicized hypothetical statements are not based on the truth of the scriptures, but on conjecture. The scriptures clearly show that God the Father had previously revealed Jesus's identity to all of the twelve disciples and not just to Peter. The assumption that Peter's profession of faith was the first genuine profession because Jesus responds solemnly with, "Flesh and blood has not revealed this to you, but my Father who is in heaven," nullifies the authenticity of the professions of faith that were previously made by the other apostles. Since only God knows the intentions of the heart, and unless it is plainly stated in God's Word, it is presumptuous to state as fact whether an individual's profession of faith is genuine (cf. Acts 1:24; Acts 15:7–9; Hebrews 4:12–13; Luke 16:15; Romans 8:27; Revelation 2:23).

It would be more reasonable to speculate or presume that the Father had previously revealed Jesus's true identity to Andrew, and that Andrew's was the first genuine profession of faith. It was immediately after having spent part of a day and the entire night with Jesus that Andrew went directly to find Peter and tell him, "We have found the Messiah" (John 1:39–42).

And what about John the Baptist, to whom it was revealed by God the Father, in AD 27 that Jesus was the Christ, *the Son of God* (John 1:25–33, 34)?

And what about the Samaritans, in AD 27 John 4:7, 25–26, 29, 39–41, 42), or Simeon in 4 BC (Luke 2:25–34) and others? If Jesus's *solemn response* is the prerequisite for determining a genuine profession of faith, then all of the above are also disqualified.

Jesus wasn't giving the Apostle Peter supreme authority and rule over his church in Matthew chapter 16; he was speaking a parable, as he most often did.[1] The rock upon which Jesus Christ is building his church is the rock of *faith*; faith in his all-sufficient sacrifice as full payment for our sins.

It is also by faith that:

*We are saved* (Ephesians 2:8; 2 Timothy 3:15; 2 Thessalonians 2:13; Luke 18:42; Luke 7:50).
We receive remission of sins (Romans 3:23–25; Acts 10:43; Acts 13:38, 39; Acts 26:18; Colossians 1:14; Mark 2:5; Revelation 1:5).

*We inherit eternal life* (John 3:15–16,36; John 5:24; 1 John 5:13; John 6:40, 47, 68, 69; 1 Timothy 1:16; John 11:25–26; Acts 13:46–48; John 20:31; etc.).

*We become the children of God* (Galatians 3:26; John 1:12–13; 1 John 5:1).

*We receive the Holy Spirit* (John 7:38–39; Galatians 3:2, 14; Ephesians 1:13; Acts 11:15–18).

*We are justified* (Acts 13:38–39; Galatians 2:16; Galatians 3:8, 24; Romans 3:28; Romans 5:1).

*We are sanctified* (Acts 26:18; Hebrews 10:10, 29; Hebrews 13:12; John 17:17; 2 Thessalonians 2:13–14; Ephesians 5:26; 1 Corinthians 1:2,30).

*We receive the gift of righteousness* (Philippians 3:9; Psalms 24:3–5; Romans 5:17; Romans 3:22; Romans 4:3,5; Romans 4:11, 21–25; Romans 9:30; Romans 10:2–4;

Romans 10:6, 10; Jeremiah 33:14–16; Jeremiah 51:10; Isaiah 54:17; Isaiah 45:22–25; 1 Corinthians 1:29–31).

*We receive the promises of God* (Hebrews 6:12; Galatians 3:2, 14, 22; Hebrews 11:33; James 2:5).

*We have access into grace* (Romans 5:2; Hebrews 4:14–16; Hebrews 10:19–23; Ephesians 3:12).

*We inherit the kingdom of God* (James 2:5; 2 Thessalonians 1:4–5; Acts 14:22).

*We are kept by the power of God* (1 Peter 1:5).

*We resist the devil and quench all the fiery darts of the wicked* (1 Peter 5: 8–9; Ephesians 6:11–12,16).

*We stand* (2 Corinthians 1:24; 1 Corinthians15:1–4; 1 Thessalonians 3:7–8; Romans 5:2).
God purifies our hearts (Acts 15:9).

If Peter is, *in fact*, the rock upon which Jesus said he was going to build his church, and if he is, *in fact*, "the only one to whom Christ specifically entrusted keys to the kingdom" (Catechism, p. 142), and there was "no possibility of the original hearers being confused about Jesus's meaning," as stated in *Born Fundamentalist* (p. 76), then why, after having heard these facts, did the disciples continue to ask Jesus, "Who is the greatest?" And why didn't Jesus answer them by saying, "Peter is the greatest"?

Compare his answer to this question in Matthew 18:1–4 with his reply to Peter's rebuke in Matthew 16:23–26. In both passages, the prerequisite for being *the greatest* in the kingdom of heaven is *self denial* and *humility*. Peter, humble?

At the same time came the disciples unto Jesus, saying, *Who is the greatest in the kingdom of heaven?* And Jesus called a little child unto him, and set him in the midst of them, And said, Verily I say unto you, Except ye be converted, and become as little children, ye shall not enter into the kingdom of heaven. Whosoever therefore shall *humble himself* as this little child, *the same is greatest in the kingdom of heaven.*

Matthew 18:1–4, emphasis added

But he turned, and said unto Peter, *Get thee behind me, Satan*: thou art an offence unto me: for *thou savourest not the things that be of God, but those that be of men.* Then said Jesus unto his disciples, If any man will come after me, *let him deny himself*, and take up his cross, and follow me. For whosoever will save his life shall lose it: and whosoever will lose his life for my sake shall find it. For what is a man profited, if he shall gain the whole world, and lose his own soul? or what shall a man give in exchange for his soul?

Matthew 16:23–26, emphasis added

Compare the following chronological order of events. In all three gospels, it was after Jesus said he was going to build his church on this *petra* that the disciples asked, "Who is the greatest?"

Matthew:
*29 a.d.* (Summer)
> Peter-*"Thou art the Christ, the Son of the living God"*-*Matthew 16:16*
> *Disciples*-Who's the greatest?-*Matthew 18:1–4*
*30 a.d.* (March)
> *James and John*-Request for their pre-eminence in Christ's kingdom-*Matthew 20:21*
*Mark:*
> Peter-*"Thou art the Christ"*-*Mark 8:29*
> *Disciples*-Who's the greatest?-*Mark 9:34*
> *James and John*-Request for their preeminence in

Christ's kingdom-*Mark 10:35–37* (*the other ten were displeased, verse 41*)

Luke:

*Peter-"Thou art the Christ"-Luke 9:20*
*Disciples-Who's the greatest?-Luke 9:46*
*Disciples-Who's the greatest?-Luke 22–24*

Even though the disciples heard Jesus say: "The kingdom of God cometh not with observation ... The kingdom of God is within you" (Luke 17:20–21), "my kingdom is not of this world," "now is my kingdom not from hence" (John 18:36)-their focus was on an *earthly kingdom* in which they all wanted to play an important part.

All of the disciples had a natural desire for preeminence, and whether Peter's desire for preeminence was more than that of the other disciples, his was definitely more pronounced because of his enthusiastic and impulsive nature. Peter undoubtedly considered himself the most worthy of a high position in Christ's kingdom; as seen in the passage of Matthew 26:31–35.

The night Jesus was betrayed, Peter blatantly and persistently contradicted Jesus. Jesus said, "All ye shall be offended because of me this night: for it is written, I will smite the shepherd, and the sheep of the flock shall be scattered abroad" (Matthew 26:31).

Peter answered, saying, "Though all men shall be offended because of thee, yet will I never be offended."

Jesus answered Peter, saying, "Verily I say unto thee, That this night, before the cock crow, thou shalt deny me thrice."

Peter not only persisted in contradicting the Lord the second time, but his persistence also influenced the others to do the same; as seen in verse 35: "Though I should die with thee, yet will I not deny thee. Likewise also said all the disciples." Peter's aggressive, take-charge personality played no small part in influencing the other disciples (cf. John 21:1–3, etc.).

144

Although Peter's motives may have been somewhat questionable, there can be no doubt as to his devotion to the Lord Jesus Christ. Nor can there be any doubt about his impetuousness. It was Peter who cut off the ear of the high priest's servant (John 18:10). It was Peter who, on the mount of Transfiguration, wanted to build tabernacles, taking charge of the situation (Matthew 17:1–4). Peter was usually the first to speak out in response to the Lord's statements and questions, and his doing so in Matthew 16:13–16 was not an uncommon occurrence. When Jesus told the disciples, "A rich man shall hardly enter the kingdom of heaven," it was Peter who responded: "Behold, we have forsaken all and followed Thee; what shall we have therefore?" (Matthew 19:23–27). In John 21:19–23, when Jesus told Peter to follow him, Peter then turned around and saw John following and asked Jesus, "What shall this man do?" Because of Peter's obvious aspiration of preeminence, Jesus rebuked him, saying, "What is that to thee? Follow thou me."

The picture that is painted of Peter in the Scriptures does not reflect or support the Roman Catholic understanding of the passage of Matthew chapter sixteen. Peter is not the only one to whom Jesus entrusted the keys of the kingdom, and he most certainly is not the *rock* upon which Jesus is building his church. Jesus was referring to the *rock of faith* in Matthew 16:18. I see Jesus's statement—"And I say also unto thee, That thou art Peter, and upon this rock I will build my church"—not as a pronouncement of authority and preeminence given to Peter, but as a rebuke of Peter's impetuousness in striving to supersede the other disciples. Jesus rebuked Peter the second time in this same passage because Peter "savourest not the things that be of God, but those that be of men."

When Jesus announced that he would be killed, Peter rebuked him. This announcement was a threat to Peter's aspirations of preeminence and authority over what he viewed as a *worldly* kingdom, a kingdom which could not be established if Christ died. Christ's response to Peter's rebuke was: "Get thee behind me Satan…for thou savourest not the things that be of God, but those that be of men."

Jesus then told his disciples that in order to follow him, one must "take up his cross and deny self," and that anyone saving his life in this world will lose it. "For what is a man profited if he shall gain the whole world" (*cf.* John 12:23–25, 26; Matthew 10:38–39; Luke 9:23–25).

The Apostle Peter was bent on saving his life in this world with his attention on an earthly kingdom in which he wanted to exercise lordship and authority. This is why Jesus said to him in Matthew 16:23, "Get thee behind me, Satan: thou art an offence unto me: for thou savourest not the things that be of God, but those that be of men," and in Luke 22:31, "Simon, Simon, behold, Satan hath desired to have you, that he may sift you as wheat."

Jesus could not have been referring to Peter as the *rock* upon which he was going to build the church in Matthew 16:16–18. The subject matter in both of these passages is *the kingdom* and *the question of preeminence in the kingdom*, and in both passages Jesus zeroed in on Peter, speaking directly to him with reference to Satan. From the time of Peter's confession of faith in the summer of AD 29 up until the very night that Jesus was betrayed, in the spring of AD 30, there was strife among the disciples as to whom was the greatest (cf. Luke 22:15–24–34).

In answer to their question of preeminence, Jesus said, "The kings of the Gentiles exercise lordship over them; and they that exercise authority upon them are called benefactors. But ye shall not be so: but he that is greatest among you, let him be as the younger; and he that is chief, as he that doth serve" (Luke 22:25–26).

It wasn't until after Peter's conversion that he, in essence, said the same thing in AD 60: "Feed the flock of God which is among you, taking the oversight thereof, not by constraint, but willingly; not for filthy lucre, but of a ready mind; Neither as being lords over God's heritage, but being ensamples to the flock" (1 Peter 5:2–3); and so did Paul: "Not for that we have dominion over your faith, but are helpers of your joy: for by faith ye stand" (2 Corinthians 1:24).

After having told his disciples that they were not to exercise lordship and authority, Jesus told not just Peter but also the other eleven disciples: "I appoint unto you a kingdom, as my Father hath appointed unto me; That ye may eat and drink at my table in my kingdom, and sit on thrones" (Luke 22:25–30). Eating and drinking at Christ's table and *sitting on thrones in his kingdom* has nothing whatsoever to do with a mandate of authority given exclusively to the apostles and so called successors. We who are *in Christ* have been translated into his kingdom and *are* seated (present tense) with Christ in his throne; "in heavenly places," and eat and drink at his table.

> …Unto him that loved us, and washed us from our sins in his own blood, And *hath made us kings* and priests unto God and his Father; to him *be* glory and dominion for ever and ever. Amen.
>
> Revelation1:5–6, emphasis added

> I John, who also am your brother, and companion in tribulation, and *in the kingdom* and patience *of Jesus Christ*…
>
> Revelation 1:9, emphasis added

> Who *hath* delivered us from the power of darkness, and *hath* translated us into the kingdom of his dear Son., emphasis added
>
> Colossians 1:13, emphasis added

> The Father raised Christ from the dead and set him at his own right hand in heavenly places … and hath raised

us up together and *made us sit together in heavenly places in Christ*...

Ephesians 1:20 & 2:6–8

If ye then be risen with Christ, seek those things which are above, where Christ sitteth on the right hand of God.

Colossians 3:1

And he opened his mouth in blasphemy against God, to blaspheme his name, and his tabernacle, and them that dwell in heaven.

Revelation 13:6

For our conversation is in heaven; from whence also we look for the Saviour, the Lord Jesus Christ.

Philippians 3:20

Jesus talked about these same things in Revelation 3:20–21, using virtually the same phraseology, and his statements are addressed to *anyone* who hears his voice and overcomes.

Behold, I stand at the door, and knock: if *any man* hear my voice, and open the door, *I will come in to him*, and *will sup with him, and he with me.* To him that overcometh will I grant to sit with me in my throne, even as I also overcame, and am set down with my Father in his throne.

Revelation 3:20–21, emphasis added

Overcoming has to do with *faith*. Christ *comes into* and/or lives in the hearts of those who believe in him, by way of his Holy Spirit (Ephesians 3:17; Galatians 4:6; Romans 8:9–10), and the Holy Spirit can only be received through faith (Galatians 3:2, 14; John 7:37–39; Ephesians 1:13; Acts 10:44–47; and Acts 11:15–18). This is what Jesus was talking about when he said that he would come into any man who heard his voice and opened the door ).[2]

Whosoever *believeth* that Jesus is the Christ *is born of God*: and every one that loveth him that begat loveth him also that is begotten of him … For *whatsoever is born of God overcometh* the world: and this is the victory that *overcometh* the world, even our faith. Who is he that *overcometh* the world, but he that *believeth* that Jesus is the Son of God.

1 John 5:1, 4–5, emphasis added

The Apostle Paul said:

The word is nigh thee, even in thy mouth, and in thy heart:[3] that is, the word of faith, which we preach; That if thou shalt confess with thy mouth the Lord Jesus, and shalt believe in thine heart that God hath raised him from the dead, thou shalt be saved. For with the heart man believeth unto righteousness; and with the mouth confession is made unto salvation" (cf. Galatians 4:6 and Romans 5:5).

Romans 10:8–10

Revelation 12:10–11 also talks about overcoming by the same confession made unto salvation.

And I heard a loud voice saying in heaven, Now is come salvation, and strength, and the kingdom of our God, and the power of his Christ: for the accuser of our brethren is cast down, which accused them before our God day and night. And they overcame him by the blood of the Lamb, and by the word of their testimony; and they loved not their lives unto the death.

Revelation 12:10–11

Without the slightest hint of supreme authority given to Peter, all of these passages are talking about the same things—the death and resurrection of Jesus Christ, the kingdom of God, and faith in the shed blood of Jesus Christ for the forgiveness of sin (Romans 3:21–26; Colossians 1:13–14), and *faith* upon which Christ is building his church. The contention as to *who is the greatest* started with the twelve apostles and still exists within the body of Christ today; even though it is emphatically stated in the Scriptures that none of God's ministers are to hold a position of *supreme* power, authority, or esteem.

A prime example is seen in Paul's chiding the church in the first four chapters of his first epistle to the Corinthians.

> For it hath been declared unto me of you, my brethren, by them which are of the house of Chloe, that there are contentions among you. Now this I say, that every one of you saith, I am of Paul; and I of Apollos; and *I of Cephas* [Peter]; and I of Christ. Is Christ divided? was Paul crucified for you? or were ye baptized in the name of Paul? I thank God that I baptized none of you... For Christ sent me not to baptize, but to preach the gospel: not with wisdom of words, lest the cross of Christ should be made of none effect.
>
> 1 Corinthians 1 11–14, 17, emphasis added

> For ye are yet carnal: for whereas there is among you envying, and strife, and divisions, are ye not carnal, and walk as men? For while one saith, I am of Paul; and another, I am of Apollos; are ye not carnal? Who then is Paul, and who is Apollos, but ministers by whom ye believed, even as the Lord gave to every man? I have planted, Apollos watered; but God gave the increase. So then neither is he that planteth any thing, neither he that watereth; but God that giveth the increase. Now he that planteth and he that watereth are one and every man shall receive his own reward according to his own labour. For we are labourers together with God: ye are God's husbandry, ye are God's building. According to the grace of God which is given unto me, as a wise masterbuilder, I have laid the foundation, and another buildeth thereon. But let every man take heed how he buildeth thereupon. *For other foundation can no man lay than that is laid, which is Jesus Christ.*
>
> 1 Corinthians 3:3–11, emphasis added

Therefore *let no man glory in men*. For all things are yours; Whether Paul, or Apollos, or *Cephas* [*Peter*], or the world, or life, or death, or things present, or things to come; all are yours.

1 Corinthians 3:21–22, emphasis added

And these things, brethren, I have in a figure transferred to myself and to Apollos for your sakes; that ye might learn in us *not to think of men above that which is written, that no one of you be puffed up for one against another*.

1 Corinthians 4:6, emphasis added

Catholic author David B. Currie says, "The insurmountable problem with the Evangelical analysis of the Greek text is that in Aramaic, the language of Jesus, there was only one word for rock (kepha)."

With due respect to Mr. David B. Currie, the "insurmountable problem" is not in the one Aramaic word for rock. The problem is in disregarding the harmony of the whole of God's Word, all of that which is *written in the volume of the book*, and building a dogma on one word or a few isolated verses.

# PETER'S BRETHREN

According to the magisterium of the Roman Catholic Church, Jesus telling Peter to "strengthen his brethren" is further proof that Peter is the rock upon which Christ's church is built (*Catechism of the Catholic Church*, p. 141). Jesus was not giving Peter supreme authority over the church when he told him to strengthen his brethren, nor was he referring to his entire church. Jesus told the Pharisees, "I lay down my life for the sheep. And other sheep I have, which are not of this fold: them also I must bring, and they shall hear my voice; and there shall be one fold, and one shepherd" (John 10:15–16).

When Jesus told Peter to *strengthen his brethren* in Luke 22:32 and *feed my sheep* in John 21:15–17, he was not referring to his entire church, but to Peter's kinsman according to the flesh, Jews. He was simply repeating to Peter what he had told the twelve disciples from the very beginning; that they were not to preach the gospel of the kingdom to the Gentiles, "Christ's other sheep," but only to the Jews, Peter's *brethren*.

These twelve Jesus sent forth, and commanded them, saying, *Go not into the way of the Gentiles*, and into any city of the Samaritans enter ye not: But *go rather to the lost sheep of the house of Israel*. And as ye go, preach, saying, "The kingdom of heaven is at hand.

Matthew 10:5–7, emphasis added

Compare the following scriptures as to why Jesus commanded the twelve apostles to "go not into the way of the Gentiles, and into any city of the Samaritans enter ye not: But go rather to the lost sheep of the house of Israel."

But he [Jesus] answered and said, I am not sent but unto the lost sheep of the house of Israel.

Matthew 15:24

Now I say that Jesus Christ was a minister of the circumcision for the truth of God, to confirm the promises made unto the fathers: And that the Gentiles might glorify God for his mercy; as it is written, For this cause I will confess to thee among the Gentiles, and sing unto thy name. And again he saith, Rejoice, ye Gentiles, with his people. And again, Praise the Lord, all ye Gentiles; and laud him, all ye people. And again, Esaias saith, There shall be a root of Jesse, and he that shall rise to reign over the Gentiles; in him shall the Gentiles trust.

Romans 15:8–12

For I am not ashamed of the gospel of Christ: for it is the power of God unto salvation to every one that believeth; *to the Jew first*, and also to the Greek.

Romans 1:16, emphasis added

Unto you *first* God, having raised up his Son Jesus, sent him to bless you, in turning away every one of you from his iniquities.

Acts 3:26, emphasis added

But when the Jews saw the multitudes, they were filled with envy, and spake against those things which were spoken by Paul, contradicting and blaspheming. Then Paul and Barnabas waxed bold, and said, It was necessary that the word of God should *first* have been spoken to you: but seeing ye put it from you, and judge yourselves unworthy of everlasting life, lo, we turn to the Gentiles.

Acts 13:45–46, emphasis added

Jesus having told Peter in Luke 22:32 to "strengthen his brethren" has absolutely nothing whatsoever to do with a mandate of authority or preeminence given to Peter. "The lost sheep of house of Israel," to whom Jesus commanded his disciples to preach the kingdom of heaven, and "the twelve tribes of Israel," that are mentioned in the same passage wherein Peter was told to strengthen his brethren, are one in the same; Peter's "brethren" his "kinsman according to the flesh," Jews, who were also the Apostle Paul's *brethren* and kinsman according to the flesh.

> For I [Paul] could wish that myself were accursed from Christ for *my brethren, my kinsmen according to the flesh*: Who are Israelites; to whom pertaineth the adoption, and the glory, and the covenants, and the giving of the law, and the service of God, and the promises...
>
> Romans 9:3–4, emphasis added

The Apostle Paul said: "In nothing am I behind the very chiefest apostles, though I be nothing" (2 Corinthians 2:11). Jesus appeared to the Apostle Paul on the road to Damascus and commanded him to preach the same "gospel of the kingdom" to the gentiles, and with no less authority than that of Peter or the other apostles.

> But rise, and stand upon thy feet: for *I have appeared unto thee for this purpose*, to make thee a minister and a witness both of these things which thou hast seen, and of those things in the which I will appear unto thee; Delivering thee from the people, and from *the Gentiles, unto whom now I send thee*, To open their eyes, and to turn them from darkness to light, and from the power of Satan unto God, that they may receive forgiveness of sins, and inheritance among them which are sanctified by faith that is in me.
>
> Acts 26:16–18, emphasis added

*Paul, an apostle,* not of men, neither by man, but *by Jesus Christ, and God the Father,* who raised him from the dead; ... But I certify you, brethren, that the gospel which was preached of me *is not after man.* For I neither received it of man, neither *was I taught it, but by the revelation of Jesus Christ.*

Galatians 1:1, 11–12, emphasis added

But the Lord said unto him, Go thy way: for *he [Paul] is a chosen vessel unto me, to bear my name before the Gentiles,* and kings, and the children of Israel.

Acts 9:15, emphasis added

Whereunto I am ordained a preacher, *and* an apostle, (I speak the truth in Christ, and lie not;) *a teacher of the Gentiles* in faith and verity.

1 Timothy 2:7, emphasis added

For I speak to you Gentiles, inasmuch as *I am the apostle of the Gentiles,* I magnify mine office.

Romans 11:13, emphasis added

... the gospel: Whereunto *I am* appointed a preacher, and *an apostle, and a teacher of the Gentiles.*

2 Timothy 1:10–11, emphasis added

For this cause I Paul, the prisoner of Jesus Christ *for you Gentiles,* If ye have heard of the dispensation of the grace of God which is given me to you-ward: How that by revelation he made known unto me the mystery; (as I wrote afore in few words)...That the Gentiles should be fellow heirs, and of the same body, and partakers of his promise in Christ by *the gospel: Whereof I was made a minister,* according to the gift of the grace of God given unto me by the effectual working of his power. Unto me, who am less than the least of all saints, is this grace given, *that I should preach among the Gentiles* the unsearchable riches of Christ.

Ephesians 3:1–3,6–8, emphasis added

*That I should be the minister of Jesus Christ to the Gentiles,* ministering the gospel of God, that the offering up of the Gentiles might be acceptable, being sanctified by the Holy Ghost.

Romans 15:16, emphasis added

Notwithstanding the Lord stood with me, and strengthened me; *that by me* the preaching might be fully known, and *that all the Gentiles might hear:* and I was delivered out of the mouth of the lion.

2 Timothy 4:17, emphasis added

The Apostle Paul said:

But of these who seemed to be somewhat, (whatsoever they were, it maketh no matter to me: God accepteth no man's person) for they who seemed to be somewhat in conference added nothing to me ... *The gospel of the uncircumcision was committed unto me, as the gospel of the circumcision was unto Peter; For he that wrought effectually in Peter to the apostleship of the circumcision, the same was mighty in me toward the Gentiles.* And when James, Cephas [Peter], and John, who seemed to be pillars, perceived the grace that was given unto me, they gave to me and Barnabas the right hands of fellowship; that we should go unto the heathen, and they unto the circumcision.

Galatians 2:6–9[1], emphasis added

Immediately after having told the Galatians that "God accepteth no man's person" and how God was as mighty in him toward the Gentiles as he was in Peter toward the Jews, Paul told the Galatians about an incident wherein Peter's behavior was not "according to the truth of the gospel" and how he had also influenced others, including Barnabas, to behave in like manner.

He said, "But when Peter was come to Antioch, I withstood Peter to the face, because he was to be blamed." Peter had been eating with Gentiles, but when a party of Jews came, he withdrew himself from them because "he feared them which were of the circumcision. And the other Jews dissembled likewise with him; insomuch that Barnabas also was carried away with their dissimulation" (Galatians 2:11–14).

Compare Peter's actions with what is written about those who *feared the Jews* and who *loved the praise of men more than the praise of God* (John 12:42–43; John 9:22; John 7:13; John 19:38).

This incident of Peter's dissimulation took place sometime between AD 54 and 58, long after Peter was *supposedly* (according to Roman Catholic dogma) declared to be the *rock* upon which Christ is building his church; and yet, Peter was still "savouring not the things that be of God, but those that be of men" (cf. Matthew 16:23).

Paul began his letter to the Galatians talking about those who were perverting the gospel of the *grace* of Christ and then said: "Do I seek to please men? For if I yet please men, I should not be the servant of Christ" (Galatians 1:3–12). Paul obviously said these things in view of what he was about to tell the Galatians concerning Peter's wavering in the faith and falling from grace (Galatians 2:11–16; Galatians 5:4). The topic of Paul's entire epistle to the Galatians is "faith and grace" as opposed to "the law and works," and he used the example of Peter's dissimulation to drive home his point.

In AD 40, several years prior to Peter's dissimulation, Peter told Cornelius and those who were with him, "Ye know how that it is an unlawful thing for a man that is a Jew to keep company, or come unto one of another nation; but God hath shewed me that I should not call any man common or unclean" (Acts 10:11–16, 28).[2] Peter had obviously reverted to, and was still practicing, the works of the law, which was why Paul told him in Galatians 2:18, "For if I build again the things which I destroyed, I make myself a transgressor" (cf. "Where no law is there is no transgression" [Romans 4:15]); "Sin is not imputed when there is no law" (Romans 5:13)].

Paul, in essence, said the same thing to the Philippians. "This one thing I do, forgetting those things which are behind, and reaching forth unto those things which are before." He had just told the Philippians of his background prior to his conversion. Among other things, he said that he had been a Pharisee and was *blameless* according to the righteousness which is of *the law* but that he suffered the loss of these things "and do count them but dung, that I may win Christ, and be found in him, not having *mine own righteousness, which is of the law,* but *that which is through the faith of Christ,* the righteousness which is of God *by faith*" (read Philippians 3:13 in context with Acts 10:9–17, 28).

It couldn't be more obvious that, at that point in time (AD 54–58), Peter was confusing the issue of *the law and works* with *faith and grace,* which is the basic message of the gospel of Christ. Peter was not *strengthening his brethren* in the faith, but was misleading them from *the truth of the gospel.* It is inconceivable that Peter's deficiency in spiritual discernment and constancy in the faith is the mark of a man upon whom Christ would build his church. It is inconceivable that Jesus would build his church upon any man! Not even Paul, who was not lacking in spiritual understanding and faith but who also had his own shortcomings (cf. Romans 7:14–25; Acts 15:36–39).

Jesus did not commit himself to any man. He didn't trust even those who believed in him because "he knew what was in man" (John 2:23–25; Romans 7:14–20).[3] He knew that Peter would deny him three times; just as he also "knew, from the beginning who they were that believed not, and who should betray him" (John 6:64).

In both passages where the subject of Jesus's discourse is that of *the kingdom* (Luke 22:15–32) and *the keys* (Matthew 16:13–26), Jesus zeroed in on Peter with reference to Satan.

When Jesus told Peter that *Satan desired to sift him* and that he would pray that *his faith would not fail,* he knew beforehand that Peter would waver in the faith. Jesus rebuked the twelve disciples numerous times for their *little faith*; once in the same chapter that supposedly proves Peter is the rock upon which Jesus is building his church (Matthew 16:8), and just prior to that, in Matthew 14:31, the rebuke of *little faith* was directed to Peter himself (Matthew 8:8–10; Matthew 8:26; Matthew 14:31; Matthew 16:8; Matthew 17:20; Matthew 21:21; Mark11:23; with Mark 8:29; Luke 17:5; Luke 18:8).

The following quotation from the *Catechism of the Catholic Church* is not in harmony with the divinely inspired Scriptures.

552 Because of the faith he confessed Peter will remain the unshakable rock of the Church. His mission will be to keep this faith from every lapse and to *strengthen his brothers in it.* emphasis added

*Catechism of the Catholic Church*, p. 141

# PETER, SON OF JONAS

Was The Apostle Peter really the son of a man named Jonas? Jesus referred to Peter as "the son of Jonah" on only three occasions. These occurrences are recorded in Matthew chapter 16 and the first and last chapters of John's gospel. There are no other writings that confirm as fact that Peter's father's name was actually Jonah.

> And Simon Peter answered and said, Thou art the Christ, the Son of the living God. And Jesus answered and said unto him, Blessed art thou, Simon Barjona: for flesh and blood hath not revealed it unto thee, but my Father which is in heaven.
>
> Matthew 16:16–17

> And he brought him to Jesus. And when Jesus beheld him, he said, Thou art Simon the son of Jona: thou shalt be called Cephas, which is by interpretation, A stone.
>
> John 1:42

> So when they had dined, Jesus saith to Simon Peter, Simon, son of Jonas, lovest thou me more than these? He saith unto him, Yea, Lord; thou knowest that I love thee. He saith unto him, Feed my lambs. He saith to him again the second time, Simon, son of Jonas, lovest thou me? He saith unto him, Yea, Lord; thou knowest that I love thee. He saith unto him, Feed my sheep. He saith unto him the third time, Simon, son of Jonas, lovest thou me? Peter was grieved because he said unto him the third time, Lovest

thou me? And he said unto him, Lord, thou knowest all things; thou knowest that I love thee. Jesus saith unto him, Feed my sheep.

John 21:15–17

Jesus, in the proverbial sense, nicknamed James and John the *sons of thunder*. However, it is stated eleven times, and unequivocally in all four gospels, that James and John were in fact the sons of Zebedee.[1]

Notice that when Matthew gave the names of the twelve apostles, he mentioned Zebedee as the father of the brothers James and John but did not mention Jona as the father of the brothers Peter and Andrew. "Now the names of the twelve apostles are these; The first, Simon, who is called Peter, and Andrew his brother; James the son of Zebedee, and John his brother" (Matthew 10:2).

The first time Peter met Jesus, Jesus's very first words to Peter were: "Thou art Simon the son of Jona" (John 1:42). The second time Jesus called Peter "son of Jona" was in his response to Peter's profession of faith. The third time he called Peter the "son of Jona" was when he appeared to the disciples the third time, after his resurrection. Jesus called Peter the "son of Jona" three times within three verses, and each time he added, "Feed my sheep."

The disciples had taken up fishing again and were on the sea of Tiberias. The sea of Tiberias is also called the Sea of Galilee and Lake of Gennesaret. There were large fisheries on the lake, and much commerce was carried on there (*Smith's Bible Dictionary*).[2]

Hypothetically, consider the possibility that Jesus may have called Peter the son of Jona in the proverbial sense as a type of the prophet Jonah. He knew Peter would deny him three times, and he also knew that Peter would be tempted to return to the profession of fishing and disregard the Lord's command to go into all the world, and preach the gospel to every creature, just as Jonah had rebelled against God's commandment to preach to Nineveh.

> Now the word of the Lord came unto Jonah the son of Amittai, saying, Arise, *go to Nineveh*, that great city, and cry against it; for their wickedness is come up before me. But Jonah rose up to flee unto Tarshish from the presence of the Lord, and went down to Joppa; and *he found a ship* going to Tarshish: so he paid the fare thereof, and went down into it, to go with them unto Tarshish *from the presence of the Lord*.
>
> Jonah 1:1–3, emphasis added

> And the word of the Lord came unto Jonah *the second time*, saying, Arise, go unto Nineveh, that great city, and *preach unto it the preaching that I bid thee*.
>
> Jonah 3:1–2, emphasis added

When Peter said to the other disciples, "I go a fishing," the other disciples, as usual, followed suit. Due to his aggressive and take-charge nature, Peter had a great deal of influence over the other disciples. According to the following, the disciples could not have been fishing for the sake of sport. The word *ship*, in John 21:3, is translated from the Greek word *ploion*, which indicates *a large ship*. This same word is used to describe the ship the disciples used in their fishing trade (Mark 1:16–20; Matthew 4:21; Luke 5:3–11).

In John 21:7, Peter is wearing a *fisher's coat*, a garment used in the fishing trade. Verse eight talks about other disciples who were in another ship, a little ship. *Little ship* is translated from the Greek word *ploiarion* (*cf.* Mark 3:9; Mark 4:36; John 6:22–23). In the following passage, it is evident in verses one through eight that the disciples were not fishing for sport.

> After these things Jesus shewed himself again to the disciples at the sea of Tiberias; and on this wise shewed

he himself. There were together Simon Peter, and Thomas called Didymus, and Nathanael of Cana in Galilee, and the sons of Zebedee, and two other of his disciples. Simon Peter saith unto them, I go a fishing. They say unto him, We also go with thee. They went forth, and entered into a *ship* immediately; and *that night they caught nothing.* But when the morning was now come, Jesus stood on the shore: but the disciples knew not that it was Jesus. Then Jesus saith unto them, Children, have ye any meat? They answered him, No. And he said unto them, *Cast the net on the right side of the ship, and ye shall find.* They cast therefore, and now they were not able to draw it for *the multitude of fishes.* Therefore that disciple whom Jesus loved saith unto Peter, It is the Lord. Now when Simon Peter heard that it was the Lord, he girt his *fisher's coat* unto him, (for he was naked,) and did cast himself into the sea. And the other disciples came in *a little ship;* (for they were not far from land, but as it were two hundred cubits,) dragging the net with fishes.

John 21:1–8, emphasis added

The scenario in the twenty-first chapter of John is virtually the same as that of Luke 5:4–11, wherein Jesus first called the disciples to preach the gospel of the kingdom. Both passages begin with an unsuccessful night of fishing and Jesus telling the disciples where to cast their nets and their catching a multitude of fish (Luke 5:4–6; John 21:3–6). Both passages end with *following Jesus* (Luke 5:11; John 21:19, 22). Compare these two passages in the following:

In Luke chapter five, it was on the Lake of Gennesaret that Jesus told Peter, "Launch out into the deep, and let down your nets for a draught." Peter said, "We have toiled all the night, and have taken nothing." When they let down their nets they "inclosed a great multitude of fishes." It was then that Jesus said: "From henceforth thou shalt catch men," and when they had brought their ships to land, "they forsook all, and followed him."

In John chapter twenty-one, the setting is the same-the Sea of Tiberias (the Sea of Galilee and/or Lake of Gennesaret). "That night they caught nothing." Jesus told the disciples *where to cast their nets* and they caught *a multitude of fishes*. After telling Peter three times *to feed his sheep*. Jesus said, "Follow thou me" (John 21:15–17). Then again in verse twenty-two, Jesus said to Peter, "Follow thou me." Jesus zeroed in on Peter in this passage, knowing that the others would follow his lead.

Peter and the others had *literally* forsaken all to follow Jesus. When Jesus said that it was hard for a rich man to enter the kingdom of heaven and told the rich young ruler to sell all that he had and give to the poor, Peter responded, "Behold, we have forsaken all, and followed thee; what shall we have therefore?" (Matthew 19:27).

It couldn't have been more obvious to Peter and the others that Jesus did not intend for them to return to their former occupation of fishing. He said that he would "make them to become fishers of men" (Mark 1:17; Matthew 4:19). He went about preaching the gospel of the kingdom (Matthew 9:35) and "sent forth and commanded" them to do the same (Matthew 10:5–7; Mark 16:15).

When they asked Jesus about the signs of his coming and the end of the world, he said, "This gospel of the kingdom shall be preached in all the world for a witness unto all nations; and then shall the end come" (Matthew 24:14). Just prior to his death, Jesus prayed to the Father, saying, "I have given unto them the words which thou gavest me; and they have received them … As thou hast sent me into the world, even so have I also sent them into the world … Neither pray I for these alone, but for them also which shall believe on me through their word" (John 17:8, 18–20).

When Jesus asked Peter, "Lovest thou me more than these?" he was not referring to *the other disciples*, but to *the multitude of fish*. The Jerusalem version of the Bible has, "Lovest thou me more than these others?" The word *others* does not appear in any of the ancient manuscripts. The addition of this word in the Jerusalem version is obviously the result of sectarian bias on the part of the translators. The addition of the word *others* to verse 15 creates the impression that Peter loved Jesus more than the other disciples loved him, and therefore lends support to "Feed my sheep," in verse 17, which is one of three verses of Scripture that is presented as "proof text" for the dogma that "Peter is the 'rock' upon which Jesus is building His church."[3] In the following passage, nine of the twelve sentences are referring to fish. With this in mind, skip the commentary and read only the *italicized* words spoken by Jesus. It's very clear that when Jesus asked Peter, "Lovest thou me more than these?" that he was not referring to the other disciples, but to the 153 great fishes. *Wuest Greek Word Studies* also has: "Do you consider me more precious and thus love me more than these fish?"

> Then Jesus saith unto them, Children, *have ye any meat?* They answered him, No. And he said unto them, *Cast the net on the right side of the ship, and ye shall find.* They cast therefore, and now they were not able to draw it *for the multitude of fishes ...* Jesus saith unto them, *Bring of the fish which ye have now caught.* Simon Peter went up, and drew the net to land *full of great fishes, an hundred and fifty and three:* and for all *there were so many,* yet was not the net broken. Jesus saith unto them, *Come and dine.* And none of the disciples durst ask him, Who art thou? knowing that it was the Lord. Jesus then cometh, and taketh bread, and giveth them, *and fish likewise.* This is now the third time that Jesus shewed himself to his disciples, after that he was risen from the dead. So *when they had dined,* Jesus saith to Simon Peter, *Simon, son of Jonas, lovest thou me more than these?* He saith unto him, Yea, Lord; thou knowest that I love thee. He saith unto him, Feed my lambs.
>
> John 21:5–6, 10–15, emphasis added

The primary issue of the twenty-first chapter of John is not the miracle of the multitude of fishes, or who loved Jesus the most. Since Jesus reconstructed virtually the same scenario as that of Luke chapter five, he had to have been relating the same message to his disciples in both passages; "His commissioning the disciples to preach the gospel." In the twenty-first chapter of John, Jesus was affirming the commission he had given them in Luke 5:1–11. In both passages, he, in essence, was telling them to preach the gospel; to be fishers of men (cf. Matthew 4:18–19; Mark 1:16–20).

Jesus zeroed in on Peter in John chapter twenty-one because his faith was waning, and his losing sight of the commission the Lord had given them to preach the gospel was likewise influencing the others. This passage in John's gospel is relevant to what Jesus told Peter in Luke 22:31–34.

> And the Lord said, Simon, Simon, behold, Satan hath desired to have you, that he may sift you as wheat: But I have prayed for thee, that thy faith fail not: and *when thou art converted*, strengthen thy brethren. And he said unto him, Lord, I am ready to go with thee, both into prison, and to death. And he said, I tell thee, Peter, the cock shall not crow this day, before that thou shalt thrice deny that thou knowest me.
>
> Luke 22:31–34, emphasis added

When Jesus asked Peter three times if he loved him and then added, "Feed my sheep," Peter was grieved. He had not only denied Jesus *three times* but had also returned to the fishing trade that he had once forsaken to preach the gospel.

Peter answered, saying, "Lord, thou knowest all things; thou knowest that I love thee" (John 21:17). Jesus already knew beforehand the degree of Peter's affection toward him, when he kept asking Peter if he loved him and kept telling him to feed his sheep. Jesus wasn't doubting Peter's affection; he was assuring Peter that he still wanted him to preach the gospel.

Peter was grieved because he, in his own strength, was unable to do what he so zealously had intended to do. He didn't realize that the commission the Lord had given him to preach the gospel was impossible to carry out without the indwelling power of the Holy Spirit. Remember what Jesus said in John 15:5, "He that abideth in me, and I in him, the same bringeth forth much fruit: for without me ye can do nothing." It was with reference to the Holy Spirit that Jesus continued assuring Peter, in verse eighteen, that he was to fulfill his commission to preach the gospel, saying:

> Verily, verily, I say unto thee, When thou wast young, thou girdedst thyself, and walkedst whither thou wouldest: but when thou shalt be old, thou shalt *stretch forth thy hands*, and *another* shall gird thee, and carry thee whither thou wouldest not. This spake he, signifying by what *death* he should glorify God. And when he had spoken this, he saith unto him, Follow me.
>
> John 21:18–19, emphasis added

The "death" by which the Apostle Peter was to "glorify God," as signified by Jesus in v. 19 above, was none other than "the crucified life in Christ"; Peter's dying to self. Jesus was not referring to someone carrying Peter off to be crucified upside down. He was referring to the Holy Spirit, who would indwell and empower him to preach the gospel, and who would also bear witness to his preaching by granting signs and wonders and miracles to be done by his hands. Jesus's last words to his disciples, before he ascended into heaven, were: "But ye shall receive power, after that the Holy Ghost is come upon you: and ye shall be witnesses unto me both in Jerusalem, and in all Judaea, and in Samaria, and unto the uttermost part of the earth" (Acts 1:8). There are many scriptures, of which the following are just a few, that make it very clear that the *another* Jesus spoke of in verse 18 was, in fact, "the Holy Spirit."

And when they were come up out of the water, the Spirit of the Lord caught away Philip, that the eunuch saw him no more: and he went on his way rejoicing. But Philip was found at Azotus: and passing through he preached in all the cities, till he came to Caesarea.

Acts 8:39–40

And they were not able to resist the wisdom and the spirit by which he spake.

Acts 6:10

Testifying both to the Jews, and also to the Greeks, repentance toward God, and faith toward our Lord Jesus Christ. And now, behold, I go bound in the spirit unto Jerusalem, not knowing the things that shall befall me there.

Acts 20:21–22

Now when they had gone throughout Phrygia and the region of Galatia, and were forbidden of the Holy Ghost to preach the word in Asia, After they were come to Mysia, they assayed to go into Bithynia: but the Spirit suffered them not.

Acts 16:6–7

Whereof I was made a minister, according to the gift of the grace of God given unto me by the effectual working of his power.

Ephesians 3:8

Not that we are sufficient of ourselves to think any thing as of ourselves; but our sufficiency is of God; Who also hath made us able ministers of the new testament.

2 Corinthians 3:5–6

The Word of God is replete with Scriptures which speak of "stretching forth hands" and that have absolutely nothing whatsoever to do with being crucified.[4] When Jesus told Peter, thou shalt "stretch forth" thy hands, he was talking about the healing power of the Holy Spirit that would work in and through Peter's hands. Jesus "put forth" his hand and touched the people and healed them, and he told his disciples that in his name, the Father would send the Holy Spirit to indwell them and in his name, they would do the same works that he does (John 14:11–17, 26). According to Abingdon's Strong's Concordance #1614, the words "stretch forth" (as pertaining to the Apostle Peter's hands in John 21:18), and the words "put forth" (as pertaining to Jesus' hands in Luke 5:13, Matthew 8:3 and Mark 1:41) are translated from the same Greek word "ekteino." Jesus *stretched forth* his hands and healed people, and in his name so did his disciples; after they had received the gift of the Holy Spirit.

> Long time therefore abode they speaking boldly in the Lord, which gave testimony unto the word of his grace, and granted signs and wonders to be done by their hands.
>
> Acts 14:3

> God also bearing them witness, both with signs and wonders, and with divers miracles, and gifts of the Holy Ghost, according to his own will?
>
> Hebrews 2:4

> And fear came upon every soul: and many wonders and signs were done by the apostles.
>
> Acts 2:43

> And by the hands of the apostles were many signs and wonders wrought among the people; and they were all with one accord in Solomon's porch.
>
> Acts 5:12

Then Peter said, Silver and gold have I none; but such as I have give I thee: In the name of Jesus Christ of Nazareth rise up and walk. And he took him by the right hand, and lifted him up: and immediately his feet and ankle bones received strength.

Acts 3:6–7

Nevertheless I tell you the truth; It is expedient for you that I go away: for if I go not away, the Comforter will not come unto you; but if I depart, I will send him unto you.

John 16:7

Verily, verily, I say unto you, He that believeth on me, the works that I do shall he do also; and greater works than these shall he do; because I go unto my Father. And whatsoever ye shall ask *in my name*, that will I do, *that the Father may be glorified in the Son.*

John 14:12–13, emphasis added

It wasn't until after Peter had been filled with the Holy Spirit that he comprehended and gave witness to the meaning of the words Jesus spoke in John 21:18–19. Peter said: "If any man speak, let him speak as the oracles of God; if any man minister, let him do it as of the ability which God giveth: that God in all things may be glorified through Jesus Christ, to whom be praise and dominion for ever and ever" (1 Peter 4:11).

The Apostles Peter and John both had been filled with the Holy Spirit prior to the time John wrote of the events in John 21, and they both understood that Jesus was not referring to Peter's *physical* crucifixion and death in verses 18 and 19, but to Peter's *living* sacrifice; his taking up his cross *daily* and dying to self, following Christ's example of suffering and thereby producing the fruit of the Holy Spirit and glorifying God. As shown by the scriptures in the previous chapter, "Peter, the Rock," denying self was definitely not Peter's strong suit.

The last few verses of John 21 give an excellent example of the unreliableness of '*living tradition*' as a source of truth.

When Jesus told Peter, "follow thou me," Peter, then turning and looking at John, said, "Lord, and what shall this man do?" Jesus said, "If I will that he tarry till I come, what is that to thee? Follow thou me." Then, in the immediate following verse, the Apostle John writes:

> Then went this saying abroad among the brethren, that that disciple should not die: yet Jesus said not unto him, He shall not die; but, If I will that he tarry till I come, what is that to thee? This is the disciple which testifieth of these things, and wrote these things: and we know that his testimony is true.
>
> John 21:23–24

There are also many other such sayings that have gone abroad among the brethren, such as the saying that "Peter was crucified upside down."

> One of the traditional symbols of St. Peter is the inverted cross (not a crucifix). It is a symbol and commemoration of the fact that St. Peter was executed by the Romans by being placed on an upside down cross. This was done at his request as he declared himself unworthy to die in the same fashion as our Lord
> (http://www.ewtnkids.net/vexperts/showmessage. asp?number=472237&Pg=Forum3&Pgnu=1&recnu=12).

> "The Alexandrian scholar Origen (d. 256) is the first to report that St. Peter 'was crucified head downward, for he had asked that he might suffer in this way' (Eusebius, History, III, 1)"
> (http://www.shasta.com/sphaws/invertedcross.html).

Also:
http://www.catholic.org/encyclopedia/
http://www.stpeter.webhero.com/st-peter-medal.htm

# THE CHURCH

There is one body, and one Spirit, even as ye are called in
one hope of your calling; One Lord, one faith, one baptism,
One God and Father of all, who is above all, and through
all, and in you all.

Ephesians 4:4–6

Jesus was talking about his *one body* in John chapter ten when
he told the Jews, "I am the good shepherd...other sheep I
have, which are not of this fold they shall hear my voice; and
there shall be one fold, and one shepherd." The *one shepherd* is
neither Peter or Paul, but Jesus Christ himself.[1] The *one fold* is
Christ's *one body*, his *universal* church which consists of both
Jews and Gentiles, all peoples universally who are the children
of God, born again by the Word of God (James 1:18; 1 Peter
1:23) "through faith in Jesus Christ" (1 John 5:1; John 1:12–13;
Galatians 3:26–29).

Catholic means *universal*. However, Jesus's reference to his
*one fold* was certainly not in view of the Roman Catholic Church,
nor any other particular church. Just prior to the passion, Jesus
prayed that everyone who believes in him through the words of
his apostles may all be one (John 17:20–21, 23). Christ's church is
built upon faith *in the words of* the apostles and prophets.[2] It is
through faith in the message God has given through his prophets
and apostles, concerning the sacrificial death and the resurrection

of his Son, that all peoples *universally* are made the children of God, are born again, inherit eternal life, and are sanctified and cleansed by the washing of water *by the Word*, and are made members of the one and only body of Christ (Ephesians 4:4–6), which is his *universal* church (Romans 10:8–9; Galatians 3:26; 1 Peter 1:23, 25; John 3:15–16, 36; Ephesians 5:25–27; 1 John 5:4–10–12). The foundation upon which the church is built is not a man but faith in the preaching of the crucifixion of Christ, who is the cornerstone of the foundation (1 Corinthians 1:17–18, 21; 2:1–2).[3]

> Now therefore ye are no more strangers and foreigners, but fellow citizens with the saints, and of the household of God; And are built upon the foundation of the apostles and prophets, Jesus Christ himself being *the chief corner stone*; In whom all the building fitly framed together groweth unto an *holy temple* [*church*] in the Lord: In whom ye also are builded together for *an habitation of God through the Spirit*.
>
> Ephesians 2:19–22, emphasis added

The Holy Spirit comes to indwell each person the very moment they believe the gospel's message of salvation through faith in Jesus Christ (John 7:38–39; Ephesians 1:13; Galatians 3:2, 14; Acts 11:15–17).

> He that believeth on me, as the scripture hath said, out of his belly shall flow rivers of living water. But this spake he of the Spirit, which they that *believe* on him should receive: for the Holy Ghost was not yet given; because that Jesus was not yet glorified.
>
> John 7:38–39, emphasis added

> In whom ye also trusted, after that ye *heard the word of truth, the gospel* of your salvation: in whom also after that ye *believed*, ye were sealed with that holy Spirit of promise.
>
> Ephesians 1:13, emphasis added

174

This only would I learn of you, *Received ye the Spirit by* the works of the law, or by the hearing of *faith?*

Galatians 3:2, emphasis added

That the blessing of Abraham might come on the Gentiles through Jesus Christ; that we might *receive the promise of the Spirit through faith.*

Galatians 3:14, emphasis added

And as I began to speak, the Holy Ghost fell on them, as on us at the beginning. Then remembered I the word of the Lord, how that he said, John indeed baptized with water; but ye shall be baptized with the Holy Ghost. Forasmuch then as God gave them the like gift as he did unto us, *who believed on the Lord Jesus Christ;* what was I, that I could withstand God?

Acts 11:15–17, emphasis added

And believers were the more added to the Lord, multitudes both of men and women.

Acts 5:14

But he that is joined unto the Lord is one spirit.

1 Corinthians 6:17

Every person, universally, who is indwelt by the Holy Spirit is a member of the *one body* of Christ, which is his one and only true church, his *spiritual house.* The Apostle Paul said that the members of Christ's one body are built together for a habitation of God through the Spirit. The Apostle Peter, in essence, said the same thing from a slightly different perspective. He said that as newborn babes Christians were to "desire the sincere milk of the word, that they may grow thereby" and that they also, "as lively stones, are built up a spiritual house, an holy priesthood, to offer up spiritual sacrifices, acceptable to God by Jesus Christ...Wherefore also it is contained in the scripture, Behold, I lay in Sion a chief cornerstone, elect, precious: and he that believeth on him shall not be confounded" (1 Peter 2:2–6).

When Jesus talked about building his church, he was not talking about an earthly religious organization governed by an hierarchy exercising authority over its members[4] (Mark10:42–44; Matthew 20:25–27; 2 Corinthians1:24; 1 Peter 5:2–3; Acts 20:29–30), nor was he talking about earthly temples made with men's hands. He was talking about the temple of God made without hands, about each individual member of his body collectively, his universal/catholic church (Ephesians 1:22–23; Colossians 1:18).

> Howbeit the most High dwelleth not in temples made with hands; as saith the prophet.
>
> Acts 7:48

> God that made the world and all things therein, seeing that he is Lord of heaven and earth, *dwelleth not in temples made with hands*; Neither is worshipped with men's hands, as though he needed any thing, seeing he giveth to all life, and breath, and all things.
>
> Acts 17:24–25, emphasis added

> What? know ye not that *your body is the temple of the Holy Ghost which is in you*, which ye have of God, and ye are not your own?
>
> 1 Corinthians 6:19, emphasis added

> Know ye not that *ye are the temple* [church] *of God*, and that the Spirit of God dwelleth in you?
>
> 1 Corinthians 3:16, emphasis added

> Now of the things which we have spoken this is the sum: We have such an high priest, who is set on the right hand of the throne of the Majesty in the heavens; A minister of the sanctuary, and of *the true tabernacle, which the Lord pitched, and not man* (cf. John 4:21, 24).
>
> Hebrews 8:1–2, emphasis added

But Christ being come an high priest of good things to come, by *a greater and more perfect tabernacle, not made with hands*, that is to say, *not of this building.*

Hebrews 9:11, emphasis added

For we are labourers together with God: ye are God's husbandry, *ye are God's building.*

1 Corinthians 3:9, emphasis added

Jesus said:

The hour cometh, when ye shall neither in this mountain, nor yet at Jerusalem, worship the Father…The true worshipers shall worship the father in spirit and in truth…God is a Spirit: and they that worship Him must worship Him in spirit and in truth.

John 4:21–24

The early church met in private homes. They did not have luxurious buildings with stained-glass windows, nor did their worship services consist of ceremonious *religious* rituals and trappings. The early church indeed worshiped God *in spirit and in truth*, and with simplicity. There were certain guidelines set by the apostles as to the requirements necessary to hold the office of a bishop or deacon, such as being husband to only one wife, etc. (1 Timothy 3:2–13; Titus 1:5–9). The requirements pertained mainly to moral conduct, and there were no directives as to bishops or pastors setting themselves apart from the rest of the congregation in any particular mode of dress, such as clerical robes or collars, etc. Choir robes were not worn, nor were records kept of each individual's giving of tithes, as we do in our churches today. Many of the practices and observances of today's church are traditions that have developed over the centuries and do not conform to or remotely resemble the practices and observances of the early church.

One of the many deviations of the Roman Catholic Church from the early church is the canonization of saints.

The word saint has undergone a significant change in meaning during the approximately 2,000 years of Christianity. In the Hebrew Bible (Old Testament) it applies to any Israelite, one of God's chosen people. In the New Testament its meaning is similar, referring to any Christian. Basically, as Paul the Apostle noted in his Epistle to the Romans, the word refers to anyone who is set apart from others for God's service … The authority to declare a person a saint is, in the Roman Catholic Church, reserved for the pope. The first step toward sainthood is beatification, which implies limited permission to venerate. The act of declaring a saint is called canonization because the procedure is done in accordance with codes of canon law (see Canon Law). Canonization imposes veneration of the saint upon the whole church, and prayers of intercession may be offered to the saint. This implies a belief that the saint is able to intercede with God on behalf of the one who prays.

*Compton's Interactive Encyclopedia*

Differentiating between Old and New Testament saints is unbiblical. According to the *Catechism of the Catholic Church*, paragraph #61, "The patriarchs, prophets and certain other Old Testament figures have been and always will be honored as saints in all the Church's liturgical traditions."

However, neither Moses, Abraham, Isaac, Jacob, nor any of the other Old Testament saints mentioned in Hebrews chapter eleven have been canonized by the Roman Catholic Church. The Old Testament saints and certain *spirits* of the dead, to whom Christ preached the gospel, are also members of Christ's *universal* church, which is his *one body* spoken of in Ephesians 4:4. The canonization of saints undermines the plain teaching of the inspired Scriptures. God is not a respecter of persons (Galatians 2:6; Acts 10:34; James 2:1, 8–9; Matthew 22:16; Romans 2:11; 1 Timothy 5:21; 1 Corinthians 4:6), and the members of the body of Christ are not to exalt one member of his body above another.

But of these who seemed to be somewhat, (whatsoever they were, it maketh no matter to me: *God accepteth no man's person:*) for they who seemed to be somewhat in conference added nothing to me.

Galatians 2:6, emphasis added

Therefore *let no man glory in men.* For all things are yours; Whether Paul, or Apollos, or Cephas [Peter], or the world, or life, or death, or things present, or things to come; all are yours; And ye are Christ's; and Christ is God's.

1 Corinthians 3:21–23, emphasis added

And these things, brethren, I have in a figure transferred to myself and to Apollos for your sakes; that ye might learn in us *not to think of men above that which is written*, that no one of you be puffed up for one against another.

1 Corinthians 4:6, emphasis added

Nay, much more those members of the body, which seem to be more feeble, are necessary: And *those members of the body, which we think to be less honourable, upon these we bestow more abundant honour*, and our uncomely parts have more abundant comeliness. For our comely parts have no need: but *God hath tempered the body together, having given more abundant honour to that part which lacked*: That there should be no schism in the body; but that *the members should have the same care one for another.*

1 Corinthians 12:22–25, emphasis added

Notice, in the following Old and New Testament scriptures, that every saint throughout the history of the world plays exactly the same role of judging at the return of Jesus Christ to earth. Also notice that the Apostle Paul refers to those who are "least esteemed in the church" as "saints."

Dare any of you, having a matter against another, go to law before the unjust, and not before the saints? Do ye not know that *the saints shall judge the world?* and if *the world shall be judged by you*, are ye unworthy to judge the smallest matters? Know ye not that *we shall judge angels?* how much more things that pertain to this life? If then ye have judgments of things pertaining to this life, set them to judge *who are least esteemed in the church.*

1 Corinthians 6:1–4, emphasis added

Praise ye the Lord. Sing unto the Lord a new song, *and* his praise in *the congregation of saints.* Let Israel rejoice in him that made him: let the children of Zion be joyful in their King. Let them praise his name in the dance: let them sing praises unto him with the timbrel and harp. For the Lord taketh pleasure in his people: he will beautify the meek with salvation. *Let the saints be joyful in glory:* let them sing aloud upon their beds. Let the high praises of God be in their mouth, and *a twoedged sword in their hand; To execute vengeance upon the heathen, and punishments upon the people;* To bind their kings with chains, and their nobles with fetters of iron; *To execute upon them the judgment written:* this honour have *all his saints.* Praise ye the Lord.

Psalm 149:1–9, emphasis added
cf. Hebrews 4:12; John 12:48; Ephesians 6:17; Revelation 19:14–15

But *the saints* of the most High shall take the kingdom, and possess the kingdom for ever, even for ever and ever. I beheld, and the same horn made war with the saints, and prevailed against them; *Until the Ancient of days came, and judgment was given to the saints* of the most High; and the time came that *the saints* possessed the kingdom.

Daniel 7:18, 21–22, emphasis added

And Enoch also, the seventh from Adam, prophesied of these, saying, Behold, *the Lord cometh with ten thousands of his saints, To execute judgment upon all,* and to convince all that are ungodly among them of all their ungodly deeds which they have ungodly committed, and of all their hard speeches which ungodly sinners have spoken against him.

Jude 14–15, emphasis added

To the end he may stablish your hearts unblameable in holiness before God, even our Father, *at the coming of our Lord Jesus Christ with all his saints.*
1 Thessalonians 3:13, emphasis added

And ye shall flee to the valley of the mountains; for the valley of the mountains shall reach unto Azal: yea, ye shall flee, like as ye fled from before the earthquake in the days of Uzziah king of Judah: and *the LORD my God shall come, and all the saints with thee.*
Zechariah 14:5, emphasis added

For if we believe that Jesus died and rose again, even so *them also which sleep in Jesus will God bring with him.*
1 Thessalonians 4:14, emphasis added

And other sheep I have, which are not of this fold: *them also I must bring*, and they shall *hear my voice*; and there shall be *one fold*, and *one shepherd*.
John 10:16, emphasis added

The above scriptures are all in view of the Lord's return to earth with his *one fold*, which includes the spirits of the dead to whom Jesus preached when he descended into the heart of the earth after his crucifixion. Those spirits who *heard his voice* and *believed* his preaching were made alive in Christ and became members of his one body, his universal church. As the Apostle Paul said, "For to this end Christ both died, and rose, and revived, that he might be Lord both of the dead and living (Romans 14:9).

Jesus said:

Verily, verily, I say unto you, He that heareth my word, and believeth on him that sent me, hath everlasting life, and shall not come into condemnation; but is passed from death unto life. Verily, verily, I say unto you, *The hour is coming, and now is, when the dead shall hear the voice of the Son of God*: and they that *hear* shall *live*.

John 5:24–25, emphasis added

For as Jonas was three days and three nights in the whale's belly; *so shall the Son of man be three days and three nights in the heart of the earth.*

Matthew 12:40, emphasis added

And there arose certain, and bare false witness against him, saying, We heard him say, I will destroy this temple that is made with hands, and *within three days I will build another made without hands.*

Mark 14:57–58, emphasis added

For Christ also hath once suffered for sins, the just for the unjust, that he might bring us to God, being put to death in the flesh, but quickened by the Spirit: By which also *he went and preached unto the spirits in prison*; Which sometime were disobedient, when once the longsuffering of God waited in the days of Noah, while the ark was a preparing, wherein few, that is, eight souls were saved by water.

1 Peter 3:18–20, emphasis added

For this cause was *the gospel preached also to them that are dead*, that they might be judged according to men in the flesh, *but live* according to God *in the spirit.*

1 Peter 4:6, emphasis added

Wherefore he saith, When he ascended up on high, he led captivity captive, and gave gifts unto men. (Now that he ascended, what is it but that *he also descended first into the lower parts of the earth*? He that descended is the same also that ascended up far above all heavens, *that he might fill all things.*

Ephesians 4:8–10, emphasis added

Jesus was in the heart of the earth three days and nights preaching to everyone who had died, from Adam to the thief on the cross-to whom he said, "Verily I say unto thee, To day shalt thou be with me in paradise" (Luke 23:43). As depicted in what some deem as the parable of the rich man and Lazarus, *paradise and the bosom of Abraham* are one and the same place, which is separated from hell by *a great gulf* (Luke 16:19–31).

The Apostle Paul said, "The scripture, foreseeing that God would justify the heathen through faith, preached before the gospel unto Abraham" (Galatians 3:8). He also said that it "was preached to every creature which is under heaven" (Colossians 1:23), which also includes the dead spirits to whom Jesus preached when he descended into the lower parts of the earth.

As pertaining to those who came out of Egypt and died in the wilderness, Paul said: "For unto us was the gospel preached, as well as unto them: but the word preached did not profit them, not being mixed with faith in them that heard it" (Hebrews 3:16–4:2).

Jesus not only preached the gospel to the disobedient spirits of the dead but also to those of faith, such as Abel, Enoch, Noah, Abraham, Isaac, and Jacob, etc. (Hebrews 11:1–10). As pertaining to these same Old Testament saints, the Apostle Paul said, "And these all, having obtained a good report through faith, received not the promise: God having provided some better thing for us, that they without us should not be made perfect" (Hebrews 11:39–40). The promise the apostle referred to is the promise of the *Holy Spirit of life*, which is received through faith in the word of truth, the gospel (Galatians 3:2–3; Galatians 3:14, 21; 1 John 2:25; Revelation 11:11; Romans 8:2; Romans 8:10; 1 Peter 4:6; Ephesians 1:13).[5]

In the very next chapter, Hebrews 12, the apostle addresses these same Old Testament saints as *spirits of just men made per-*

*fect* and members of the general assembly and church of Jesus Christ, saying,

> But ye are come unto mount Sion, and unto the city of the living God, the heavenly Jerusalem, and to an innumerable company of angels, To *the general assembly and church* of the firstborn, which are written in heaven, and to God the judge of all, and to *the spirits* of just men *made perfect*, And *to Jesus* the mediator of *the new covenant*, and *to the blood of sprinkling*, that speaketh better things than that of Abel.
> Hebrews 12:22–24, emphasis added

The "members of the *general assembly and church of Jesus Christ*" in Hebrews 12:22–24 are the same "*family of God in heaven and earth*" the Apostle Paul referred to in Ephesians 3:14–16. The same family of God that Paul described as "the mystery of God" in Ephesians 1:9–10 and Colossians 1:26–28

> For this cause I bow my knees unto the Father of our Lord Jesus Christ, Of whom *the whole family in heaven and earth* is named, That he would grant you, according to the riches of his glory, to be strengthened with might by his Spirit in the inner man;
> Ephesians 3:14–16, emphasis added

> Having made known unto us *the mystery* of his will ... that in the dispensation of the fulness of times he might gather together in one all things in Christ, both *which are in heaven, and which are on earth; even in him*
> Ephesians 1:9–10, emphasis added

> Even *the mystery* which hath been hid from ages and from generations, but *now* is *made manifest to his saints*: To whom God would make known what is the riches of the glory of this mystery among the Gentiles; which is *Christ in you*, the hope of glory: Whom we preach, warning every man,

and teaching every man in all wisdom; that we may present every man *perfect in Christ Jesus.*

Colossians 1:26–28, emphasis added

This is precisely what Jesus was talking about when, just before the passion, he prayed to the Father regarding his apostles, saying,

> For I have given unto them the words which thou gavest me; and they have received them, and have known surely that I came out from thee, and they have believed that thou didst send me ... *Sanctify them* through thy truth: *thy word is truth* ... Neither pray I for these alone, but for them also which shall *believe* on me through their word; *That they all may be one;* as thou, Father, art in me, and I in thee, *that they also may be one in us:* that the world may believe that thou hast sent me ... I in them, and thou in me, that they may be *made perfect in one;* and that the world may know that thou hast sent me, and *hast loved* them, as thou hast loved me.
>
> John 17:8, 20–21, 23, emphasis added

This is the same Word of Truth, the same *gospel* Jesus preached to the spirits of the dead (1 Peter 4:6). Those who believed his preaching were *sanctified* and made perfect in one. "Both he that sanctifieth and they who are sanctified are all of one" (Hebrews 2:11–12). Being made perfect in one through faith in Christ's sacrificial blood for the remission of our sins is the essence of the new covenant message of the gospel of Christ. The same gospel where *by faith* we are saved, justified, sanctified, inherit God's promise of the Holy Spirit of eternal life, and become members of His *one* and *only body*, Christ's one true church.

Compare the following scriptures:

Then said he, Lo, I come to do thy will, O God. *He taketh away the first, that he may establish the second.* By the which will *we are sanctified through the offering of the body of Jesus Christ once for all.* And every priest standeth daily ministering and offering oftentimes the same sacrifices, which can never take away sins: But this man, after he had *offered one sacrifice for sins for ever,* sat down on the right hand of God; From henceforth expecting till his enemies be made his footstool. For by one offering he *hath perfected for ever* them that are *sanctified.*

Hebrews 10:9–14, emphasis added

But we are bound to give thanks alway to God for you, brethren beloved of the Lord, because God hath from the beginning chosen you to *salvation through sanctification of the Spirit* and *belief of the Truth*: Whereunto he called you by our gospel, to the obtaining of the glory of our Lord Jesus Christ.

2 Thessalonians 2:13–14, emphasis added

Wherefore *Jesus* also, that he might *sanctify the people with his own blood,* suffered without the gate.

Hebrews 13:12, emphasis added

The Gentiles, unto whom now I send thee [Paul] To open their eyes, and to turn them from darkness to light, and *from the power of Satan* unto God, that they may receive *forgiveness of sins,* and *inheritance* among them which are *sanctified by faith that is in me.*

Acts 26:17–18, emphasis added

Being *justified freely* by his grace through the redemption that is in Christ Jesus: Whom God hath set forth to be a propitiation *through faith in his blood,* to declare his righteousness for the remission of sins that are past, through the forbearance of God.

Romans 3:24–25, emphasis added<br>cf. 1 Peter 1:18,19–23–25

Much more then, being *now justified by his blood*, we shall be saved from wrath through him.

Romans 5:9, emphasis added

Be it known unto you therefore, men and brethren, that through this man is preached unto you the forgiveness of sins: And by him *all* that *believe* are *justified* from all things, from which ye could not be justified by the law of Moses.

Acts 13:38–39, emphasis added

The teaching of the Roman Catholic Church, as pertaining to the body of Christ, does not conform to that which is taught in the Scriptures. According to the inspired Word of God, "both he that sanctifieth and they who are sanctified are all of one: for which cause he is not ashamed to call them brethren" (Hebrews 2:11). As seen in the above, *all* who *by faith in Jesus Christ*, that is, *by faith in his shed blood* for the remission of sins, are *sanctified* and *justified and* thus become members of his one and only body; which is his *universal/catholic* church. According to the catechism, it is not by faith in Christ but by *faith in water baptism* that we are *incorporated into* and made members of the body of Christ. The spirits of the dead who believed Christ's preaching were not baptized in water but are nevertheless members of the one body of Christ, his *universal* church.

*Catechism of the Catholic Church*

818 However, one cannot charge with the sin of the separation those who at present are born into these communities [that resulted from such separation] and in them are brought up in the faith of Christ, and the Catholic Church accepts them with respect and affection as brothers ... All who have been *justified by faith in Baptism* are *incorporated into Christ*; they therefore have a right to be called Christians, and with good reason are accepted

as brothers in the Lord by the children of the Catholic Church. , emphasis added

*Catechism of the Catholic Church*, p.216

1271 Baptism constitutes the foundation of communion among all Christians, including those who are *not yet in full communion with the Catholic Church*: "For *men who believe in Christ* and have been properly baptized are put in some, though *imperfect*, COMMUNION with the Catholic Church. *Justified by faith in Baptism, they are incorporated into Christ;* they therefore have a right to be called Christians, and with good reason are accepted as brothers by the children of the Catholic Church." "*Baptism* therefore constitutes the sacramental bond of unity existing among *all who through it are reborn.*"

*Catechism of the Catholic Church* p. 323

According to the above, Christians who *believe* in Christ but are not members of the Roman Catholic Church are *put in some, though imperfect, communion with the Catholic Church.* However, they are nevertheless *incorporated into Christ* and are accepted as brothers by the children of the Catholic Church. This is not speaking of one body but two.

Now this I say, that every one of you saith, I am of Paul; and I of Apollos; and I of Cephas; and I of Christ. *Is Christ divided?* was Paul crucified for you? or were ye baptized in the name of Paul?

i Corinthians 1:12–13, emphasis added

For as *the body is one*, and hath many members, and all the members of that *one body*, being many, are *one body: so also is Christ*. For *by one Spirit* are we *all* baptized into *one body*, whether we be Jews or Gentiles, whether we be bond or free; and have been all made to drink into one Spirit. For the body is not one member, but many.

i Corinthians 12:12–14, emphasis added

There is *one body*, and one Spirit, even as ye are called in one hope of your calling; one Lord, one faith, *one baptism*.

Ephesians 4:4–5, emphasis added

If the *Roman Catholic Church* and the *one body* in Ephesians 4:4 are, in fact, one and the same body of Christ, those who through faith in Christ have been incorporated into Christ and made *perfect in one* cannot be put in *imperfect* communion with the Roman Catholic Church. The statements in the catechism point to two different entities: (1) The *members of the earthly Roman Catholic Church*, collectively, and (2) the *members of the whole family of God in heaven and earth*, collectively, which is the one and only body of Christ, the true church, the *spiritual* habitation and temple of God; which also includes those members of the Roman Catholic Church who believe the gospel's basic message of salvation in Christ Jesus and who love the Lord but are unaware of the fact that many doctrines of Roman Catholicism are false—including doctrines on *water baptism*.

There are various *baptisms* mentioned in Holy Scripture but, as stated in Ephesians 4:5, there is only *one* baptism. According to the Word of God, and contrary to Roman Catholic doctrine, this *one* baptism is not *water* baptism but *Holy Spirit* baptism. "By one Spirit are we all baptized into one body" (1 Corinthians 12:13). In the baptism into Christ, Jesus Christ, God almighty himself, is the baptizer (John 1:33, 34). In water baptism, man is the baptizer.

I [John] *indeed baptize you with water* unto repentance: but he that cometh after me is mightier than I, whose shoes I am not worthy to bear: *he shall baptize you with the Holy Ghost*, and with fire.

Matthew 3:11, emphasis added

Wait for the promise of the Father, which, saith he, ye have heard of me. For *John truly baptized with water*, but *ye shall be baptized with the Holy Ghost* not many days hence.

Acts 1:4–5, emphasis added

*Can any man forbid water*, that these should not be *baptized*, which *have received the Holy Ghost* as well as we?

Acts 10:47, emphasis added

And *as I began to speak, the Holy Ghost fell on them*, as on us at the beginning. Then remembered I the word of the Lord, how that he said, *John indeed baptized with water*, but *ye shall be baptized with the Holy Ghost.*

Acts 11:15–16, emphasis added

Water baptism is the outward expression of our faith in Jesus Christ's death, burial, and resurrection and symbolizes our identification with the *one* body of Christ. The moment we believe the gospel's message of salvation, the Lord Jesus baptizes us with his Holy Spirit (John 7:38–39; Galatians 3:2, 14; Ephesians 1:13) and we are *born again*. This is the *one* and only baptism spoken of in Ephesians 4:6. Water baptism does not save. We are saved by grace and *born of God* through faith in his Word concerning the sacrifice of his Son as full payment for our sins—past, present, and future.

The Apostle Paul said:

I thank God that I baptized none of you ... For Christ sent me not to baptize, but to preach the gospel: not with wisdom of words, lest the cross of Christ should be made of none effect. For the preaching of the cross is to them that perish foolishness; but unto us which are saved it is the power of God ... The world by wisdom knew not God, it pleased God by the foolishness of preaching to save them that believe.

1 Corinthians 1:14, 16–18, 21

This is the same gospel the Apostle Peter was preaching when the Holy Ghost fell on those who heard and believed his preaching (Acts 11:16). If read in context (Acts 10:34 through 11:16), it is very clear that the Holy Spirit is not received by way of water baptism but by faith in the preaching of the cross of Jesus Christ. As seen in the following excerpt, the Roman Catholic Church's teaching on salvation is quite different from the gospel the Apostle Paul preached.

> 1257 The Lord himself affirms that Baptism is necessary for salvation...The Church does not know of any means other than Baptism that assures entry into eternal beatitude...She has received from the Lord to see that all who can be baptized are "reborn of water and the Spirit." God has bound salvation to the sacrament of baptism.
>
> *Catechism of the Catholic Church*, p.320

Water baptism is not necessary for salvation. The Roman Catholic Church's teaching on water baptism is based on 1 Peter 3:20–21, John 3:5, and the one and only verse in all of holy Scripture that mentions both baptism and salvation within the same context, Mark 16:16. "He that believeth and is baptized shall be saved; but he that believeth not shall be damned." Mark 16:16 is not speaking of water baptism but of Holy Spirit baptism. We are saved by grace through faith, which precedes water baptism.

If salvation were by way of water baptism, the Apostle Paul would never have said: "I thank God that I baptized none of you...For Christ sent me not to baptize, but to preach the gospel...It pleased God by the foolishness of preaching to save them that believe" (1 Corinthians 1:16–17, 21).

Nor was the Apostle Peter referring to *water* baptism in 1 Peter 3:20–21 when he talked about the days of Noah and the eight souls that were *saved by water*. He said that water is "the like figure whereunto even baptism doth also now save us." *The like figure?* The Apostle Peter was talking about Holy Spirit baptism of which *water* is *the like figure*. This is made indisputably clear in John 7:38–39 and John 4:10 and 14. Notice in John 4:10 that Jesus referred to living water as *the gift of God*. The gift of God is the Holy Spirit of life.[6]

> If any man thirst, let him come unto me, and drink. He that *believeth on me*, as the scripture hath said, out of his belly shall flow *rivers of living water*. (But *this spake he of the Spirit*, which they that *believe* on him should receive: for *the Holy Ghost* was not yet given; because that Jesus was not yet glorified.)
>
> John 7:37–39, emphasis added

> Jesus answered and said unto her, If thou knewest *the gift of God*, and who it is that saith to thee, Give me to drink; thou wouldest have asked of him, and he would have given thee *living water*... But whosoever drinketh of the water that I shall *give* him shall *never thirst*; but the water that I shall give him shall be in him a well of *water springing up into everlasting life.*
>
> John 4:10 and 14, emphasis added

The Lord Jesus and the Apostle Peter were both talking about the same thing: *living water/the Holy Spirit*. Peter spoke of the *like figure* in the very same passage wherein he said that Jesus preached the gospel to the spirits of the dead: "For this cause was *the gospel preached* also to them that are dead, that they might be judged according to men in the flesh, but *live* according to God *in the spirit*" (1 Peter 3:18–19 and 4:6). Those who *heard* and *believed* Jesus's preaching were given *living water/the Holy Spirit*. There can be absolutely no doubt that what Jesus preached to the spirits of the dead was the gospel's message of salvation and eternal life through faith in his blood of the new covenant, the same *preaching of the cross* the Apostle Paul talked about in 1 Corinthians 1:18.

Notice the beautiful harmony of the inerrant Word of God in the following. The prophet Isaiah talks about the new covenant and God's free gift of eternal life, about coming to the *waters* with *no money, without price*. God's gift of eternal life is just that…totally free! We are "saved by God's grace through faith; and that not of yourselves: it is the gift of God: *Not of works*, lest any man should boast" (Ephesians 2:8–9; 2 Timothy 1:9–10). There's absolutely nothing anyone can do to earn or gain eternal life but to hear and believe the gospel of Jesus Christ and to know in our hearts that Jesus did it all. He died in our place to pay for our sins because the wages of sin is death. But the gift of God is eternal life through faith in Jesus Christ (Romans 6:22–23). We are justified *freely* through faith in the blood he shed as full payment for our sins (Romans 3:24–25).

> Ho, every one that thirsteth, come ye to *the waters*, and he that hath *no money*; come ye, buy, and eat; yea, come, buy wine and milk without money and *without price*. Wherefore do ye spend money for that which is not bread? and your labour for that which satisfieth not? hearken diligently unto me, and eat ye that which is good, and let your soul delight itself in fatness. *Incline your ear*, and come unto me: *hear, and your soul shall live*; and I will make an *everlasting covenant* with you, even the sure mercies of David.
> Isaiah 55:1–3, emphasis added

> But now *being made free from sin*, and become servants to God, ye have your fruit unto holiness, and the end everlasting life. For *the wages of sin is death*; but *the gift of God is eternal life* through Jesus Christ our Lord.
> Romans 6:22–23, emphasis added

> Being *justified freely* by his grace through the redemption that is in Christ Jesus: Whom God hath set forth to be a propitiation *through faith in his blood*, to declare his righteousness for the remission of sins that are past, through the forbearance of God.
> Romans 3:24–25, emphasis added

He that spared not his own Son, but delivered him up for us all, how shall he not with him also *freely* give us *all things*? Who shall lay any thing to the charge of God's elect? It is God that justifieth.

Romans 8:32–33, emphasis added

The *waters* in Isaiah 55:1, as seen in the above, is the same *living water* that the Apostle John identified as *the Holy Spirit,* and that Jesus said would be given to those who *believe* in him (John 7:37–39). Jesus, in essence, repeated the same thing in Revelation 21:6–7, saying, "I will give unto him that is athirst of the fountain of the water of life freely. He that overcometh shall inherit all things; and I will be his God, and he shall be my son." Thus, he that overcometh, is he who believes that Jesus is the Christ" and is given *living water,* which is the Holy Spirit and is therefore *born again* of the Spirit of God:

> Whosoever *believeth* that Jesus is the Christ *is born of God*…For whatsoever is *born of God* overcometh the world: and this is the victory that overcometh the world, even our *faith.* Who is *he that overcometh* the world, but he that *believeth* that Jesus is the Son of God?
>
> 1 John 5:1, 4–5, emphasis added

In John 3:3–8 Jesus talked about being *born of God and the kingdom of God* saying, "Except a man be born of water and of the Spirit, he cannot enter into the kingdom of God. In light of the aforementioned Scriptures it is evident that Jesus was not referring to *literal* water but to the Holy Spirit." His reference to the kingdom of God in verses 3 and 5, is also indicative of the Holy Spirit because "the kingdom of God cometh not with observation … The kingdom of God is within you" (Luke 17:20–21).

Jesus referred to the Holy Spirit the third time in verse 8, saying, "The wind bloweth where it listeth, and thou hearest the sound thereof, but canst not tell whence it cometh, and whither it goeth: so is every one that is born of the Spirit." This is precisely what occurred on the day of Pentecost. "…There came *a sound* from heaven as of a rushing *mighty wind*… And they were all *filled* with *the Holy Ghost*…" (Acts 2:1–4, emphasis added)

> Jesus answered and said unto him, Verily, verily, I say unto thee, Except a man be born again, *he cannot see the kingdom of God*. Nicodemus saith unto him, How can a man be born when he is old? can he enter the second time into his mother's womb, and be born? Jesus answered, Verily, verily, I say unto thee, Except a man be *born of water and of the Spirit*, he cannot *enter into the kingdom of God*. That which is born of the flesh is flesh; and that which is *born of the Spirit* is *spirit*. Marvel not that I said unto thee, Ye must be born again. *The wind* bloweth where it listeth, and thou *hearest the sound* thereof, but *canst not tell whence it cometh*, and whither it goeth: so is every one that is *born of the Spirit*.
>
> John 3:3–8, emphasis added

According to *Vine's Expository Dictionary of New Testament Words* and *Strong's Concordance,* the word *and* in John 3:5 and the word *even* in the following scriptures are both translated from the same Greek word *KAI*.

> Jesus answered, Verily, verily, I say unto thee, Except a man be born of water *and* of the Spirit, he cannot enter into the kingdom of God.
>
> John 3:5 5, emphasis added

> Then cometh the end, when He shall have delivered up the kingdom to God, *even* the Father
>
> 1 Corinthians 15:24, emphasis added

To the end He may stablish your hearts unblameable in holiness before God *even* our Father at the coming of our Lord Jesus with all His saints.

1 Thessalonians 3:13, emphasis added

Therewith bless we God, *even* the Father; and therewith curse we men, which are made after the similitude of God.

James 3:9, emphasis added

In the above scriptures, if the Greek word *kai* were to be translated *and* instead of *even*, the verses would read: "... God, *and* the Father..." thus indicating two separate entities which would not conform to what the rest of what the Word of God says about the one and only God, our Father. In order for John 3:5 to conform to the rest of what the Word of God says about baptism, the word *and* must also be rendered the same as the above scriptures, *even* and/or *namely*—(born of water "namely" of the Spirit). Compare the following excerpts.

*Strong's:* (in part)
"*KAI*"-appar. a prim. particle, having a *copulative* and sometimes a *cumulative force*
*Vines':*
"*KAI*"-conjunction, is usually a mere connective meaning "and"; it frequently, however, has an *ascensive or climatic* use, signifying "even," the thing that is added being out of the ordinary, and producing a climax. The determination of this meaning depends on the context. The epexegetic or explanatory use of KAI followed by a noun *in opposition*, and meaning "namely" or "even" is comparatively rare ... some think it has this sense in John 3:5, "water, even the Spirit," and Galatians 6:16, "even the Israel of God."

Peace be on *them* and mercy, *"even"* upon the Israel of God.

Galatians 6:16, emphasis added

Except a man be born of water, *"even" (namely)* *of the Spirit*... That which is born of the flesh is flesh; and that which is *born of the Spirit* is spirit.

John 3:5, 6, emphasis added

We are *born again through faith in God's Word*. Through faith in Jesus Christ's death and resurrection; faith in the *blood* he shed as an all sufficient sacrifice in full payment for our sins. The moment we believe, we receive God's Holy Spirit (Ephesians 1:13; Galatians 3:2, 14; Acts 11:17). His spirit is joined to our spirit and we become one with him (1 Corinthians 6:17; Jeremiah 50:5; Hebrews 2:11; John 17:21, 23; Ephesians 5:30–32; Mark 10:7–9); he in us and we in him (John 14:20). His spirit indwells our spirit forever ( John 14:16–17; 2 John 1:2). In receiving *the Holy Spirit*, we inherit *eternal life* and become new creatures, created in Christ Jesus (2 Corinthians 5:17, 21; Ephesians 2:10; Ephesians 4:24; Galatians 6:15; Colossians 3:9–10). At which time we are *translated into the kingdom of God* (Colossians 1:12–14; Acts 26:18). All of this and more, *through faith* in the *Word of God*.

Being *born again,* not of corruptible seed, but of incorruptible, *by the word of God*, which liveth and abideth for ever.

1 Peter 1:23, emphasis added

*Whosoever believeth that Jesus is the Christ is born of God*: and every one that loveth *him that begat* loveth him also that is begotten of him.... For whatsoever is *born of God* overcometh the world: and this is the victory that overcometh the world, even our *faith*. Who is he that overcometh the world, but he that *believeth* that Jesus is the Son of God?

1 John 5:1, 4–5, emphasis added

For ye are all the *children* of God *by faith* in Christ Jesus.
Galatians 3:26, emphasis added

But as many as received him, to them gave he power to become *the sons of God*, even to them that *believe* on his name: *Which were born*, not of blood, nor *of the will of the flesh*, nor of *the will of* man, but *of God*.
John 1:12–13, emphasis added

*Of his own will begat he us with the word of truth*, that we should be a kind of firstfruits of his creatures.
James 1:18, emphasis added

In whom ye also trusted, after that ye heard the *word of truth*, the *gospel of your salvation*: in whom also *after that ye believed*, ye were sealed with that *holy Spirit of promise*.
Ephesians 1:13, emphasis added

But we are bound to give thanks always to God for you, brethren beloved of the Lord, because God hath from the beginning chosen you to *salvation through sanctification of the Spirit* and *belief of the truth*: Whereunto he called you *by our gospel*, to the obtaining of the glory of our Lord Jesus Christ.
2 Thessalonians 2:13–14, emphasis added

But he answered and said, It is written, Man shall not *live* by bread alone, but by *every word* that proceedeth *out of the mouth of God*.
Matthew 4:4, emphasis added

The words *water* and *wash(-ed)* in Scripture are often symbolic of the *Holy Spirit* and also of *the Word of God*. In John 15:3, Jesus told the disciples that they were *clean* through the *Word* he had spoken to them. In Ephesians 5:25, 26, the Apostle Paul said that Christ gave himself that he might sanctify and *cleanse* the church by the *washing* of *water by the Word*, and in 2 Thessalonians 2:13, that "God hath from the beginning chosen you to salvation through sanctification of the Spirit and belief of the truth." In 1 Corinthians 6:11, it's … "ye are washed, but ye are sanctified, but ye are justified in the name of the Lord Jesus, and by the Spirit of our God." Titus 3:5–6 says that God "saved us, by the washing of regeneration, and renewing of the Holy Ghost; which he shed on us abundantly through Jesus Christ our Saviour."

The word *regeneration* in Titus 3:5 is translated from the Greek word *paliggenesia.*

> #3824 paliggenesia {pal-ing-ghen-es-ee'-ah: (spiritual) rebirth (the state of the act), i.e. (fig.) spiritual renovation; spec. Messianic restoration: -regeneration.
> *Abingdon's Strong's Concordance, #3824*

Titus 3:5–6 clearly reveals the fact that the *washing* of regeneration and renewing of the Holy Spirit, by which we are born again is Holy Spirit baptism which is *shed on us abundantly through Jesus Christ*; the one who baptizes with the Holy Spirit (John 1:33). As Jesus said in Revelation 21:6–7, "I will give unto him that is athirst of the fountain of the water of life freely. He that overcometh shall inherit all things; and I will be his God, and he shall be my son." The symbolism used in Scripture of water and *wash (-ed)* is pointing to the cleansing of sin through faith in Christ's blood of the new covenant.

> Whom God hath set forth to be a propitiation *through faith in his blood*, to declare his righteousness for the *remission of sins* that are past, through the forbearance of God
> Romans 3:25, emphasis added

> Unto *him that loved us, and washed us from our sins in his own blood.*
> Revelation 1:5, emphasis added

Peter saith unto him, Thou shalt never wash my feet. Jesus answered him, *If I wash thee not, thou hast no part with me.*
John 13:8, emphasis added

But if we walk in the light, as he is in the light, we have fellowship one with another, and *the blood of Jesus Christ his Son cleanseth us from all sin.*
1 John 1:7, emphasis added

These are they which came out of great tribulation, and have washed their robes, and made them white *in the blood of the Lamb.*
Revelation 7:14, emphasis added

And they *overcame* him *by the blood of the Lamb*, and *by the word of their testimony*; and they loved not their lives unto the death.
Revelation 12:11, emphasis added

Let us draw near with a true heart *in full assurance of faith*, having our hearts sprinkled from an evil conscience, and our bodies *washed* with *pure water*. Let us hold fast the profession of our *faith* without wavering (for he is faithful that promised).
Hebrews 10:22–23, emphasis added

Then will I sprinkle *clean water* upon you, and ye shall be clean: from all your filthiness, and from all your idols, will I cleanse you. A new heart also will I give you, and *a new spirit will I put within you*: and I will take away the stony heart out of your flesh, and I will give you an heart of flesh. And *I will put my spirit within you*, and *cause you to walk in my statutes*, and ye shall keep my judgments, and do them.
Ezekiel 36:25–27, emphasis added

Now the God of peace, that brought again from the dead our Lord Jesus, that great shepherd of the sheep, *through the blood of the everlasting covenant*, Make you perfect in every good work to do his will, *working in you that which is wellpleasing in his sight, through Jesus Christ*, to whom be glory for ever and ever. Amen.

Hebrews 13:20–21, emphasis added

The Roman Catholic Church's teaching on water baptism belies the divine authority of the inspired Scriptures. The members of the body of Christ are chosen to salvation through sanctification of the Spirit and belief of the truth, not through faith in water baptism.[7]

2813 In the waters of Baptism, we have been washed … sanctified … justified in the name of the Lord Jesus Christ and in the Spirit of our God.

*Catechism of the Catholic Church*, p. 674

1271 Justified by faith in Baptism, [they] are incorporated into Christ; they therefore have a right to be called Christians, and with good reason are accepted as brothers by the children of the Catholic Church. Baptism therefore constitutes the sacramental bond of unity existing among all who through it are reborn.

*Catechism of the Catholic Church*, p. 323

For my people have committed two evils; they have forsaken me the fountain of living waters, and hewed them out cisterns, broken cisterns, that can hold no water.

Jeremiah 2:13

# GRACE

For by grace are ye saved through faith; and that not of yourselves: it is the gift of God: Not of works, lest any man should boast.

Ephesians 2:8–9

Due to much of the gibberish within the scope of Catholicism's various doctrines and dogmas, there is a common misunderstanding of Catholic terminology. For instance, Catholicism's meaning of the phrase *saved by grace through faith, not of works* is quite different from the biblical meaning of the gospel of grace as taught by the Apostle Paul. Catholicism's salvation is based upon God's grace by faith *plus good works*; not one's own works, but the good works of God, God working in him/her-which is the result of God's grace having been obtained by that person through his/her participation in the sacraments of the Roman Catholic Church. In other words, one has to perform the required action of participating in the sacraments in order to receive the grace of God which enables that person to collaborate with God's good works. This is not *free* grace. It's doing something for something. It's meritorious *works* and contrary to the teaching of Scripture.

Therefore *being justified by faith*, we have peace with God through our Lord Jesus Christ: By whom also *we have access by faith into this grace* wherein we stand, and rejoice in hope of the glory of God.

Romans 5:1–2, emphasis added

For *through him we* both *have access by one Spirit* unto the Father.

Ephesians 2:18, emphasis added

In whom *we have boldness and access with confidence by the faith of him.*

Ephesians 3:12, emphasis added

The Word of God tells us that we are to "come boldly to the throne of grace that we may obtain mercy, and find grace to help in time of need" (Hebrews 4:16). Nothing is required to receive the grace of God's *help in time of need* but to pray in faith, asking the Father in Jesus' name and to yield to the Holy Spirit.

The Apostle Paul said he had received of the Lord Jesus "the ministry to testify the gospel of the grace of God" (Acts 20:24). He said he was an apostle "not of men, neither by man, but by Jesus Christ, and God the Father...that the gospel which was preached of me is not after man. For I neither received it of man, neither was I taught it, but by the revelation of Jesus Christ" (Galatians 1:1, 11–12).

Paul wrote about "the riches of God's grace" (Ephesians 1:7; 2:7; 3:8), "the word of the truth of the gospel," and "knowing the grace of God in truth" (Colossians 1:5–6) but never mentioned anything anywhere in any of his epistles that would remotely resemble the Roman Catholic Church's teaching on the grace of God or the so-called Seven Sacraments.

Compare the following:

MARLENE C. CROUCH

And how *I [Paul] kept back nothing that was profitable unto you*, but have shewed you, and have taught you publicly, and from house to house.

Acts 20:20, emphasis added

For *I have not shunned to* declare unto you *all the counsel of God.*

Acts 20:27, emphasis added

Who hath saved us, and called us with an holy calling, *not according to our works*, but according to *his own purpose and grace*, which was given us in Christ Jesus before the world began, But is now made manifest by the appearing of our Saviour Jesus Christ, who hath abolished death, and hath brought life and immortality to light through the gospel: *Whereunto I am appointed a preacher, and an apostle, and a teacher of the Gentiles.*

2 Timothy 1:9–11, emphasis added

## The Apostle Paul wrote to the Galatians, saying,

I marvel that ye are so soon removed from Him that called you into the grace of Christ unto another gospel: which is not another; but there be some that trouble you and would *pervert the gospel of Christ.* But though we, or an angel from heaven, preach any other gospel unto you than that which we have preached unto you, let him be accursed. As we said before, so say I now again, If any man preach any other gospel unto you than that ye have received, let him be accursed.

Galatians 1:6–9, emphasis added

The following excerpts from the *Catechism of the Catholic Church* are presented as an example of Catholicism's perversion of the gospel of God's grace and in lieu of a lengthy dissertation on the mumbo jumbos of the Catechism and its erroneous teaching on obtaining not only the grace of God but also eternal life through the sacraments and meritorious works. Simply put, we are saved by grace and inherit eternal life through faith, not of works (Ephesians 2:8–9), not through the so-called sacraments and certainly not by commandment-keeping.[1]

2068 The Council of Trent teaches that *the Ten Commandments* are *obligatory* for Christians and that the justified man is still bound to keep them; the Second Vatican Council confirms: "The bishops, successors of the apostles, receive from the Lord ... the mission of teaching all peoples, and of preaching the Gospel to every creature, so that all men may *attain salvation through* faith, Baptism *and the observance of the Commandments.*, emphasis added

1345 As early as the second century we have the witness of St. Justin Martyr ... Then we all rise together and offer prayers for ourselves ... and for all others, wherever they may be, so that we may be found righteous *by our life and actions,* and *faithful to the commandments, so as to obtain eternal salvation.*, emphasis added

1129 The Church affirms that for believers the *sacraments* of the New Covenant *are necessary for salvation.* "Sacramental grace" is the grace of the Holy Spirit, given by Christ and proper to each sacrament. The Spirit heals and transforms those who receive him by conforming them to the Son of God. The fruit of the sacramental life is that the Spirit of adoption makes the faithful partakers in the divine nature by uniting them in a living union with the only Son, the Savior. , emphasis added

1113 *The whole liturgical life of the Church revolves around the Eucharistic sacrifice and the sacraments.* There are seven sacraments in the Church: Baptism, Confirmation or Chrismation, Eucharist, Penance, Anointing of the Sick, Holy Orders, and Matrimony. , emphasis added

2010 Since the initiative belongs to God in the order of grace, no one can merit the *initial* grace of forgiveness and

206

justification, at the beginning of conversion. Moved by the Holy Spirit and by charity, *we can then merit for ourselves and for others the graces needed for our sanctification*, for the increase of grace and charity, and *for the attainment of eternal life*. Even temporal goods like health and friendship can be merited in accordance with God's wisdom. These graces and goods are the object of Christian prayer. Prayer attends to the grace we need for *meritorious actions.*, emphasis added

2027 No one can merit the initial grace which is at the origin of conversion. Moved by the Holy Spirit, *we can merit for ourselves and for others all the graces needed to attain eternal life,* as well as necessary temporal goods., emphasis added

1843 By hope we desire, and with steadfast trust await from God, *eternal life and the graces to merit it.*, emphasis added

1533 Baptism, Confirmation, and Eucharist are sacraments of Christian initiation. They ground the common vocation of all Christ's disciples, a vocation to holiness and to the mission of evangelizing the world. They confer the graces needed for the life according to the Spirit during this life as pilgrims on the march towards the homeland. , emphasis added

2003 Grace is first and foremost the gift of the Spirit who justifies and sanctifies us. But grace also includes the gifts that the Spirit grants us to associate us with his work, to enable us to collaborate in the salvation of others and in the growth of the Body of Christ, the Church. *There* are sacramental graces gifts proper to the different sacraments., emphasis added

1131 *The sacraments* are efficacious signs of grace, instituted by Christ and entrusted to the Church, *by which divine life is dispensed to us.* The visible rites by which the sacraments are celebrated signify and make present the graces proper to each sacrament. They bear fruit in those who receive them with the required dispositions. , emphasis added

1075 Liturgical catechesis aims to initiate people into the mystery of Christ (It is "mystagogy.") by proceeding *from the visible to the invisible*, from the sign to the thing signified, *from the "sacraments" to the "mysteries."* Such catechesis is to be presented by local and regional catechisms. This Catechism, which aims to serve the whole Church in all the diversity of her rites and cultures, will present what is fundamental and common to the whole Church in the liturgy as mystery and as celebration. emphasis added

2008 *The merit of man* before God in the Christian life *arises from the fact that God has freely chosen to associate man with the work of His grace.* The fatherly action of God is first on his own initiative, and then follows man's free acting through his collaboration, so that the merit of good works is to be attributed in the first place to the grace of God, then to the faithful. Man's merit, moreover, itself is due to God, for his good actions proceed in Christ, from the predispositions and assistance given by the Holy Spirit. emphasis added

2009 The merits of our good works are gifts of the divine goodness. "Grace has gone before us; *now we are given what is due*... Our merits are God's gifts. emphasis added

1210 *Christ instituted the sacraments of the new law. There are seven*: Baptism, Confirmation (or Chrismation), the Eucharist, Penance, the Anointing of the Sick, Holy Orders and Matrimony. The seven sacraments touch all the stages and all the important moments of Christian life: they give birth and increase, healing and mission to the Christian's life of faith. emphasis added

1211 This order, while not the only one possible, does allow one to see that the sacraments form an organic whole in which each particular sacrament has its own vital place. In this organic whole, *the Eucharist occupies a unique place as the "Sacrament of sacraments"*: "all the other sacraments are ordered to it as to their end. emphasis added

1407 The Eucharist is the heart and the summit of the Church's life, for in it Christ associates his Church and all her members with his sacrifice of praise and thanksgiving offered once for all on the cross to his Father; by this sacrifice he pours out the graces of salvation on his Body which is the Church. emphasis added

2014 Spiritual progress tends toward *ever more intimate union with Christ.* This union is called "*mystical*" because it participates in *the mystery of Christ* through *the sacraments - "the holy mysteries"* - and, in him, in the mystery of the Holy Trinity. God calls us all to this intimate union with him, even if the special graces or extraordinary signs of this mystical life are granted only to some for the sake of manifesting the gratuitous gift given to all. emphasis added

1310 To receive the sacrament of Confirmation one must be in *a state of grace.* One should receive *the sacrament of Penance in order to be cleansed for the gift of the Holy Spirit.* More intense prayer should prepare one to receive the strength and graces of the Holy Spirit with docility and readiness to act. emphasis added

There is much said in the New Testament about those who were distorting the truth of God's Word concerning *the grace of God.* In Hebrews 10:29, we read about those "who hath trodden under foot the Son of God, and hath counted the blood of the covenant, wherewith he was sanctified, an unholy thing, and hath done despite unto the Spirit of grace." In Jude 1:4, we read about "certain men turning the grace of our God into lasciviousness, and denying the only Lord God, and our Lord Jesus Christ."

The Catechism's erroneous teaching and perversion of the gospel of God's grace is not surprising in view of the examples given herein of the false teachings of some of the earliest church fathers and alleged successors of the apostles. There most certainly is truth to be derived from the writings of the church fathers, but with regard to what is truth and what is not, there can also be found their personal opinions, which are not consistent one with another, and therefore their writings are not absolute *truth*; which is precisely why, *sola scriptura*, the Bible only, is the only guaranteed source of unadulterated truth.[2]

In John chapter 17, Just prior to his crucifixion, Jesus prayed to the Father, referring to his apostles as "the men which thou gavest me," saying: "I have given unto them the words which thou gavest me (v. 8). Then again, in verse 14, "I have given them thy word ... Sanctify them through thy truth: thy word is truth" (verse 17). "As thou hast sent me into the world, even so have I also sent them into the world" (verse 18). "Neither pray I for these alone, but for them also which shall believe on me through their word" (verses 8, 17, 18, 20).

Not through the word of just anyone (early church fathers, or so called *successors*, nor sincere but mistaken followers of the faith), but through the unadulterated oral and written words of the apostles.

However, as predicted numerous times by Jesus Christ and his apostles, the oral teachings of the apostles were soon corrupted, falling prey to false teachers "in sheep's clothing" (Matthew 7:15; Acts 20:29–31; Matthew24:4–5, 11, 24; 2 Peter 2:1–2). Church leaders blending the adulterated apostolic teachings with Greek philosophical concepts further corrupted the apostles oral teachings and resulted in speculative theology. Hence, the original oral teachings of the apostles have been lost and the one and only genuine source of unadulterated truth left to the church is the inspired written word of God contained in both the Old and New Testaments.

Jude admonished those who were sanctified, preserved in Jesus Christ and called, to "remember the words which *were spoken before* of the apostles of our Lord Jesus Christ," and to "earnestly contend for *the faith* which was *once delivered* unto the saints."

> Jude, the servant of Jesus Christ, and brother of James, to *them that are sanctified* by God the Father, and preserved in Jesus Christ, and called: Mercy unto you, and peace, and love, be multiplied. Beloved, when I gave all diligence to write unto you of the common salvation, it was needful for me to write unto you, and exhort you that ye should *earnestly contend for the faith which was once delivered unto the saints.* For there are certain men crept in unawares, who were before of old ordained to this condemnation, ungodly men, *turning the grace of our God into lasciviousness, and denying the only Lord God, and our Lord Jesus Christ.* I will therefore put you in remembrance, though ye once knew this, how that the Lord, having saved the people out of the land of Egypt, afterward *destroyed them that believed not* ... But, beloved, *remember ye the words which were spoken before of the apostles of our Lord Jesus Christ.*
>
> Jude 1:1–5, 17, emphasis added

The Apostle Peter said, "desire the sincere milk of the word, that ye may grow thereby" (1 Peter 2:2). The Roman Catholic Church's spurious teachings on the grace of God can not stand in the light of the inspired Word of God contained in the Old and the New Testaments. The word *grace* is mentioned 122 times in the New Testament and not once is it used in connection with Catholicism's so-called *sacraments.*

According to the Apostle Peter, *the grace of God is "mul-tiplied" to us*, not through seven sacraments but, *"through the knowledge of God, and of Jesus Christ our Lord."*

It is through the Old Testament scriptures of the proph-ets as revealed to the apostles by Jesus Christ that we have the knowledge of God, and of Jesus Christ our Lord. The fundamental truth of the Gospel message of Jesus Christ is contained in the Old Testament scriptures of the prophets and in the words Jesus gave to his apostles, which were later written down.

> *Search the scriptures*; for in them ye think ye have eternal life: and they are they which testify of me [Jesus Christ].
>
> John5:39 , emphasis added

> *God*, who at sundry times and in divers manners spake in time past unto the fathers *by the prophets, Hath in these last days spoken unto us by his Son.*
>
> Hebrews 1:1–2, emphasis added

> Now to him that is of power to stablish you according to my gospel, and the preaching of Jesus Christ, according to *the revelation of the mystery*, which was kept secret since the world began, but *now* is *made manifest*, and *by the scriptures of the prophets* ...
>
> Romans 16:25–26, emphasis added

> And he [Jesus] said unto them, These *are the words which I spake unto you*, while I was yet with you, that *all things* must be fulfilled, *which were written* in the law of Moses, and *in* the prophets, and *in* the psalms, *concerning me*. Then opened he their understanding, that they might *understand the scriptures*,
>
> Luke24:44–45, emphasis added

> And *this is life eternal*, that they might *know thee the only true God, and Jesus Christ*, whom thou hast sent ... For *I*

*have given unto them the words which thou gavest me;* and they have received them, and have known surely that I came out from thee, and they have believed that thou didst send me ... *I have given them thy word.*

John 17:3, 8, 14, emphasis added

And we know that *the Son of God* is come, and *hath given us an understanding,* that we may *know him* that is true, and we are in him that is true, even in his Son Jesus Christ. *This is the true God, and eternal life.*

1 John 5:20, emphasis added

*Grace* and peace *be multiplied* unto you *through the knowledge of God, and of Jesus our Lord,* According as his divine power hath given unto us all things that pertain unto life and godliness, *through the knowledge of him* that hath called us to glory and virtue.

2 Peter 1:2–3, emphasis added

Be not carried about with *divers and strange doctrines.* For it is a good thing that the heart be established with *grace;* not with meats, which have not profited them that have been occupied therein.

Hebrews 13:9, emphasis added

Which they that are unlearned and unstable wrest, as they do also the other Scriptures, unto their own destruction. Ye therefore, beloved, seeing ye know these things before, *beware* lest ye also, being led away with the *error* of the wicked, fall from your own steadfastness. But *grow in grace,* and *in the knowledge of our Lord and Saviour Jesus Christ.*

2 Peter 3:16–18, emphasis added

Now our Lord Jesus Christ Himself, and God, even our Father, which *hath loved us,* and hath given us *everlasting* consolation and good hope *through grace,* comfort your hearts, and *stablish you* in every good word and work.

2 Thessalonians 2:16–17, emphasis added

# TRANSUBSTANTIATION

St. Augustine [354–430], one of the most influential church fathers said, "Christ bore himself in his hands, when he offered his body saying,
"This is my body."

According to the tradition of the Roman Catholic Church, the bread and wine of the Eucharist are changed into the actual body and blood of Jesus Christ, and it is by eating and drinking Christ's flesh and blood that we receive remission of sins, eternal life, and special graces. This doctrine is referred to as *Transubstantiation* and/or *The Real Presence* and is based primarily on a literal interpretation of the parable in John 6:26–69 with reference to the gospel accounts of the Lord's supper in Matthew 26:26–28; Mark 14:22–24; Luke 22:15–20; and also 1 Corinthians 11:23–26.

The perfect harmony of God's Word throughout the Holy Scriptures negates any possibility of a literal interpretation of the parable in John chapter six. Shortly after Jesus arose from the dead, he appeared to his disciples and said,

These are the words which I spake unto you, while I was yet with you, that all things must be fulfilled, which were written in the law of Moses, and in the prophets, and in the psalms, concerning me. Then opened he their understanding, that they might understand the scriptures.

Luke 24:44–45

There is not the slightest hint of *transubstantiation* within the context of anything which is written in the Law of Moses, the prophets, and the Psalms, concerning Jesus Christ. *Thus,* Transubstantiation, the transformation of bread and wine into Christ's flesh and blood, is not included in the *all things written in the Scriptures* that Jesus said were to be *fulfilled* concerning him.

This is an extremely critical factor when considering that according to The *Catechism of The Catholic Church*, the Eucharistic 'real presence' of Christ's flesh and blood is "the source and summit of the Christian life," "the whole spiritual good of the Church," and "the sum and summary of our faith" (p.334, #1324 and #1327), "the center of the Church's life" (p.339, #1343). Those who partake of the Eucharist are "united to all the faithful in one body" (p.341, #1353 and p.352, #1396). It "reconciles us with the Father" (p.341, #1354), and it "fills us with every heavenly blessing and grace" (p.349, #1383), "cleanses us from past sins and preserves us from future sins" (p.351, #1393), "strengthens our charity" (p.352, #1394), and it is "especially in the Eucharist, that Christ Jesus works in fullness for the transformation of men" (p.279, #1074) (cf. 2 Corinthians 3:18).[1]

Not one of the Catechism's statements in the above can be validated by the inspired written Word of God; and yet the Apostle Paul said, "whatsoever things were written aforetime were written for our learning" (Romans 15:4). He "persuaded people concerning Jesus, both out of the law of Moses, and out of the prophets, from morning till evening" (Acts 28:23). He "believed all things that are written in the law and the prophets" and taught nothing else, concerning Jesus Christ, other than what was written (Acts 24:14, 26:22). He said, "I kept back nothing that was profitable unto you, but have shewed you, and have taught you publickly, and from house to house." He taught absolutely nothing that would remotely hint of literally eating Christ's flesh and blood to receive remission of sins, eternal life, and *special graces;* nor did Moses, the prophets, Jesus, Peter, James, John, or Jude.

216

But those things, which God before had shewed by the mouth of all his prophets, that Christ should suffer, he hath so fulfilled ... Which God hath spoken by the mouth of all his holy prophets since the world began.

Acts 3:18, 21

O fools, and slow of heart to believe all that the prophets have spoken: Ought not Christ to have suffered these things, and to enter into his glory? And beginning at Moses and *all the prophets*, he (Christ) expounded unto them *in all the scriptures* the things concerning himself.

Luke 24:25–27, emphasis added

These are the words which I spake unto you, while I was yet with you, that *all things* must be fulfilled which was written in the law of Moses and in the prophets and in the psalms, *concerning me*. Then opened he their understanding, that they might understand the scriptures. Thus it is written, and thus it behoved Christ to suffer, and to rise from the dead the third day: And that repentance and remission of sins should be preached in his name among all nations, beginning at Jerusalem.

Luke 24:44–47, emphasis added

To him give all the prophets witness, that through his name whosoever *believeth* in him shall receive remission of sins.

Acts 10:43, emphasis added

From a child thou hast known the Holy Scriptures, which are able to make thee wise unto salvation *through faith* which is in Christ Jesus. *All Scripture* is given by inspiration of God, and is profitable for doctrine, for reproof, for correction, for instruction in righteousness ... Preach the Word; be instant in season, out of season; reprove, rebuke, exhort with all longsuffering and doctrine; for the time will come when they will not endure sound doctrine, but after their own lusts shall they heap to themselves teachers, having itching ears. And they shall turn away their ears from the truth, and shall be turned unto fables.

2 Timothy 3:15–16; 4:2–4, emphasis added

Paul's warning to the elders of the Church (AD 58):

For I have not shunned to declare unto you *all the counsel of God.* Take heed therefore unto yourselves, and to all the flock, over the which the Holy Ghost hath made you overseers, to feed the church of God, which he hath purchased with his own blood. For I know this, that after my departing shall grievous wolves enter in among you, not sparing the flock. *Also of your own selves* shall men arise, speaking perverse things, to draw away disciples after them. Therefore watch, and remember, that by the space of three years I ceased not to warn every one night and day with tears. And now, brethren, *I commend you to God, and to the word of his grace,* which is able to build you up, and to give you an inheritance among all them which are *sanctified.*

Acts 20:27–32, emphasis added

St. Jerome (347–420) said, "If an offense comes out of the truth, it is better that the offense come than the truth be concealed." [2] Pope Innocent III (1198–1216) not only decreed Transubstantiation but he also concealed the truth by forbidding the reading of God's Word in the vernacular.

Jesus prayed to the Father, saying, "Sanctify them through thy truth: thy word is truth" (John 17:17). The Apostle Paul said: "God hath from the beginning chosen you to salvation through sanctification of the Spirit and belief of the truth" (2 Thessalonians 2:13).

With the exception of the parable in John chapter six, nowhere in all of Holy Scripture is it stated that we receive eternal life by *literally* eating and drinking Christ's flesh and blood. According to the inspired Word of God it is by *God's grace,* through *faith in* Jesus Christ's bloody, sacrificial death at Calvary and his resurrection that we receive remission of sins and eternal life.

And ye have not *his word* abiding in you: for *whom he hath sent,* him ye *believe not. Search the scriptures;* for in them ye think ye have ETERNAL LIFE: and they are *they which testify of me.*

John 5:38–39, emphasis added

He that *believeth* on the Son of God hath the witness in himself: he that *believeth not God hath made him a liar,* because he *believeth not the record that God gave of his Son.* And *this is the record,* that God hath given to us *eternal life,* and this *life* is in his Son. He that hath the Son hath life; and he that hath not the Son of God hath not life. These things have I written unto you that *believe* on the name of the Son of God; that ye may *know* that ye *have eternal life,* and that ye may believe on the name of the Son of God.

1 John 5:10–13, emphasis added

Verily, verily, I say unto you, He that heareth *my word,* and *believeth* on him that sent me, *hath everlasting life,* and shall not come into condemnation; but *is passed from death unto life.*

John 5:24, emphasis added

But these are *written,* that ye might *believe* that *Jesus is the Christ, the Son of God;* and that *believing* ye might have *life* through his name.

John 20:31, emphasis added

But what saith it? *The word* is nigh thee, even in thy mouth, and in thy heart: that is, *the word of faith, which we preach;* That if thou shalt confess with thy mouth the Lord Jesus, and shalt *believe* in thine heart that God hath raised him from the dead, thou shalt be *saved.* For with the heart man *believeth* unto righteousness; and with the mouth confession is made unto salvation. For *the scripture saith*, Whosoever *believeth* on him shall not be ashamed.

Romans 10:8–11, emphasis added

Moreover, brethren, I declare unto you *the gospel which I preached* unto you, which also ye have received, and wherein ye stand; *By which also ye are saved*, if ye keep in memory what I preached unto you, unless ye have *believed* in vain. For I delivered unto you first of all that which I also received, how that *Christ died for our sins according to the scriptures*; And that he was buried, and that he rose again the third day *according to the scriptures*.

1 Corinthians 15:1–4, emphasis added

It is witnessed by the Law and the Prophets... that all who *believe* are justified freely by God's *grace* through the redemption that is in Christ Jesus: Whom God hath set forth to be a propitiation *through faith in his blood*, for the *remission of sins*.

Romans 3:21–25, emphasis added

That they may receive *forgiveness of sins*, and inheritance among them which are *sanctified by faith that is in me*.

Acts 26:18, emphasis added

For *the wages of sin is death*; but the *gift* of God is *eternal life* through Jesus Christ our Lord.

Romans 6:23, emphasis added

For by *grace* are ye saved through *faith*; and that not of yourselves: it is the *gift* of God. *Not of works*, lest any man should boast.

Ephesians 2:8–9, emphasis added

I said therefore unto you, that *ye shall die in your sins*: for *if ye believe not that I am he*, ye shall *die* in your sins.

John 8:24, emphasis added

220

And *when he is come*, he will reprove the world of sin, and of righteousness, and of judgment: Of *sin, because they believe not on me.*

John 16:8–9, emphasis added

And as Moses lifted up the serpent in the wilderness, even so must the Son of man be lifted up: That *whosoever believeth* in him should not perish, but *have eternal life.* For God so loved the world, that he gave his only begotten Son, that *whosoever believeth* in him should not perish, but *have everlasting life*...He that *believeth* on the Son *hath everlasting life*: and he that *believeth* not the Son *shall not see life*; but the *wrath* of God abideth on him.

John 3:14–16, 36, emphasis added

Howbeit for this cause I obtained mercy, that in me first Jesus Christ might shew forth all longsuffering, for a pattern to them which should hereafter *believe* on him to *life everlasting.*

1 Timothy 1:16, emphasis added

Then Paul and Barnabas waxed bold, and said, It was necessary that *the word of God* should first have been spoken to you: but seeing ye put it from you, and judge yourselves unworthy of *everlasting life*, lo, we turn to the Gentiles. For so hath the Lord commanded us, saying, I have set thee to be a light of the Gentiles, that thou shouldest be for *salvation* unto the ends of the earth. And when the Gentiles heard this, they were glad, and glorified the *word of the Lord*: and *as many as* were ordained to *eternal life believed.*

Acts 13:46–48, emphasis added

*It* is written, *The just shall live by faith.*

Romans 1:17, emphasis added

But as many as received him, to them gave he power to become *the sons of God*, even to them that *believe* on *his name*.

John 1:12, emphasis added
cf. 1 John 3:1–2 with John 3:16

And *because ye are sons, God hath sent forth the Spirit of his Son into your hearts*, crying, Abba, Father.

Galatians 4:6, emphasis added

For ye are all the *children of God by faith in Christ Jesus*.

Galatians 3:26, emphasis added

Whosoever *believeth* that *Jesus is the Christ is born of God*: and every one that loveth him that begat loveth him also that is begotten of him.

1 John 5:1, emphasis added

*Neither can they die any more*: for they are ... *the children of God*, being the *children of the resurrection*.

Luke 20:36, emphasis added

Martha saith unto him, I know that he shall rise again in the resurrection at *the last day*. Jesus said unto her, *I am the resurrection, and the life*: he that *believeth* in me, though he were dead, yet shall he live: And whosoever liveth and *believeth* in me *shall never die*. Believest thou this? she saith unto him, Yea, Lord: *I believe that thou art the Christ, the Son of God, which should come into the world*.

John 11:24–27, emphasis added

And this is the Father's will which hath sent me, that of all which he hath given me I should lose nothing, but should raise it up again at *the last day*. And this is the will of him that sent me, that every one which seeth the Son, and *believeth* on him, may have *everlasting life*: and I will raise him up at *the last day* ... Verily, verily, I say unto you, He that *believeth* on me *hath everlasting life*.

John 6:39–40, 47, emphasis added

If eating Christ's flesh and blood is, in fact, the means by which forgiveness of sins and eternal life is received, this fact most certainly would have been stated along with at least one of the aforementioned or following scriptures. Jesus was not speaking in the literal sense in John 6:26–69; he was speaking a parable. There is not the slightest indication anywhere else in the holy Scriptures that even remotely hints that eternal life is related in any way to literally eating Christ's flesh and blood. Nor is there anywhere in the Scriptures that suggests that Jesus is an actual door, other than the parable in John chapter 10:1–9. The subject matter *eternal life* is the same in both parables, and so was the reaction of those who heard the parables

In John 6:51, Jesus said he *came down from heaven* to give *his flesh* for the life of the world. In John 10:10–11, he said he *came* to give *his life* for his sheep that they may have life more abundantly. In John 10:15, he *lays down his life* for the sheep. In John 10:17, he *lays down his life* that he might take it again. In John 10:18, Jesus said, "No man taketh it from me, but *I lay it down of myself*. I have power *to lay it down*, and I have power to take it again..." Notice the similar phraseology in each of the following comparisons between the verses in John chapter six and chapter ten. It couldn't be more obvious that Jesus was speaking a parable in both passages.

> *I am the door*: by me if any man enter in, he shall be saved, and shall go in and out, and find pasture...*I am come* that they might have *life*, and that they might have it *more abundantly*. I am the good shepherd: the good shepherd *giveth his life* for the sheep.
>
> John 10:9–11, emphasis added

> *I* am the living bread which came *down from heaven*: if any man *eat* of this bread, he shall *live for ever*: and the bread that *I will give* is *my flesh*, which *I will give for the life of the world*.
>
> John 6:51, emphasis added

*I lay down my life* for the sheep.

John 10:15, emphasis added

~~~~~~~~~~~~~~~~~~~~~~~~

But I said unto you, That *ye also have seen me, and believe not.*

<div align="right">John 6:36, emphasis added</div>

*If thou be the Christ,* tell us plainly. Jesus answered them, *I told you, and ye believed not.*

<div align="right">John 10:24–25, emphasis added</div>

Then Simon Peter answered him, Lord, to whom shall we go? *thou hast the words of eternal life.* And *we believe* and are sure that *thou art that Christ,* the Son of the living God.

<div align="right">John 6:68–69, emphasis added</div>

~~~~~~~~~~~~~~~~~~~~~~~~

It is the spirit that quickeneth; the flesh profiteth nothing: the *words that I* speak unto you, they are spirit, and they *are life.*

John 6:63, emphasis added

My sheep *hear my voice,* and I know them, and they follow me: And *I* give unto them *eternal life;* and they shall never perish, neither shall any man pluck them out of my hand.

John 10:27–28, emphasis added

~~~~~~~~~~~~~~~~~~~~~~~~

*All that the Father giveth me* shall come to me; and him that cometh to me I *will in no wise cast out...* And this is the Father's will which hath sent me, that of *all which he hath given me I should lose nothing,* but should *raise it up again* at the last day.

<div align="right">John 6:37, 39, emphasis added</div>

And I give unto them *eternal life;* and they shall never perish, *neither shall any man pluck them out of my hand. My*

*Father, which gave them me,* is greater than all; and no man is able to pluck them out of my Father's hand.

John 10:28–29, emphasis added

~~~~~~~~~~~~~~~~~~~~~~~~~~

The Jews therefore strove among themselves, saying, *How can* this man give us his flesh to eat ... Many therefore of his disciples, when they had heard this, said, *This is an hard saying; who can hear it?*

<div align="right">John 6:52, 60, emphasis added</div>

*Therefore* speak I to them in parables: because they seeing see not; and *hearing they hear not, neither do they understand.*

<div align="right">Matthew 13:13, emphasis added</div>

*This parable spake* Jesus unto them: but *they understood not* what things they were which he spake unto them.

<div align="right">John 10:6, emphasis added</div>

~~~~~~~~~~~~~~~~~~~~~~~~~~

From that time *many of his disciples* went back, and *walked no more with him.* Then said Jesus unto the twelve, *Will ye also go away?*

John 6:66–67, emphasis added

There was a *division* therefore again among the Jews for *these sayings.*

John 10:19, emphasis added

If the parable in John 6 were to be taken literally, Jesus contradicted himself by using identical words and phrases to explain two entirely different prerequisites for obtaining eternal life: "believing" and "consuming flesh and blood." Compare the following excerpts.

And this is the will of him that sent me, that every one

which seeth the Son, and *believeth* on him, may *have everlasting life*: and *I will raise him up at the last day.*

John 6:40, emphasis added

Whoso *eateth my flesh*, and *drinketh my blood*, hath *eternal life*; and *I will raise him up at the last day.*

John 6:54, emphasis added

~~~~~~~~~~~~~~~~~~

Verily, verily, I say unto you, He that *believeth* on me *hath everlasting life.*

John 6:47, emphasis added

Verily, verily, I say unto you, Except *ye eat the flesh* of the Son of man, and *drink his blood*, ye *have no life in you.*

John 6:53, emphasis added

Eternal life is either obtained by *faith* in the flesh and blood Christ shed on the cross as full payment for our sins, or it's by literally eating his flesh and blood; it cannot be both! According to all of the many other passages of scripture that pertain to this subject, *faith in the flesh and blood* Christ sacrificed *for the remission of sins* is the prerequisite for obtaining eternal life. Since Jesus could not have contradicted himself, the seeming contradictions of his statements in John 6:40 through 6:54 were due to the fact that he was speaking a parable, as he most often did.

Jesus was not talking to a select few, in John chapter six; he was speaking to a great company of people, *a great multitude.* These people were following him because of the miracle of the five loaves and two fishes they had witnessed the previous day (John 6:2, 5, 23–26). Jesus *always, without exception,* spoke to *the multitudes* in parables. [3]

All these things spake Jesus unto the multitudes in parables: and *without a parable spake He not unto them* That it might be fulfilled which was spoken by the prophet, saying, I will

open my mouth in parables; I will utter things which have
been kept secret from the foundation of the world.

*Matthew* 13:34–35, emphasis added

And, with *many such parables* spake He *the Word* unto them
as they were able to hear it. But *without a parable spake he
not unto them…*

*Mark* 4:33–34, emphasis added

The whole multitude was by the sea on the land. And he
taught them *many things by parables,* and said unto them
*in his doctrine…* And when he was alone, they that were
about him with the twelve asked of him the parable. And
he said unto them, unto you it is given to know *the mystery
of the kingdom of God:* but unto them that are without, all
these things are done in parables: that seeing they may
see and not perceive; and hearing they may hear, and not
understand; lest at any time they should be converted,
and their sins should be forgiven them. Know ye not this
parable? and how will ye know *all parables?*

*Mark* 4:1–2, 10–13, emphasis added

When Jesus said, "Know ye not this parable? and how will ye
know all parables?" he was referring to things that had been
*kept secret* "from *the foundation of the world,* concerning God's
promise of eternal life; his eternal plan to redeem mankind by
the remission of sins through 'faith' in the blood of the Lamb
slain *from the foundation of the world"* (Romans 3:24–25; Revelation 13:8).

The following scriptures are all talking about the *mystery* of
God's hidden promise of eternal life being made manifest by
the Scriptures of the prophets and apostles, which are totally
void of any mention of Transubstantiation. Notice the similar
words and phrases in each of the following excerpts (secret,
hidden, mystery/crucified, suffer, sacrifice/from the foundation of the world, before the world began, from ages and gen-

erations/eternal life, made manifest by the scriptures, made manifest through the gospel):

> And I, brethren, when I came to you, came not with excellency of speech or of wisdom, declaring unto you the testimony of God. For I determined not to know any thing among you, save Jesus Christ, and him crucified ... But we speak the wisdom of God in a *mystery*, even *the hidden wisdom*, which God ordained *before the world* unto our glory: Which none of the princes of this world knew: for had they known it, they would not have crucified the Lord of glory.
>
> 1 Corinthians 2:1–2, 7–8, emphasis added

> Now to him that is of power to stablish you according to my gospel, and the preaching of Jesus Christ, according to the revelation of *the mystery*, which was *kept secret since the world began*, But now is *made manifest, and by the scriptures of the prophets*, according to the commandment of the everlasting God, made known to all nations for the obedience of faith.
>
> Romans 16:25–26, emphasis added

> Even *the mystery* which hath been *hid from ages and from generations*, but now is made manifest to his saints: To whom God would make known what is the riches of the glory of this mystery among the Gentiles; which is Christ in you, the hope of glory.[4]
>
> Colossians 1:26–27, emphasis added

> Who hath saved us, and called us with an holy calling, not according to our works, but according to his own purpose and grace, which was given us in Christ Jesus *before the world began*, But is now made manifest by the appearing of our Saviour Jesus Christ, who hath abolished death, and hath brought life and immortality to light through the gospel ...
>
> 2 Timothy 1:9–10, emphasis added

In hope of eternal life, which God, that cannot lie, promised before the world began;

Titus 1:2, emphasis added

Nor yet that he should offer himself often, as the high priest entereth into the holy place every year with blood of others; For then must he often have suffered since *the foundation of the world*: but now once in the end of the world hath he appeared to put away sin by the sacrifice of himself.

Hebrews 9:25–26, emphasis added

All these things spake Jesus unto the multitudes in parables: and without a parable spake he not unto them That it might be fulfilled which was spoken by the prophet, saying, I will open my mouth in parables; I will utter things which have been kept secret from *the foundation of the world*.

Matthew 13:34–35, emphasis added

The Apostle Peter said we were "redeemed with the precious blood of Christ, as of a Lamb who was foreordained before *the foundation of the world*...This is the Word of the Lord which by the gospel is preached unto you" (1 Peter 1:18–25). This is also the same Word of the Lord which Jesus spoke by parable in John chapter six concerning the sacrifice of his body and blood at Calvary for the remission of sins.

# The New Covenant

Jesus's entire discourse in the parable of John chapter six was in view of his impending sacrifice of the new covenant, which is explained in detail in the book of Hebrews, chapters 6:1 through 11:29. In John 6:51, Jesus said, "I am the living bread which came down from heaven: if any man eat of this bread, he shall live for ever: and the bread that I will give is my flesh." He wasn't talking about eating his flesh but about *dying*, about the *once* and for all sacrifice of *his body of flesh* "which taketh away the sin of the world" (John 1:29; 1 Corinthians 15:1–3). In showing the comparison between the old and the new covenants, the author of the book of Hebrews said, "Nor yet that he should offer himself *often*, as the high priest entereth into the holy place every year with blood of others; for then must he *often* have suffered since *the foundation of the world*: but now *once* in the end of the world hath he appeared to put away sin by the sacrifice of himself" (Hebrews 9:25–26, emphasis added).

The comparison that is made between the old and the new covenants makes it perfectly clear that Jesus was speaking a parable in John Chapter six. The main focus is on Christ's suffering and death as payment for our sins and again, is totally void of the slightest reference to Transubstantiation.

> For *I came down from heaven*, not *to do mine own will*, but *the will of him that sent me*.
>
> John 6:38, emphasis added

> Wherefore *when he cometh into the world*, he saith, Sacrifice and offering thou wouldest not, but a body hast thou prepared me: In burnt offerings and sacrifices for sin thou hast had no pleasure. Then said I, Lo, *I come* (in the volume of the book it is written of me,) *to do thy will*, O God. Above when he said, Sacrifice and offering and burnt offerings and offering for sin thou wouldest not, neither hadst pleasure therein; which

are offered by the law; Then said he, Lo, *I come to do thy will,
O God.* He taketh away *the first*, that he may establish *the
second.*

Hebrews 10:5–9, emphasis added

For even hereunto were ye called: because Christ also
suffered for us, leaving us an example, that ye should follow
his steps: Who did no sin, neither was guile found in his
mouth: Who, when he was reviled, reviled not again; when
he suffered, he threatened not; but committed himself to
him that judgeth righteously: Who his own self bare our
sins in *his own body on the tree* , that we, being dead to sins,
should live unto righteousness: by whose stripes ye were
healed.

1 Peter 2:21–24, emphasis added

Surely he hath borne our griefs, and carried our sorrows: yet
we did esteem him stricken, smitten of God, and afflicted.
But he was wounded for our transgressions, he was bruised
for our iniquities: the chastisement of our peace was upon
him; and with his stripes we are healed. All we like sheep
have gone astray; we have turned every one to his own
way; and the Lord hath laid on him the iniquity of us all.
He was oppressed, and he was afflicted, yet *he opened not
his mouth*: he is brought as a lamb to the slaughter, and as
a sheep before her shearers is dumb, so he openeth not
his mouth. He was taken from prison and from judgment:
and who shall declare his generation? for he was cut off
out of the land of the living: for the transgression of my
people was he stricken. And he made his grave with the
wicked and with the rich in his death; because he had done
no violence, neither was any deceit in his mouth. Yet it
pleased the Lord to bruise him; he hath put him to grief:
when thou shalt make his soul an offering for sin, he shall
see his seed, he shall prolong his days, and the pleasure
of the Lord shall prosper in his hand. He shall see of the
travail of his soul, and shall be satisfied: by his knowledge
shall my righteous servant justify many; for he shall bear

their iniquities. Therefore will I divide him a portion with the great, and he shall divide the spoil with the strong; because he hath poured out his soul *unto death*: and he was numbered with the transgressors; and he bare the sin of many, and made intercession for the transgressors.

Isaiah 53:4–12, emphasis added

The doctrine of Transubstantiation undermines the basic teaching of Scripture concerning the relationship of Christ's *suffering and death* to the New Covenant. In John 6:51, when Jesus said he was going to *give his flesh for the life of the world*, he wasn't talking about eating flesh and drinking blood but about faith in his blood for the remission of sin and eternal life (Romans 3:25). He was talking about that which was written in the above prophecy. About laying down his life.⁵ He was talking about suffering *in the flesh*, shedding his blood, and dying for the remission of sins "for the life of the world." As it is written, "the wages of sin is death; but the gift of God is eternal life through Jesus Christ our Lord" (Romans 6:23), and "he died for our sins, according to the Scriptures" (1 Corinthians 15:3).

But God commendeth his love toward us, in that, while we were yet sinners, Christ died for us. Much more then, being now justified by his blood, we shall be saved from wrath through him. For if, when we were enemies, we were reconciled to God *by the death* of his Son, much more, being reconciled, we shall be saved by his life.

Romans 5:8–10, emphasis added

For Christ also hath once suffered for sins, the just for the unjust, that he might bring us to God, being *put to death* in the *flesh*, but quickened by the Spirit...

1 Peter 3:18, emphasis added

And you, that were sometime alienated and enemies in your mind by wicked works, yet now hath he reconciled in the body of his *flesh through death*, to present you holy and unblameable and unreproveable in his sight.

Colossians 1:21–22, emphasis added

He was made a little lower than the angels *for the suffering of death*, that he by the grace of God should taste death for every man ... Forasmuch then as the children are partakers of flesh and blood, he also himself likewise took part of the same; *that through death* he might destroy him that had the power of death, that is, the devil; And deliver them who through fear of death were all their lifetime subject to bondage.

Hebrews 2:9, 14–15, emphasis added

Nor yet that he should offer himself often, as the high priest entereth into the holy place every year with blood of others; For then must he often have *suffered* since the foundation of the world: but now *once* in the end of the world hath he appeared to put away sin *by the sacrifice of himself.*

Hebrews 9:25–26, emphasis added

For the bodies of those beasts, whose blood is brought into the sanctuary by the high priest for sin, are burned without the camp. Wherefore Jesus also, that he might sanctify the people with his own blood, *suffered* without the gate.

Hebrews 13:11–12, emphasis added
cf. John 17:17

Sanctify them through thy truth: *thy word is truth.*

John 17:17, emphasis added

In Luke's gospel account of the Lord's supper, Jesus said, With desire I have desired to eat this Passover with you before I suffer ... He took bread, and gave thanks, and brake it, and gave unto them, saying, This is my body which is given for you: this do in remembrance of me. Likewise also the cup after supper, saying, This cup is the new testament in my blood, which is shed for you (Luke 22:15, 19–20). Jesus, in essence, was telling his disciples that they were to *remember* his suffering and death, to keep in mind the *once and for all sacrifice* that he was about to make for the remission of sins.

According to *Abingdon's Strong's Concordance*, #364, the word *remembrance* in Luke 22:19 is translated from the Greek word *anamnesis* and is used only four times in Scripture (Luke 22:19; 1 Corinthians 11:24- 25; Hebrews 10:3). All four occurrences are in reference to the old and new covenants. When Jesus said "this do in remembrance of me," he meant exactly that and no more.

Notice in the following excerpt that the Apostle Paul, in his account of the Lord's Supper uses this same phrase twice: this do in remembrance of me. Then he expounds, "For as often as ye eat this bread, and drink this cup, ye do shew the Lord's death till he come." Paul not only clarifies the purpose of partaking of the Lord's Supper as a commemoration of Christ's sacrifice, but he also reveals the necessity of the Lord's bloody death in consummating the New Covenant of redemption and eternal inheritance; as seen in Hebrews chapter nine below.

> For I have received of the Lord that which also I delivered unto you, That the Lord Jesus the same night in which he was betrayed took bread: And when he had given thanks, he brake it, and said, Take, eat: this is my body, which is broken for you: this do in remembrance of me. After the same manner also he took the cup, when he had supped, saying, This cup is the new testament in my blood: this do ye, as oft as ye drink it, in remembrance of me. For as often as ye eat this bread, and drink this cup, ye do *shew the Lord's death* till he come.
>
> 1 Corinthians 11:23–26 , emphasis added

> Neither by the blood of goats and calves, but by his own blood he entered in once into the holy place, having obtained eternal redemption for us … And for this cause he

is the mediator of the new testament, that *by means of death*, for the redemption of the transgressions that were under the first testament, they which are called might receive the promise of eternal inheritance. For where a testament is, there must also *of necessity be the death* of the testator. For a testament is of force after men are dead: otherwise it is of no strength at all while the testator liveth.

Hebrews 9:12, 15–17, emphasis added

A brief study of Hebrews chapters nine and ten further reveals the significance of the Lord's words "this do in remembrance of me." As seen in the following, under the Old Testament law, the blood of animal sacrifices that were made year by year could never take away the sins of the people. Thus, leaving a remembrance again of sin. Contrariwise, under the New Testament, our remembrance is to be of the sacrificial blood of Jesus Christ, his *once and for all* sacrifice for sin, "the Lamb of God, which *taketh away* the sin of the world" (John 1:29; 1 Peter 1:19; 1 John 3:5; Hebrews 10:17–18).

For the law having a shadow of good things to come, and not the very image of the things, can never with those sacrifices which they offered year by year *continually* make the comers thereunto *perfect*. For then would they not have ceased to be offered? because that the worshippers once purged should have had no more *conscience of sins*. But in those sacrifices there is a remembrance again made of sins every year For it is not possible that the blood of bulls and of goats should *take away* sins.

Hebrews 10:1–4, emphasis added

And every priest standeth daily ministering and offering oftentimes the same sacrifices, which can never take away sins: But this man, after he had offered *one* sacrifice for sins *for ever*, sat down on the right hand of God ... For by *one* offering he *hath perfected for ever* them that are sanctified. Whereof the Holy Ghost also is a witness to us: for after that he had said before, This is the covenant that I will make with them after those days, saith the Lord, I will put my laws into their hearts, and in their minds will I write them; And their sins and iniquities will I remember no more. Now where remission of these is, there is no more offering for sin.

Hebrews 10:11–12, 14–18

Let us draw near with a true heart in full assurance of *faith*, having our hearts sprinkled from an *evil conscience*, and our bodies washed with pure water. Let us hold fast the profession of our faith without wavering; for he is faithful that promised.[6]

Hebrews 10:22–23, emphasis added

The Apostle Paul told the Corinthians,

Christ sent me not to baptize, but to preach the gospel: not with wisdom of words, lest the cross of Christ should be made of none effect... And I, brethren, when I came to you, came not with excellency of speech or of wisdom, declaring unto you the testimony of God. For I determined not to know any thing among you, save Jesus Christ, and him crucified.

1 Corinthians 1:17; 2:1–2

The subject matter in Hebrews chapters nine and ten is that of Jesus Christ's sacrifice of the New Covenant for the remission of sins, "Jesus Christ, and him crucified," the plain and simple truth of the gospel of our salvation. Contrary to the statements of the Catechism the Catholic Church (#1393), these chapters are totally void of any mention of an ongoing daily sacrifice or of eating Christ flesh and drinking his blood in order to receive the forgiveness of our sins.

The divinely inspired Word of God repeatedly states that Christ "offered *one* sacrifice for sins *forever*" (Hebrews 10:12, emphasis added), that "by his own blood he entered in once into the holy place, having obtained eternal redemption for us (Hebrews 9:12). Jesus Christ, our high priest "needeth not daily, as those high priests, to offer up sacrifice, first for his own sins, and then for the people's: for this he did *once*, when he offered up himself" (Hebrews7:27, emphasis added). "Nor yet that he should offer himself *often*" (Hebrews 9:25, emphasis added). "So Christ was *once* offered to bear the sins of many" (Hebrews 9:28, emphasis added). "By the which will we are sanctified through the offering of the body of Jesus Christ *once* for all" (Hebrews 10:10, emphasis added).

Do not the following excerpts from the *Catechism of the Catholic Church* make the Cross of Christ of no effect?

> 1367 The sacrifice of Christ and the sacrifice of the Eucharist are one single sacrifice: The victim is one and the same: the same *now offers* through the ministry of priests, *who then offered* himself on the cross; only the manner of offering is different." "In this divine sacrifice which is celebrated in the Mass, the same Christ who offered himself once in a bloody manner on the altar of the cross is contained and is offered in an unbloody manner. ,emphasis added
> *Catechism of the Catholic Church*, p. 344

> 1393 Holy Communion separates us from sin. The body of Christ we receive in Holy Communion is *"given up for us,"* and the blood we drink "shed for the many for the forgiveness of sins." For this reason the Eucharist cannot unite us to Christ without at the same time cleansing us from past sins and preserving us from future sins: For as often as we eat this bread and drink the cup, we proclaim the death of the Lord. If we proclaim the Lord's death, we proclaim the forgiveness of sins. If, *as often as* his blood is poured out, it is poured for the forgiveness of sins, I should always receive it, so that it may always forgive my sins. Because I always sin, *I should always have a remedy.* ,emphasis added
> *Catechism of the Catholic Church*, pp. 351, 352

The statements in the above excerpts definitely make the Cross of Christ of no effect! The excerpts read like a sequel to Hebrews 10:1–4, the Old Testament sacrifices of the law, wherein it is stated that the sacrifices were *offered continually* but could *never continually* make the worshipers *perfect* because *once purged* they should have had *no more conscience of sins*. But in those sacrifices there was *a remembrance again* made of sin. Likewise, the sacrifice of the Catholic mass is also offered *continually (daily)* but *never continually* makes the worshipers *perfect;* because there's *a constant remembrance again of sin* and the need to repeat the same sacrifice over and over again-as stated in the above excerpt.

Those who are in Christ are to have their hearts sprinkled from *an evil conscience of sins* "in full assurance of faith" (Hebrews 10:22). "For by one offering he hath perfected for ever them that are sanctified" (Hebrews 10:14). According to *Abingdon's Strong's Concordance*, #5048, the word *perfect* in Hebrews 10:14 is the same word that is used in Hebrews 10:1 and also in Hebrews 7:19, which tells us: "For the law made nothing perfect, but the bringing in of a better hope did." The Apostle Paul confirmed the fact that we are "perfect in Christ" in his epistle to the Colossians. He said:

> You, that were sometime alienated and enemies in your mind by wicked works, yet now hath he reconciled in the body of his flesh through death, to *present* you holy and unblameable and unreproveable in his sight... Christ in you, the hope of glory: Whom we preach, warning every man, and teaching every man in all wisdom; that we may *present* every man perfect in Christ Jesus.
>
> Colossians 1:21–22, 27–28, emphasis added

The Apostle Paul's preaching and teaching were, in effect, to prove every man perfect *in* Christ Jesus.

Christ's one offering having "perfected for ever" those who are sanctified is not talking about our flesh but about our spirits; spirits which are referred to in the Word of God as "the new man" (Ephesians 4:24; Colossians 3:9–10), "a new creature" (2 Corinthians 5:16–17; Galatians 6:15), "the hidden man of the heart … that which is not corruptible …" (1Peter 3:4), "the inner man" (Romans 7:22; Ephesians 3:16); "Spirits of just men made perfect" (Hebrews 12:23–24; 1 Peter 3:18–19; 1 Peter 4:6).

The Word of God also tells us that "he that is joined unto the Lord is one spirit" (1 Corinthians 6:17). This is what Jesus was talking about when he said: " … that which is born of the Spirit is spirit … Ye must be born again" (John 3:6–7). This is also what the Apostle John meant when he wrote: "Whosoever is born of God doth not commit sin; for his seed remaineth in him: and he cannot sin, because he is born of God" (1 John 3:9; 1 John 5:18).

The Apostle John was not contradicting himself in 1 John 1:9 when he said: "If we confess our sins, he is faithful and just to forgive us our sins, and to cleanse us from all unrighteousness." Nor was he talking about confessing sins to a Roman Catholic priest. Contrary to the Catechism's remedy of drinking Christ's blood for the forgiveness of sins, the Apostle John was giving us the biblical remedy for the sins of the flesh. He understood that it is not the flesh but the spirits of those who are sanctified that are "made perfect forever." He understood that as long as we are in our earthly bodies, we must contend with the sin in our flesh and come boldly to the throne of grace, confessing the sins of our flesh that we may obtain mercy and find grace to help in time of need (Hebrews 4:16).

In his epistle to the Romans, the Apostle Paul explained in detail the difference between *the sinful flesh* and the *sinless spirits* of those of us who have been sanctified through faith in Jesus Christ.

> If then I do that which I would not, I consent unto the law that it is good. *Now then it is no more I that do it,* but *sin that dwelleth in me.* For I know that in me (that is, *in my flesh,*)

dwelleth no good thing: for to will is present with me; but how to perform that which is good I find not ... Now *if I do that I would not, it is no more I that do* it, but sin that dwelleth in me. I find then a law, that, when I would do good, evil is present with me. For I delight in the law of God after *the inward man*: But I see another law in *my members*, warring against the law of my mind, and bringing me into captivity to the law of sin which is in *my members* ... O wretched man that I am! Who shall deliver me from *the body* of this death? I thank God *through Jesus Christ our Lord*. So then with the mind *I myself* serve the law of God; but with the *flesh* the law of sin. There is therefore now *no condemnation* to them which are *in Christ Jesus*, who walk not after *the flesh*, but after *the Spirit*. For the law of *the Spirit of life in Christ Jesus* hath made me free from the law of sin and death. For what the law could not do, in that it was weak through the *flesh*, God sending his own Son *in the likeness of sinful flesh*, and for sin, condemned sin in the flesh.

Romans 7:16–8:3, emphasis added

Romans 8:3 talks about what the law could not do because it was weak through the flesh. Hebrews 7:18–19 talks about the disannulling of the law of the commandment because of the weakness and un-profitableness thereof, "for the law made nothing perfect, but the bringing in of a better hope did." It couldn't be more obvious that both passages are talking about the same thing: "Christ's one bloody sacrifice of the new covenant," by which " ... he hath perfected for ever them that are sanctified" (Hebrews 10:14). Per *Abingdon's Strong's Concordance*, #37, the word *sanctify(-ied)* is translated from the Greek word *hagiazo* {hag-ee-ad'-zo},which means to purify by expiation: free from the guilt of sin, to purify internally by renewing of the soul, to cleanse.

Unto him that loved us, and washed us from our sins in his own blood.

Revelation 1:5

... If I [Jesus] wash thee not, thou hast no part with me.

John 13:8

... have washed their robes, and made them white in the blood of the Lamb.

Revelation 7:14

And they overcame him by the blood of the Lamb, and by the word of their testimony; and they loved not their lives unto the death.

Revelation 12:11

Christ also loved the church, and gave himself for it; that he might sanctify and cleanse it with the washing of water by the word,

Ephesians 5:25–26

The doctrine of Transubstantiation totally rejects that which is written in Word of God concerning the suffering and death of Christ's one and only bloody sacrifice for sins. Christ's sacrifice at Calvary and the sacrifice of the mass *are not* one and the same sacrifice. There is no suffering, no shedding of blood, and no death in the sacrifice of the mass (see Catechism #1366; #1367; #1369). "... without shedding of blood is no remission" (Hebrews 9:22). "Now where remission of these is, there is no more offering for sin" (Hebrews 10:18). Yet Roman Catholics continually resort to the spurious sacrifice of the mass that their sins may be forgiven over and over and over again. Catholicism's denial of the efficacy of Christ's suffering and the blood he shed while on the cross most assuredly does "despite unto the Spirit of Grace" (Hebrews 10:29).

Transubstantiation's un-bloody sacrifice of the mass does not forgive sins. Nor does it reconcile us with God, as stated in the Catechism (#1354; #737). We *were*—past tense—justified and reconciled to God through the bloody suffering and death of Christ's sacrifice on the cross at Calvary.

For Christ also hath once suffered for sins, the just for the unjust, that he might bring us to God, being put to death in the flesh, but quickened by the Spirit ...

1 Peter 3:18

Much more then, being now justified by his blood, we shall be saved from wrath through him. For if, when we were enemies, we were reconciled to God by the death of his Son, much more, being reconciled, we shall be saved by his life.

Romans 5:9–10

And, having made peace through the blood of his cross, by him to reconcile all things unto himself; by him, I say, whether they be things in earth, or things in heaven. And you, that were sometime alienated and enemies in your mind by wicked works, yet now hath he reconciled In the body of his flesh through death, to present you holy and unblameable and unreproveable in his sight: If ye continue in the faith grounded and settled, and be not moved away from the hope of the gospel, which ye have heard, and which was preached to every creature which is under heaven; whereof I Paul am made a minister;

Colossians 1:20–23

A brief study of Hebrews chapter 7:19 through 10:23 negates any possibility of a literal interpretation of the parable Jesus spoke in John chapter six. Those who heard the parable said, "How can this man give us his flesh to eat ... This is an hard saying; who can hear it?" (John 6:52, 60). This is what Jesus meant when he said, "Therefore speak I to them in parables: because ... hearing they hear not, neither do they understand" (Matthew 13:13).

Those who heard the parable in John chapter six but did not understand the underlying meaning had to have deemed Jesus's statements ridiculous. No more ridiculous, however, than the many unbiblical statements that are made in support of the doctrine of Transubstantiation, such as Jesus Christ wanting to come into our lives so bad that he wants us to eat him up in order to have the closest possible union with him. This statement, in essence, was made on one of the teaching tapes of Mr. Scott Hahn, a Roman Catholic theologian and apologist who is held in very high esteem by many practicing Roman Catholics.

Over the years, I've listened to several of Mr. Hahn's teaching tapes on various biblical subjects. In the very beginning, because many of his statements not only contradicted the Word of God but were also ridiculous, the thought crossed my mind, *Could Mr. Hahn possibly be a plant in the Roman Catholic Church in order to bring unsuspecting Christians out from under the rule of Romanism?* Shortly thereafter, the answer to my question was a resounding *no!* For the purpose of refutation, and because his teachings were/are extremely contrary to the Word of God, I began cataloging, word for word, portions of these tapes. The following presentation is set forth as an example of Mr. Hahn's teaching on the Eucharist and not a word-for-word presentation. To preface my comments on Mr. Hahn's erroneous teachings, let it be known as fact that the words *verily* and *amen* are both translated from the same Greek word *am-ane* (*Strong's Greek and Hebrew Lexicon #281*).

In John 6:47 Jesus said, "Verily, verily, I say unto you, He that believeth on me hath eternal life." In John 6:53 he said, "Verily, verily, I say unto you, Except ye eat the flesh of the Son of man, and drink his blood, ye have no life in you."

According to Mr. Hahn, the Greek word for *verily/amen* is an oath formula that transforms prayers into to a sworn oath. He insisted that Jesus had to have been speaking literally in John chapter six because he was swearing an oath in John 6:53, when he said, "Verily, verily, I say unto you, Except ye eat the flesh of the Son of man, and drink his blood, ye have no life in you." If Jesus was swearing an oath in John 6:53, he also had to have been swearing an oath in John 6:47 when he said, "Verily, verily, I say unto you, He that believeth on me hath eternal life." This would leave us to conclude one of two things. He was either speaking a parable, which agrees with holy Scripture, or he contradicted himself, which is impossible.

Jesus was not swearing an oath when he said, *Amen, amen/ verily, verily.* Mr. Hahn alluded to Numbers 5:22 to confirm his statement of an oath formula. However, upon consulting *Abingdon's Strong's Concordance,* I discovered that the woman in Numbers 5:22 was not swearing an oath when she said *amen*; she was simply saying, *so be it* to the oath that is made by the priest. I also discovered that the word *oath* (Grk. #3727 -*kapporeth kap-po'-reth*) and (Grk. #3728 -*kaphash kaw-fash'*) is nowhere to be found in the entire book of John, let alone chapter six. *Abingdon's Strong's Concordance,* # 281 and #3727, shows two entirely different meanings between the words *verily {amen}* and *oath.*[7]

Mr. Hahn continually referred to his higher education—his attending seminary, triple majoring in his second year of college, his doctorate, etc. However, his presentation of John 6:53 does not comply with the principles and laws of sound exegesis, which is expected of one who has a doctorate in theology.

In Mark 7:13, Jesus told the religious leaders of his day that they made the Word of God "of none effect" through their tradition. They were blinded from the underlying spiritual truth of God's Word because they placed the utmost importance on their *tradition.* Mr. Hahn also places the utmost importance on tradition. In support of his erroneous teaching that the word *covenant* means a sacred family bond, Mr. Hahn recommended his source materials, which consisted of an endless reference to books *written by man* and the four gospels only; which are void of any explanation or definition of the meaning of the word *covenant.* Likewise, in his determination to teach and substantiate the doctrines handed down by the oral and written *tradi-*

*tion of man,* Mr. Hahn chose and presented only those parts of the inspired written Word of God that seemed suitable for sanctioning the validity of the doctrine of Transubstantiation.

Mr. Hahn insisted that John chapter six was to be taken literally because Jesus said four times in four different ways that we must literally eat his flesh and blood in order to be raised the last day and to receive eternal life. For whatever reason, whether intentionally or inadvertently, he neglected to mention within the same passage the eight times and the several different ways in which the Lord's emphasis, concerning eternal life, was on believing.

> Jesus answered and said unto them, This is the work of God, that ye believe on him whom he hath sent.
>
> John 6:29

> They said therefore unto him, What sign shewest thou then, that we may see, and believe thee? what dost thou work?
>
> John 6:30

> And Jesus said unto them, I am the bread of life: he that cometh to me shall never hunger; and he that believeth on me shall never thirst.
>
> John 6:35

> But I said unto you, That ye also have seen me, and believe not.
>
> John 6:36

> And this is the will of him that sent me, that every one which seeth the Son, and believeth on him, may have everlasting life: and I will raise him up at the last day.
>
> John 6:40

> Verily, verily, I say unto you, He that believeth on me hath everlasting life.
>
> John 6:47

> But there are some of you that believe not. For Jesus knew from the beginning who they were that believed not, and who should betray him.
>
> John 6:64

> And we believe and are sure that thou art that Christ, the Son of the living God.
>
> John 6:69

Nor did Mr. Hahn mention any of the many other scriptures throughout the Bible wherein it is plainly stated that we receive eternal life by grace, through faith in the sacrifice of Christ's flesh and blood at Calvary as full payment for the sins of the world. I sincerely believe that those who are following Scott Hahn's teachings are seriously lacking in the knowledge of the truth of God's Word concerning the love of God and eternal life in Christ and are being dangerously misled. Jesus said: "For God so loved the world that he gave his only begotten Son, that whosoever believeth in him should not perish, but have everlasting life."

Anything that diverts our attention from the plain teaching of scripture concerning the love of God onto something else is not truth. According to Scott Hahn's teaching on Transubstantiation, it's not through an in-depth knowledge of the love of Christ that we come into the closest possible union with him; it's by "eating him up." According to the inspired Word of God, Christ dwells in our hearts by faith, and we are "filled with all the fulness of God" by comprehending "what is the breadth, and length, and depth, and height; and to know the love of Christ."

> For this cause I bow my knees unto the Father of our Lord Jesus Christ, Of whom the whole family in heaven and earth is named, That he would grant you, according to the riches of his glory, to be strengthened with might by his Spirit in the inner man; That Christ may dwell in your

hearts by faith; that ye, being rooted and grounded in love, May be able to comprehend with all saints what is the breadth, and length, and depth, and height; And to know the love of Christ, which passeth knowledge, that ye might be *filled with all the fulness of God.* Now unto him that is able to do exceeding abundantly above all that we ask or think, according to the power that worketh in us, Unto him be glory in the church by Christ Jesus throughout all ages, world without end. Amen

Ephesians 3:14–21, emphasis added

The Catholic interpretation of the Apostle Paul's account of the Lord's Supper is a typical example of man's reasoning obscuring the truth of God's Word and undermining the gospel's basic message of God's love. With total disregard for the context of the entire passage of 1 Corinthians 11:17 through 13:13, the words *unworthily* and *guilty of the body and of the blood of the Lord* are commonly presented as text proof of the doctrine of Transubstantiation.

> Therefore whosoever shall eat this bread, or drink the chalice of the Lord unworthily, shall be guilty of the body and of the blood of the Lord...For he that eateth and drinketh unworthily, eateth and drinketh judgement to himself, not discerning the body of the Lord."
>
> 1 Corinthians 11:27, 29 (Douay Bible)

Transubstantiation is not the subject of this passage. When read in context, it couldn't be more obvious that 1 Corinthians 11:27–29 has nothing whatsoever to do with Transubstantiation. Beginning with 1 Corinthians 11:17 and going all the way through to 1 Corinthians 13:13, Paul was talking about divisions and/or schism in the church, and his main focus was on *brotherly love.*[8]

The Apostle Paul was chiding the Corinthians because of the alleged pre-eminence of some members of the body of Christ over the others. In verses 18 and 19, he wrote: "For first of all, when ye come together in the church, I hear that there be divisions among you; and I partly believe it. For there must be also heresies among you that they which are approved may be made manifest among you."[9]

When Paul talked about eating the Lord's Supper, he wasn't talking about *eating* Christ. When he talked about "discerning the body of the Lord," he wasn't talking about Christ's "flesh and blood body" but about his body, "the church."

He said, "For in eating every one taketh before other his own supper: and one is hungry, and another is drunken. What? have ye not houses to eat and to drink in? or *despise ye the church of God, and shame them that have not?* What shall I say to you? shall I praise you in this? I praise you not" (1 Corinthians 11:20–22), emphasis added.

Paul was rebuking those of the body of Christ who were not walking in love toward the others. This is what he meant when he said, "Wherefore whosoever shall eat this bread, and drink this cup of the Lord, unworthily, shall be guilty of the body and blood of the Lord … For he that eateth and drinketh unworthily, eateth and drinketh damnation to himself, not discerning the Lord's body" (verse 29). In other words: *guilty of the body and blood of the Lord that was sacrificed for those you are mistreating.* "The church of God, which he hath purchased with his own blood" (Acts 20:28). "For whom Christ died" (Romans 14:15; 1 Corinthians 8:11).

When Paul was persecuting the church Jesus appeared to him and asked, "Saul, Saul, why persecutest thou me?" Jesus, in essence, said the same thing in Matthew 25:40, 45. "Inasmuch as ye have done it unto one of the least of these my brethren, ye have done it unto me," and "Inasmuch as ye did it not to one of the least of these, ye did it not to me."

I repeat, Paul was not talking about discerning Christ's *physical* body of flesh and blood, but about discerning the

248

members of the body of Christ; "the church" for whom Christ died and who were being mistreated.

Compare the following excerpts from chapters eleven and thirteen with correlative scriptures.

> Now in this that I declare unto you I praise you not, that ye come together not for the better, but for the worse. For first of all, when ye come together in the church, I hear that there be divisions among you; and I partly believe it. For there must be also heresies among you, that they which are approved may be made manifest among you. When ye come together therefore into one place, this is not to eat the Lord's Supper. For in eating every one taketh before other his own supper: and one is hungry, and another is drunken.
>
> 1 Corinthians 11:17–21

> For I was an hungred, and ye gave me no meat: I was thirsty, and ye gave me no drink... Verily I say unto you, Inasmuch as ye did it not to one of the least of these, ye did it not to me.
>
> Matthew 25:42, 45

> He that oppresseth the poor reproacheth his Maker: but he that honoureth him hath mercy on the poor.
>
> Proverbs 14:31

> What? have ye not houses to eat and to drink in? or despise ye the church of God, and shame them that have not?
>
> 1 Corinthians 11:22

> He that heareth you heareth me; and he that despiseth you despiseth me; and he that despiseth me despiseth him that sent me.
>
> Luke 10:16

… Verily I say unto you, Inasmuch as ye have done it unto one of the least of these my brethren, ye have done it unto me.

Matthew 25:40

He therefore that despiseth, despiseth not man, but God, who hath also given unto us his holy Spirit. But as touching brotherly love ye need not that I write unto you: for ye yourselves are taught of God to love one another.

1 Thessalonians 4:8–9

Wherefore, my brethren, when ye come together to eat, tarry one for another. And if any man hunger, let him eat at home; that ye come not together unto condemnation. And the rest will I set in order when I come.

1 Corinthians 11:33–34

In 1 Corinthians 12:1, after having expounded on the *unloving* behavior in which some of the Corinthians were partaking of the Lord's supper, the Apostle Paul immediately reverts to his previous statements made concerning *divisions* and/or *schisms, heresies*, and the *assumed pre-eminence* of some members of the body of Christ over the others (1 Corinthians 11:18–19). He continues in 1 Corinthians 12:1, saying, "Now concerning spiritual gifts, brethren, I would not have you ignorant." From 1 Corinthians 12:1 all the way through to the end of chapter 12, verse 31, Paul is still talking about the same body of Christ, the church. In order to preclude any false notion of the pre-eminence of one member of the body of Christ over another, he goes into great detail in explaining the division of spiritual gifts which are given to each individual member of Christ's body. The underlying meaning of Paul's statement in 1 Corinthians 11:29, of not discerning the Lord's body, is made perfectly clear in the following verses.

And there are diversities of operations, but it is the same God which worketh all in all. But the manifestation of the Spirit is given to every man to profit withal.

1 Corinthians 12:6–7

But all these worketh that one and the selfsame Spirit, dividing to every man severally as he will. For as the body is one, and hath many members, and *all the members of that one body*, being many, *are one body: so also is Christ*. For by one Spirit are we all baptized into one body, whether we be Jews or Gentiles, whether we be bond or free; and have been all made to drink into one Spirit. For the body is not one member, but many.

1 Corinthians 12:11–14, emphasis added

If the foot shall say, Because I am not the hand, I am not of the body; is it therefore not of the body?

1 Corinthians 12:15

If the whole body were an eye, where were the hearing? If the whole were hearing, where were the smelling? But now hath God set the members every one of them in the body, as it hath pleased him. And if they were all one member, where were the body?

1 Corinthians 12:17–19

And those members of the body, which we think to be less honourable, upon these we bestow more abundant honour; and our uncomely parts have more abundant comeliness. For our comely parts have no need: but God hath tempered the body together, having given more abundant honour to that part which lacked: That there should be no schism in the body; but that the members should have the same care one for another.

1 Corinthians 12:23–25

Now *ye are the body of Christ*, and members in particular.
1 Corinthians 12:27, emphasis added

Have all the gifts of healing? do all speak with tongues? do all interpret? But covet earnestly the best gifts: and yet shew I unto you a more excellent way.
1 Corinthians 12:30–31

Though I speak with tongues … and have not charity … And though I have the gift of prophecy … and have not charity, I am nothing … And though I bestow all my goods to feed the poor, and though I give my body to be burned, and have not charity, it profiteth me nothing … Charity suffereth long, is kind, envieth not, is not puffed up … Charity seeketh not her own, thinketh no evil … And now abideth faith, hope, charity, but the greatest of these is charity.
1 Corinthians 13:1–13

As previously stated, 1 Corinthians 11:27–29 is taken out of context and cited as proof text for Transubstantiation. The above is one of many examples of false doctrines spawned by man's reason and tradition. False doctrines stemming from man's tradition can not stand in the light of the whole Word of God. Truth can not contradict truth! Thus, the importance of *sola Scriptura*. The pick-and-choose method of presenting a couple or so verses of scripture out of context in support of man's tradition is a very sad state of affairs for those who profess to love God. When read in context, it couldn't be more obvious that from 1 Corinthians 11:17 all the way through to 1 Corinthians 13:13 the Apostle Paul's main focus throughout his entire treatise is on brotherly love and has nothing whatsoever to do with the erroneous doctrine of Transubstantiation.

Jesus said: "Whatsoever entereth in at the mouth goeth into the belly, and is cast out into the draught" (Matthew15:17). The decomposition of that which enters the stomach during the process of the digestive system is an extremely critical issue for Roman Catholics who insist on a literal interpretation of the parable in John chapter six. This digestive process would degrade our precious Lord and Saviour, the Creator of all that is, to nothing more than a putrid elimination into the draught and at the same time render void the promise of God almighty to never allow his holy Son to see decay (Acts 2:27; Psalm 16:10).

> 1377 The Eucharistic presence of Christ begins at the moment of the consecration and endures as long as the Eucharistic species subsist. Christ is present whole and entire in each of the species and whole and entire in each of their parts, in such a way that the breaking of the bread does not divide Christ.
>
> *Catechism of the Catholic Church*, p.347

> Because thou wilt not leave my soul in hell, neither wilt thou suffer thine Holy One to see corruption.
>
> Acts 2:27

> For thou wilt not leave my soul in hell; neither wilt thou suffer thine Holy One to see corruption.
>
> Psalm16:10

The blasphemous contradictions and inconsistencies in Catholicism's teaching on Transubstantiation couldn't be more obvious. Even though it is clearly stated in the Catechism that the Eucharistic presence of Christ endures only as long as the Eucharistic species subsist, and even though Jesus said "whatsoever entereth in at the mouth goeth into the belly, and is cast out into the draught," and even though Jesus began the parable in John 6:27 saying, "Labour not for the meat which perisheth, but for that meat which endureth unto everlasting life," John 6:55–56 is, nevertheless, presented as text proof for the doctrine of Transubstantiation:

Labour not for the meat which perisheth, but for that meat which endureth unto everlasting life.

John 6:27

My flesh is meat indeed, and my blood is drink indeed. He that eateth my flesh, and drinketh my blood, dwelleth in me, and I in him.

John 6:55–56

According to *Abingdon's Strong's Concordance* #3306, the words *endureth* in John 6:27 and *dwelleth* in John 6:56 are both translated from the same Greek word *meno* meaning "to remain, abide; not to depart; to continue to be present; to continue to be, not to perish, to last, endure."

Therefore, Jesus could not have been speaking of his flesh and blood as literal meat and drink "which perisheth." He was *spiritually* speaking of the impending sacrifice of his flesh and blood of the new covenant in symbolic terms, just as he did in John 4:32–34 and Matthew 26:42. Compare the following.

But he said unto them, I have meat to eat that ye know not of. Therefore said the disciples one to another, Hath any man brought him ought to eat? Jesus saith unto them, My meat is to do the will of him that sent me, and to finish his work.

John 4:32–34

He went away again the second time, and prayed, saying, O my Father, if this cup may not pass away from me, except I drink it, thy will be done.

Matthew 26:42

Wherefore when he cometh into the world, he saith, Sacrifice and offering thou wouldest not, but a body hast thou prepared me: In burnt offerings and sacrifices for sin thou hast had no pleasure. Then said I, Lo, I come (in the

volume of the book it is written of me) to do thy will, O
God.

Hebrews 10:5–7

For I came down from heaven, not to do mine own will,
but the will of him that sent me.

John 6:38

Jesus Christ indwells all who believe in him. Not by way of
eating his flesh and drinking his blood, but by way of his Holy
Spirit; and not for just a few hours, but continually, forever.
Thus, it is by way of his indwelling Holy Spirit of life that we
live and that we dwell in Christ and him in us:

> And I will pray the Father, and he shall give you another
> Comforter that he may abide with you for ever; Even the
> Spirit of truth; whom the world cannot receive, because it
> seeth him not, neither knoweth him: but ye know him; for
> he dwelleth with you, and shall be in you. I will not leave
> you comfortless: I will come to you. Yet a little while, and the
> world seeth me no more; but ye see me: because I live, ye shall
> live also. At that day ye shall know that I am in my Father,
> and ye in me, and I in you.

John 14:16–20

And hereby we know that he abideth in us, by the Spirit
which he hath given us.

1 John 3:24

Hereby know we that we dwell in him, and he in us,
because he hath given us of his Spirit.

1 John 4:13

Whosoever shall confess that Jesus is the Son of God, God
dwelleth in him, and he in God.

1 John 4:15

In whom ye also trusted, after that ye heard the word of truth, the gospel of your salvation: in whom also after that ye believed, ye were sealed with that Holy Spirit of promise.

Ephesians 1:13<br>cf. Galatians 3:21–22

And because ye are sons, God hath sent forth the Spirit of his Son into your hearts, crying, Abba, Father.

Galatians 4:6

The Spirit of him that raised Christ from the dead will also quicken our mortal bodies by his Spirit that dwelleth in us.

Romans 8:11

For the law of the Spirit of life in Christ Jesus hath made me free from the law of sin and death.

Romans 8:2

The Holy Spirit is "the Spirit of Life" (Romans 8:2,10; Revelation 11:11; 2 Corinthians 3:6; Galatians 3:14, 21–22; Galatians 6:8). The moment we believe in Christ's sacrificial death and resurrection as full payment for our sins, we receive the gift of the Holy Spirit (Ephesians 1:13; Galatians 3:2; Galatians 3:14; Acts 11:14, 17–18; Romans 10:8–9), which is God's gift of eternal life (Romans 6:23; Acts 13:46–48). Jesus said:

... If any man thirst let him come unto me, and drink. He that believeth on me, as the scripture hath said, out of his belly shall flow rivers of living water. But this spake he of the Spirit, which they that believe on him should receive: for the Holy Ghost was not yet given; because that Jesus was not yet glorified.

John 7:37–39

... he that believeth on me shall never thirst.

John 6:35

The Holy Spirit and living water are one in the same—God's gift of eternal life. Jesus told the woman at the well:

> If thou knewest the gift of God, and who it is that saith to thee, Give me to drink; thou wouldest have asked of him, and he would have given thee living water ... Whosoever drinketh of this water shall thirst again: But whosoever drinketh of the water that I shall give him shall never thirst; but the water that I shall give him shall be in him a well of water springing up into everlasting life.
>
> John 4:10, 13–14

It is within this same passage that Jesus said, "I have meat to eat that ye know not of ... My meat is to do the will of him that sent me, and to finish his work" (John 4:32, 34).

Look closely at the following: Jesus said, "It is finished" and then bowed his head and "gave up the ghost" (John 19:30). In Revelation 21:6, he said, "It is done ... I will give unto him that is athirst of the fountain of the water of life freely." In Revelation 22:17, he said, "Let him that is athirst come. And whosoever will, let him take the water of life freely." In the parable of John 6:35, when Jesus said, "I am the bread of life: he that cometh to me shall never hunger; and he that believeth on me shall never thirst," he was not talking about eating flesh and drinking blood, but about faith in his impending sacrifice of flesh and blood at Calvary for the "remission of sins" (Romans 3:24–25) and about his resurrection, ascension, and his subsequent gift of the Holy Spirit, the water of life, the spirit of eternal life.

Just prior to his passion, Jesus said: "Now I go my way to him that sent me ... It is expedient for you that I go away: for if I go not away, the Comforter will not come unto you: but if I depart, I will send him unto you" (John 16:5–7). Jesus's ascension and subsequent gift of the Holy Spirit is precisely what he was talking about in John 6:62–64, when he said: "What and if ye shall see the Son of man ascend up where he was before?

It is the spirit that quickeneth; the flesh profiteth nothing: the words that I speak unto you, they are spirit, and they are life. But there are some of you that believe not." Those who believe not, receive not the Holy Spirit of life.

From that time on, many of Jesus's followers stopped following him. When he asked the twelve disciples if they would also leave him, the Apostle Peter answered, saying, "Lord, to whom shall we go? Thou hast the words of eternal life. And we believe and are sure that thou art that Christ, the Son of the living God."

Jesus's focus in John 6 was definitely not on literally eating flesh. He unequivocally said, "The flesh profiteth nothing." His focus was on faith in his words. Compare what Jesus said in the parable about eternal life, believing, and the last day with the previous and subsequent chapters, wherein he spoke of these same things and virtually used the same words and phrases but said nothing about eating his flesh and drinking his blood. The emphasis in all of these chapters is on faith in Christ's words.

Jesus repeatedly said that the words he spoke were not his words but his Father's words and that he spoke only that which the Father commanded him to speak. The paramount importance of believing the words of Christ regarding eternal life and his return and judgment on the last day cannot be overemphasized. The importance of believing Christ's words is prophesied in Deuteronomy 18:18–20 and referred to throughout the scriptures.

> I will raise them up a Prophet from among their brethren, like unto thee, and will put my words in his mouth; and he shall speak unto them all that I shall command him. And it shall come to pass, that whosoever will not hearken unto my words which he shall speak in my name, I will require it of him. But the prophet, which shall presume to speak a word in my name, which I have not commanded him to

speak, or that shall speak in the name of other gods, even that prophet shall die.

Deuteronomy 18:18–20

For Moses truly said unto the fathers, A prophet shall the Lord your God raise up unto you of your brethren, like unto me; him shall ye hear in all things whatsoever he shall say unto you. And it shall come to pass, that every soul, which will not hear that prophet, shall be destroyed from among the people.

Acts 3:22–23

For he whom God hath sent speaketh the words of God: for God giveth not the Spirit by measure unto him ... He that believeth on the Son hath everlasting life: and he that believeth not the Son shall not see life; but the wrath of God abideth on him.

John 3:34–36

He that believeth on me, believeth not on me, but on him that sent me ... He that rejecteth me, and receiveth not my words, hath one that judgeth him: the word that I have spoken, the same shall judge him in *the last day*. For I have not spoken of myself; but the Father which sent me, he gave me a commandment, what I should say, and what I should speak. And I know that his commandment is life everlasting: whatsoever I speak therefore, even as the Father said unto me, so I speak.

John 12:44, 48–50, emphasis added

And this is the will of him that sent me, that every one which seeth the Son, and believeth on him, may have everlasting life: and I will raise him up at *the last day*.

John 6:40, emphasis added

Martha saith unto him, I know that he shall rise again in the resurrection at *the last day*. Jesus said unto her, I am the resurrection, and the life: he that believeth in me, though he were dead, yet shall he live: And whosoever liveth and *believeth* in me *shall never die*. Believest thou this?

John 11:24–26, emphasis added

I have many things to say and to judge of you: but he that sent me is true; and I speak to the world those things which I have heard of him … When ye have lifted up the Son of man, then shall ye know that I am he, and that I do nothing of myself; but as my Father hath taught me, I speak these things.

John 8:26–28

Verily, verily, I say unto you, If a man keep my saying, he shall never see death.

John 8:51

The words that I speak unto you I speak not of myself: but the Father that dwelleth in me, he doeth the works … He that loveth me not keepeth not my sayings: and the word which ye hear is not mine, but the Father's which sent me.

John 14:10, 24

Jesus answered them, and said, My doctrine is not mine, but his that sent me. If any man will do his will, he shall know of the doctrine, whether it be of God, or whether I speak of myself.

John 7:16–17

Verily, verily, I say unto you, He that heareth my word, and believeth on him that sent me, hath everlasting life, and shall not come into condemnation; but is passed from death unto life.

John 5:24

Whosoever therefore shall be ashamed of me and of my words in this adulterous and sinful generation; of him also shall the Son of man be ashamed, when he cometh in the glory of his Father with the holy angels.

Mark 8:38

The resurrection at the last day, the day of the Lord's return, and the day of judgment are all one and the same day. All who are in the graves shall hear his voice and rise; some to eternal life and some to eternal damnation (1 Thesalonians 4:16; John 5:28, 29; Daniel 12:1–3; Matthew 13:40–43). The Holy Scriptures presented herein clearly show the consequences of believing or not believing the Word of God regarding the resurrection of eternal life on the last day, the day of judgment. These scriptures also invalidate the Roman Catholic's false doctrine of Transubstantiation.

I repeat! The emphasis Jesus placed on eating in the parable of John chapter six was not on *literally* eating his flesh and blood to obtain eternal life. His emphasis was on *spiritually* eating, consuming, the Word of God concerning his flesh and blood of the new covenant. Isaiah 55 is prophetic of the new covenant and talks about *hearing* and *spiritually eating* the Word of God.

Notice the phrases "hear, and your soul shall live" and "So shall my word be that goeth forth out of my mouth."

Ho, every one that thirsteth, *come ye to the waters*, and he that hath no money; come ye, buy, and eat; yea, come, buy wine and milk without money and without price. Wherefore do ye spend money for that which is not bread? and your labour for that which satisfieth not? *hearken diligently unto me*, and *eat* ye that which is good, and let your soul delight itself in fatness. *Incline your ear*, and come unto me: *hear, and your soul shall live*; and I will make an *everlasting covenant* with you, even the sure mercies of David...Let the wicked forsake his way, and the unrighteous man his thoughts: and let him return unto the Lord, and he will have mercy upon him; and to our

261

God, for he will abundantly pardon. For my thoughts are not your thoughts, neither are your ways my ways, saith the Lord. For as the heavens are higher than the earth, so are my ways higher than your ways, and my thoughts than your thoughts. For as the rain cometh down, and the snow from heaven, and returneth not thither, but watereth the earth, and maketh it bring forth and bud, that it may give seed to the sower, and bread to the eater: *So shall my word be that goeth forth out of my mouth:* it shall not return unto me void, but it shall accomplish that which I please, and *it shall prosper in the thing whereto I sent it.*

Isaiah 55:1–11, emphasis added
(cf. Acts 13:32–34, "the sure mercies of David,"
"Eternal life")

The above prophecy is talking about hearing and believing, *spiritually* eating the Word of God, in order to obtain forgiveness of sins and eternal life. Jesus said, "My sheep hear my voice … and I give unto them eternal life; and they shall never perish" (John 10:27–28). Eating God's Word is to hear the Word and believe it in our hearts. Jesus talked about the Word of God in the hearts of men, saying, "Those by the way side are they that hear; then cometh the devil, and taketh away the word out of their hearts, lest they should believe and be saved" (Luke 8:12, 15; Mark 4:15). And so did the Apostle Paul, saying, "The word is nigh thee, even in thy mouth, and in thy heart: that is, the word of faith, which we preach; That if thou shalt confess with thy mouth the Lord Jesus, and shalt believe in thine heart that God hath raised him from the dead, thou shalt be saved … So then faith cometh by hearing, and hearing by the word of God" (Romans 10:8–9, 17).

Compare the many scriptures in the following which speak of *spiritually* eating God's Word:

But he answered and said, It is written, Man shall not live by bread alone, but by every word that proceedeth out of the mouth of God.

Matthew 4:4

I am the Lord thy God, which brought thee out of the land of Egypt: open thy mouth wide and I will fill it. But my people would not hearken to my voice; and Israel would none of me.

Psalm 81:10–11

The entrance of thy words giveth light; it giveth understanding unto the simple. I opened my mouth, and panted: for I longed for thy commandments.

Psalm 119:130–131

And take not the word of truth utterly out of my mouth; for I have hoped in thy judgments.

Psalm 119:43

And I have put my words in thy mouth, and I have covered thee in the shadow of mine hand, that I may plant the heavens, and lay the foundations of the earth, and say unto Zion, Thou art my people.

Isaiah 51:16<br>(cf. Hebrews 12:22–25; 2 Corinthians 6:16; Romans<br>9:25–26; Hosea 2:19–20, 23 with 1 Peter 2:10)

As for me, this is my covenant with them, saith the Lord; My spirit that is upon thee, and my words which I have put in thy mouth, shall not depart out of thy mouth, nor out of the mouth of thy seed, nor out of the mouth of thy seed's seed, saith the Lord, from henceforth and for ever.

Isaiah 59:21

Then the Lord put forth his hand, and touched my mouth. And the Lord said unto me, Behold, I have put my words in thy mouth.

Jeremiah 1:9

Thy words were found, and I did eat them; and thy word was unto me the joy and rejoicing of mine heart: for I am called by thy name, O Lord God of hosts.

Jeremiah 15:16

And thou shalt speak my words unto them, whether they will hear, or whether they will forbear: for they are most rebellious. But thou, son of man, hear what I say unto thee; Be not thou rebellious like that rebellious house: open thy mouth, and eat that I give thee. And when I looked, behold, an hand was sent unto me; and, lo, a roll of a book was therein; And he spread it before me; and it was written within and without: and there was written therein lamentations, and mourning, and woe.

Ezekiel 2:7–10

But unto the wicked God saith, What hast thou to do to declare my statutes, or that thou shouldest take my covenant in thy mouth? Seeing thou hatest instruction, and castest my words behind thee.

Psalm 50:16–17

O taste and see that the Lord is good: blessed is the man that trusteth in him.

Psalm 34:8

How sweet are thy words unto my taste! yea, sweeter than honey to my mouth!

Psalm 119:103

And I, brethren, could not speak unto you as unto *spiritual*, but as unto carnal, even as unto babes in Christ. *I have fed you with milk*, and not with meat: for hitherto ye were not able to bear it, neither yet now are ye able. For ye are yet carnal: for whereas there is among you envying, and strife, and divisions, are ye not carnal, and walk as men?

1 Corinthians 3:1–3, emphasis added

MARLENE C. CROUCH

Of whom we have many things to say, and hard to be uttered, seeing ye are *dull of hearing*. For when for the time ye ought to be teachers, ye have need that one teach you again which be the first principles of *the oracles of God*; and are become such as have *need of milk, and not of strong meat*. For every one that useth milk is unskilful in the word of righteousness: for he is a babe. But strong meat belongeth to them that are of full age, even those who by reason of use have their senses exercised to discern both good and evil.

Hebrews 5:11–14, emphasis added

As *newborn babes*, desire the sincere *milk of the word* that ye may grow thereby: If so be ye have *tasted* that the Lord is gracious.

1 Peter 2:2–3, emphasis added

But as many as received him, to them gave he power to become the *sons of God*, even to them that *believe* on his name: Which were *born*, not of blood, nor of the will of the flesh, nor of the will of man, but *of God*.

John 1:12–13

Whosoever *believeth* that Jesus is the Christ *is born of God*: and every one that loveth *him that begat* loveth him also that is begotten of him.

1 John 5:1, emphasis added

Of his own will *begat he us* with *the word of* truth, that we should be a kind of firstfruits of his creatures.

James 1:18, emphasis added

It is the spirit that quickeneth; the flesh profiteth nothing: *the words* that I speak unto you, they *are spirit*, and they *are life*.

John 6:63, emphasis added

But he answered and said, It is written, *Man shall* not *live* by bread alone, but *by every word* that proceedeth out of the mouth of God.

Matthew 4:4, emphasis added

Wherefore do ye spend money for that which is not bread? and your *labour for that which satisfieth not? hearken diligently* unto me, and *eat* ye that which is good, and let your soul delight itself in fatness...hear, and your soul shall live...

Isaiah 55:2–3, emphasis added

*Labour not for the meat which perisheth*, but for that meat which *endureth* unto *everlasting life*, which the Son of man shall give unto you: for him hath God the Father sealed.

John 6:27, emphasis added

Being *born again*, not of corruptible seed, but of incorruptible, *by the word of God*, which liveth and abideth for ever...but the word of the Lord endureth for ever. And this is the word which by the gospel is preached unto you.

1 Peter 1:23–25, emphasis added

Heaven and earth shall pass away, but my words shall not pass away.

Matthew 24:35

Mary, sat at Jesus' feet, and heard his word...one thing is needful: and Mary hath chosen that good part, which shall not be taken away from her.

Luke 10:39–42

My sheep hear my voice, and I know them, and they follow me: And I give unto them eternal life; and they shall never perish, neither shall any man pluck them out of my hand.

John 10:27–28

*Whose voice are you listening to?*

# Endnotes:

Mary's Consent

1    The Virgin Mary Is Not The Church's Source Of Holiness:

> Behold, the days come, saith the LORD, that I will raise unto David a righteous Branch, and a King shall reign and prosper, and shall execute judgment and justice in the earth. In his days Judah shall be saved, and Israel shall dwell safely: and this is his name whereby he shall be called, THE LORD OUR RIGHTEOUSNESS.
>
> Jeremiah 23:5–6, emphasis added

> I have sworn by myself, the word is gone out of my mouth in righteousness, and shall not return, That unto me every knee shall bow, every tongue shall swear. Surely, shall one say, *in the* LORD *have I righteousness* and strength: even to him shall men come; and all that are incensed against him shall be ashamed.
>
> Isaiah 45:23–24,emphasis added

> I will go in the strength of the Lord God: I will make mention of thy righteousness, even of thine only.
>
> Psalm 71:16

> For I bear them record that they have a zeal of God, but not according to knowledge. For they being ignorant of God's righteousness, and going about to establish their

own righteousness, have not submitted themselves unto the righteousness of God.

Romans 10:2, 3

And be found in him, not having mine own righteousness, which is of the law, but that which is through the faith of Christ, the righteousness which is of God by faith:

Philippians 3:9

Even the righteousness of God which is by faith of Jesus Christ unto all and upon all them that believe: for there is no difference:

Romans 3:22

But seek ye first the kingdom of God, and his righteousness; and all these things shall be added unto you.

Matthew 6:33

No weapon that is formed against thee shall prosper; and every tongue that shall rise against thee in judgment thou shalt condemn. This is the heritage of the servants of the LORD, and their righteousness is of me, saith the LORD.

Isaiah 54:17

But of him are ye in Christ Jesus, who of God is made unto us wisdom, and righteousness, and sanctification, and redemption:

1 Corinthians 1:30

And that ye put on the new man, which after God is created in righteousness and true holiness.

Ephesians 4:24

For he hath made him to be sin for us, who knew no sin; that we might be made the righteousness of God in him.

2 Corinthians 5:21

The LORD hath brought forth our righteousness: come,
and let us declare in Zion the work of the LORD our God
Jeremiah 51:10

## Marian Apparitions

1   (*From: 'The Thunder of Justice'*):
Since the abolition of Canon 1399 and 2318 of the former
Canonical Code, publications about new appearances, revelations, prophecies, miracles, etc., have been allowed to be dis-
tributed and read by the faithful without the express permission of the Church, providing they contain nothing which
contravenes faith and morals. This means no imprimatur is
necessary when distributing information on new apparitions
not yet judged by the Church. The authors wish to manifest
unconditional submission to the final and official judgment of
the Magisterium of the Church regarding any events presently
under investigation.

In *Lumen Gentium*, Vatican II, Chapter 12, the Council Fathers
urged the faithful to be open and attentive to the ways in which
the Holy Spirit continues to guide the Church, including private revelations. We hear; "Such gifts of grace, whether they
are of special enlightenment or whether they are spread more
simply and generally, must be accepted with gratefulness and
consolation, as they are specially suited to and useful for, the
needs of the Church.... Judgments as to their genuiness and
their correct use lies with those who lead the Church and those
whose special task is not to extinguish the Spirit but to examine
everything and keep that which is good.

2   [http://www.miraclehunter.com/marian_apparitions/
approved_apparitions/index.html#fatima ]

3   *Abingdon's Strong's* Concordance: OBEY -#5219 hupakouo {hoop-
ak-oo'-o} from 5259 and 191; TDNT - 1:223,34; v, ; AV - obey 18,

be obedient to 2, hearken 1; 21. 1) to listen, to harken 1a) of one who on the knock at the door comes to listen who it is,

Compare John 10:3, 16, 27 -(*"My sheep hear my voice"*), Rev. 3:20 -(*"I stand at the door and knock"*)

4

For whatsoever is born of God *overcometh* the world: and this is the victory that overcometh the world, *even* our faith. Who is he that overcometh the world, but he that believeth that Jesus is the Son of God?

1 John 5:4–5

But as many as received him, to them gave he power to become the sons of God, even to them that believe on his name:

John 1:12

Being born again, not of corruptible seed, but of incorruptible, by the word of God, which liveth and abideth for ever.

1 Peter 1:23

## Mary's Immaculate Conception?

1    Websters:
Philosophy: - a study of the processes governing *thought* and conduct; investigation of the principles that regulate the universe and underlie all reality.

Abingdon's Strongs Concordance: #5385
Philosophy:- *philosophia* {fil-os-of-ee'-ah}
1) love of wisdom
1a) used either of zeal for or skill in any art or science, any branch of knowledge. Used once in the NT of the theology, or rather theosophy, of certain Jewish Christian ascetics, which busied itself with refined and speculative enquiries into the nature and classes of angels, into the ritual of the Mosaic law and the regulations of Jewish tradition respecting practical life

Beware lest any man spoil you through *philosophy* <#5385> and vain deceit, after the tradition of men, after the rudiments <#4747> of the world <#2889>, and not after Christ.

Colossians 2:8

*[Abingdon's Strong's #4747-stoicheion; #2889-kosmos]*

2    God is not a respecter of persons:
[Acts 10:34*; Romomans 2:11; Ephesians 6:9; Galatians 2:6*; Colossians 3:25; 1 Petter 1;17; 2 Chronicles 19:7; Job 34:19; 2 Samuel 14:14]

While he yet talked to the people, behold, his mother and his brethren stood without, desiring to speak with him. Then one said unto him, Behold, thy mother and thy brethren stand without, desiring to speak with thee. But he answered and said unto him that told him, Who is my mother? and who are my brethren? And he stretched forth his hand toward his disciples, and said, Behold my mother and my brethren! For whosoever shall do the will of my Father which is in heaven, the same is my brother, and sister, and mother. [Also: Mk. 3:31–35 & Lk. 8:19–21]

Matthew 12:46–50

And it came to pass, as he spake these things, a certain woman of the company lifted up her voice, and said unto him, Blessed is the womb that bare thee, and the paps which thou hast sucked. But he said, Yea rather, blessed are they that hear the word of God, and keep it.

Luke 11:27–28

And both Jesus was called, and his disciples, to the marriage. And when they wanted wine, the mother of Jesus saith unto him, They have no wine. Jesus saith unto her, Woman, what have I to do with thee? mine hour is not yet come.

John 2:2–4

3    Mary's purification according to the law of Moses

And when eight days were accomplished for the circumcising of the child, his name was called JESUS, which was so named of the angel before he was conceived in the womb. And when the days of her *purification* according to the law of Moses were accomplished, they brought him to Jerusalem, to present him to the Lord; (As it is written in the law of the Lord, Every male that openeth the womb shall be called holy to the Lord;) And to offer a sacrifice according to that which is said in the law of the Lord, A pair of turtledoves, or two young pigeons.

Luke 2:21–24

And if she be not able to bring a lamb, then she shall bring two turtles, or two young pigeons; the one for the burnt offering, and *the other for a sin* <#2403> offering: and the priest shall make an atonement for her, and she shall be clean.

Leviticus 12:8

## Mary, Ever Virgin

1    James the son of Alphaeus, one of the twelve apostles (Matt. 10:3):

Whether or not this James is to be identified with James the Less, the son of Alphaeus, the brother of our Lord, is one of the most difficult questions in the gospel history. By comparing Matt. 27:56 and Mark 15:40 with John 19:25, we find that the Virgin Mary had a sister named, like herself, Mary, who was the wife of Clopas or Alpheaus -(varieties of the same name), and who had two sons, James the Less and Joses. By referring to Matt. 13:55 and Mark 6:3 we find that a James and a Joses, with two other brethren called Jude and Simon, and at least three sisters, were living with the Virgin Mary at Nazareth. By referring to Luke 6:16 and Acts 1:13 we find that there were two brethren named James and Jude among the apostles. It would certainly be natural to think that we had here but one family of four brothers and three or more sisters, the children of Clopas and Mary, nephews and neices of the Virgin Mary. There are difficulties, however, in the way of the conclusion into which we cannot here enter; but in reply to the objection that the four brethren in Matt. 13:35 are described as the brothers of Jesus, not as his cousins, it must be recollected that the Greek word "ADELPHOS" which is here translated "brethren," may also signify cousins. (SOURCE: *SMITHS BIBLE DICTIONARY* -(p. 277).

2 Definitions of the word "before" and the phrase "come together," according to Strong's concordance:

before: <#4250> from 4253;; adv
AV - before 11, before that 2, ere 1; 14; 1) before, formerly come together: #4905 sunerchomai {soon-er'-khom-ahee}; from 4862 and 2064; TDNT - 2:684,257; v
1) to come together - 1a) to assemble; 1b) *of conjugal cohabitation*
2) to go (depart) or come with one, to accompany one

3 Reader's Edition' of *The Jerusalem Bible*:

... he took his wife to his home and, though he had not had intercourse with her, she gave birth to a son; and he named him Jesus.

Matthew 1:25

4 Old Testament Examples: "Firstborn and Only"
The following Hebrew definitions are quoted from *Abingdon's Strong's* exhaustive concordance of the Bible:

FIRSTBORN -#1060 - {Hebrew} b@kowr {bek-ore'}
from 01069; TWOT - 244a; n m
AV - firstborn 101, firstling 10, eldest 4, firstborn + 01121 1, eldest
son 1; 117
1) firstborn, firstling 1a) of men and women 1b) of animals 1c)
noun of relation (fig.)


ONLY - #3173 -{Hebrew}-yachiyd {yaw-kheed'}
from 03161; AV - only 6, darling 2, only child 1, only son 1, deso-
late 1, solitary 1; 12
adj
1) only, only one, solitary, one 1a) only, unique, one 1b) solitary
1c) (TWOT) only begotten 2) one
Judges 11:34 - And Jephthah came to Mizpeh unto his house,
and, behold, his daughter came out to meet him with timbrels
and with dances: and she was his *only child* [#3173]; *beside her he had
neither son nor daughter.*


And it came to pass, that at midnight the LORD smote all
the *firstborn* [#1060] in the land of Egypt, from the firstborn
[#1060]of Pharaoh that sat on his throne unto the *firstborn*
[#1060] of the captive that was in the dungeon; and all the
*firstborn* [#1060] of cattle.

Exodus 12:29


And I will pour upon the house of David, and upon
the inhabitants of Jerusalem, the spirit of grace and of
supplications: and they shall look upon me whom they have
pierced, and they shall mourn for him, as one mourneth
for his *only son* [#3173], and shall be in bitterness for him, as
one that is in bitterness for his *firstborn* [#1060].

Zechariah 12:10

Keys to the Kingdom and Power of God
1    The Holy Spirit - The Spirit Of Christ In You.
Ezekiel 36:27; John 7:38–39; Romans 8:9–11; Colossians 1:27;

MARLENE C. CROUCH

John 14:16–17, 20; John 17:23; 1 John 4:13; 2 John1:2; 1 John 2:27; Corinthians 13:5; Galatians 2:20; Ephesians 3:16–17; Ephesians. 4:6; 1 Corinthians 3:16; 1 Corinthians 6:19; 1 Corinthians 14:25; 2 Timothy 1:14.

The Kingdom Of God In You
Luke. 17:20–21; John 3:3 & 8; Romans 14:17; Romans 15:13

The Holy Spirit And "Joy"
John 15:11; John 16:22–24; John 17:13; Romans 14:17; 1 Thessalonians 1:6; Romans 15:13; Palsm.16:11
Raised With Christ In Heavenly Places:
Psalm 110:1–4; Hebrews 10:12; Ephesians 1:18–20; Ephesians 2:6–10; Psm. 16:11; Colossians 3:1; Colossians 2:12; John 12:26; John 14:3; John 17:24 {w/-2 Corinthians 3:18 & 2 Corinthians 4:6}; John 14:23–24 {w/-Psalm 91:14–16}; Revelation 3:21 {w/-Revelation.12:10–12 & 1 Jn. 5:1, 4,5}; Revelation. 13:6; Philippians 3:20; Ephesians 1:3

One Spirit - Together With Christ
1 Corinthians 6:17; Ephesians 5:30–32; 1 John 3:2–3; 1 John 3:5, 6, 9; Romans 8:1, 9–10; John 17:22–23; Colossians 1:27–28; Hebrews 10:14; Ephesians 4:13–15

2  And whatsoever ye shall ask in my name, that will I do, that the Father may be glorified in the Son.
John 14:13

If ye shall ask any thing in my name, I will do it.
John 14:14

Ye have not chosen me, but I have chosen you, and ordained you, that ye should go and bring forth fruit, and that your fruit should remain: that whatsoever ye shall ask of the Father in my name, he may give it you.

John 15:16-

And in that day ye shall ask me nothing. Verily, verily, I say unto you, Whatsoever ye shall ask the Father in my name, he will give it you.

John 16:23

Hitherto have ye asked nothing in my name: ask, and ye shall receive, that your joy may be full.

John 16:24

At that day ye shall ask in my name: and I say not unto you, that I will pray the Father for you:

John 16:26

3

Jesus saith unto them, Did ye never read in the scriptures, The stone which the builders rejected, the same is become the head of the corner: this is the Lord's doing, and it is marvellous in our eyes? Therefore say I unto you, The kingdom of God shall be taken from you, and given to a nation bringing forth the fruits thereof.

Matthew 21:42–43

Wherefore also it is contained in the scripture, Behold, I lay in Sion a chief corner stone, elect, precious: and he that believeth on him shall not be confounded. Unto you therefore which believe he is precious: but unto them which be disobedient, the stone which the builders disallowed, the same is made the head of the corner, And a stone of stumbling, and a rock of offence, even to them which stumble at the word, being disobedient: whereunto also they were appointed. But ye are a chosen generation, a royal priesthood, an holy nation, a peculiar people; that ye should shew forth the praises of him who hath called you out of darkness into his marvellous light:

1 Peter 2:6–9

And are built upon the foundation of the apostles and prophets, Jesus Christ himself being the chief corner stone; In whom all the building fitly framed together groweth unto an holy temple in the Lord: In whom ye also are builded together for an habitation of God through the Spirit.

Ephesians 2:20–22

That ye might walk worthy of the Lord unto all pleasing, being fruitful in every good work, and increasing in the knowledge of God; Strengthened with all might, according to his glorious power, unto all patience and longsuffering with joyfulness; Giving thanks unto the Father, which hath made us meet to be partakers of the inheritance of the saints in light: Who hath delivered us from the power of darkness, and hath translated us into the kingdom of his dear Son:

Colossians 1:10–13

4

For what the law could not do, in that it was weak through the flesh, God sending his own Son in the likeness of sinful flesh, and for sin, condemned sin in the flesh: That *the righteousness of the law might be fulfilled in us*, who walk not after the flesh, but after the Spirit.

Romans 8:3–4

For there is verily a disannulling of the commandment going before for the weakness and unprofitableness thereof. For the law made nothing perfect, but the bringing in of a better hope did; by the which we draw nigh unto God.

Hebrews 7:18–19

Blotting out the handwriting of ordinances that was against us, which was contrary to us, and took it out of the way, nailing it to his cross;

Colossians 2:14

5    Jesus repeatedly said that the words He spoke were not his words but the Father's and that the Father's Word is truth.

Jesus cried and said, He that believeth on me, believeth not on me, but on him that sent me.

John 12:44

For I have not spoken of myself; but the Father which sent me, he gave me a commandment, what I should say, and what I should speak. And I know that his commandment is life everlasting: whatsoever I speak therefore, even as the Father said unto me, so I speak.

John 12:49–50

Believest thou not that I am in the Father, and the Father in me? the words that I speak unto you I speak not of myself: but the Father that dwelleth in me, he doeth the works.

John 14:10

He that loveth me not keepeth not my sayings: and the word which ye hear is not mine, but the Father's which sent me.

John 14:24

For he whom God hath sent speaketh the words of God: for God giveth not the Spirit by measure unto him.

John 3:34

I will raise them up a Prophet from among their brethren, like unto thee, and will put my words in his mouth; and he shall speak unto them all that I shall command him.

Deuteronomy 18:18

For Moses truly said unto the fathers, A prophet shall the Lord your God raise up unto you of your brethren, like unto me; him shall ye hear in all things whatsoever he shall say unto you. [also: Acts 7:36]

Acts 3:22

For I have given unto them the words which thou gavest me; and they have received them, and have known surely that I came out from thee, and they have believed that thou didst send me. Sanctify them through thy truth: thy word is truth.

John 17:8 & 17

6    The King James Version of the Bible is free of *sectarian bias* and the translators were more consistent in using the same words and phrases throughout the Bible in describing related circumstances and subjects; thus making it easier to see the harmony between the Old and New Testament Scriptures. This is especially true regarding the subject of eschatology.

7

Seated In Heavenly Places In Christ
Behold, I stand at the door, and knock: if any man hear my voice, and open the door, I will come in to him, and will sup with him, and he with me. To him that overcometh will I grant to sit with me in my throne, even as I also overcame, and am set down with my Father in his throne.

Revelation 3:20–21

For whatsoever is born of God overcometh the world....

1 John 5:4

If ye then be risen with Christ, seek those things which are above, where Christ sitteth on the right hand of God. Set your affection on things above, not on things on the earth.

Colossians 3:1–2

Blessed and holy is he that hath part in the first resurrection: on such the second death hath no power, but they shall be priests of God and of Christ, and shall reign with him a thousand years.

Revelation 20:6

... One day is with the Lord as 1000 years.... (cf. Psalm 50;10; Psalm 90:4; Deuteronomy 7:9 )

2 Peter 3:8

... washed us from our sins in his own blood, And hath made us kings and priests

Revelation 1:5–6

Buried with him in baptism, wherein also ye are risen with him through the faith of the operation of God, who hath raised him from the dead.

Colossians 2:12

But this man, after he had offered one sacrifice for sins for ever, sat down on the right hand of God;

Hebrews 10:12

A Psalm of David. The LORD said unto my Lord, Sit thou at my right hand, until I make thine enemies thy footstool. The LORD shall send the rod of thy strength out of Zion: rule thou in the midst of thine enemies. Thy people shall be willing in the day of thy power, in the beauties of holiness from the womb of the morning: thou hast the dew of thy youth.

Psalm 110:1–3

And I heard a loud voice saying in heaven, Now is come salvation, and strength, and the kingdom of our God, and the power of his Christ: for the accuser of our brethren is cast down, which accused them before our God day and night. And they overcame him by the blood of the Lamb, and by the word of their testimony; and they loved not their lives unto the death. Therefore rejoice, ye heavens, and ye that dwell in them. Woe to the inhabiters of the earth and of the sea! for the devil is come down unto you, having great wrath, because he knoweth that he hath but a short time.

Revelation 12:10–12

And he opened his mouth in blasphemy against God, to blaspheme his name, and his tabernacle, and them that dwell in heaven.

Revelation 13:6

For our conversation is in heaven; from whence also we look for the Saviour, the Lord Jesus Christ:

Philippians 3:20

He that hath an ear, let him hear what the Spirit saith unto the churches.

Revelation3:13

8

All things that the Father hath are mine: therefore said I, that he shall take of mine, and shall shew it unto you.

John 16:15

That ye may eat and drink at my table in my kingdom, and sit on thrones judging the twelve tribes of Israel.

Luke 22:30

Jesus answered, My kingdom is not of this world: if my kingdom were of this world, then would my servants fight, that I should not be delivered to the Jews: but now is my kingdom not from hence.

John 18:36

9

But he that is joined unto the Lord is one spirit.

1 Corinthians6:17

For both he that sanctifieth and they who are sanctified *are all of one*: for which cause he is not ashamed to call them brethren,

Hebrews2:11, emphasis added

For we are members of his body, of his flesh, and of his bones. For this cause shall a man leave his father and mother, and shall be joined unto his wife, and they *two shall be one flesh*. This is a great mystery: but I speak *concerning Christ and the church*.

Ephesians5:30–32, emphasis added

And said, For this cause shall a man leave father and mother, and shall cleave to his wife: and they twain shall be one flesh? Wherefore *they are no more twain, but one flesh*. What therefore God hath joined together, let not man put asunder.

Matthew19:5–6, emphasis added

And I will betroth thee unto me *for ever*; yea, I will betroth thee unto me in righteousness, and in judgment, and in lovingkindness, and in mercies. I will even betroth thee unto me in faithfulness: and thou shalt know the Lord.

Hosea 2:19–20, emphasis added

10

*Abingdon's Strong's Concordance:* Eternal:
166 aionios {ahee-o'-nee-os}
from 165; TDNT - 1:208,31; adj
AV - eternal 42, everlasting 25, the world began + 5550 2, since the world began + 5550 1, for ever 1; 71
1) without beginning and end, that which always has been and always will be

2) without beginning
3) without end, never to cease, everlasting
For Synonyms see entry 5801

In hope of eternal life, which God, that cannot lie, promised before the world began; But hath in due times manifested his word through preaching, which is committed unto me according to the commandment of God our Saviour;

Titus1:2–3

He that believeth on the Son of God hath the witness in himself: he that believeth not God hath made him a liar; because he believeth not the record that God gave of his Son. And this is the record, that God hath given to us eternal life, and this life is in his Son.

1 John 5:10–11

That whosoever believeth in him should not perish, but have eternal life. For God so loved the world, that he gave his only begotten Son, that whosoever believeth in him should not perish, but have everlasting life... He that believeth on the Son hath everlasting life: and he that believeth not the Son shall not see life; but the wrath of God abideth on him.

John 3:15–16, 36

Verily, verily, I say unto you, He that heareth my word, and believeth on him that sent me, hath everlasting life, and shall not come into condemnation; but is passed from death unto life.

John 5:24

And whosoever liveth and believeth in me shall never die. Believest thou this?

John 11:26

For the wages of sin is death; but the gift of God is eternal life through Jesus Christ our Lord.

Romans 6:23

For the gifts and calling of God are without repentance.

Romans 11:29

And this is the will of him that sent me, that every one which seeth the Son, and believeth on him, may have everlasting life: and I will raise him up at the last day.

John 6:40

Then Paul and Barnabas waxed bold, and said, It was necessary that the word of God should first have been spoken to you: but seeing ye put it from you, and judge yourselves unworthy of everlasting life, lo, we turn to the Gentiles ... And when the Gentiles heard this, they were glad, and glorified the word of the Lord: and as many as were ordained to eternal life believed.

Acts 13:46, 48

And I give unto them eternal life; and they shall never perish, neither shall any man pluck them out of my hand. My Father, which gave them me, is greater than all; and no man is able to pluck them out of my Father's hand.

John 10:28–29

All that the Father giveth me shall come to me; and him that cometh to me I will in no wise cast out. For I came down from heaven, not to do mine own will, but the will of him that sent me. And this is the Father's will which hath sent me, that of all which he hath given me I should lose nothing, but should raise it up again at the last day.

John 6:37–39

These things have I written unto you that believe on the name of the Son of God; that ye may know that ye have eternal life, and that ye may believe on the name of the Son of God.

1 John 5:12–13

And this is the promise that he hath promised us, even eternal life.

1 John 2:25

For the LORD loveth judgment, and forsaketh not his saints; they are *preserved for ever*: but the seed of the wicked shall be cut off.

Psalm 37:28, emphasis added

Jude, the servant of Jesus Christ, and brother of James, to them that are sanctified by God the Father, and *preserved in Jesus Christ*, and called:

Jude 1, emphasis added

And be found *in him*, not having mine own righteousness, which is of the law, but that which is through the *faith* of Christ, the *righteousness* which is of God *by faith*:

Philippians 3:9, emphasis added

And *the work of righteousness* shall be peace; and *the effect of righteousness* quietness and *assurance for ever*.
Cf "Righteousness" Isaiah 61:10; Isaiah 32:1; Isaiah 54:17

Isaiah 32:17, emphasis added

11

For we have not an high priest which cannot be touched with the feeling of our infirmities; but was in all points tempted like as we are, yet without sin. Let us therefore come boldly unto the throne of grace, that we may obtain mercy, and find grace to help in time of need.

Hebrews 4:15–16

For we through the Spirit wait for the hope of righteousness by faith. For in Jesus Christ neither circumcision availeth any thing, nor uncircumcision; but faith which worketh by love.

Galatians 5:5–6

I am the vine, ye are the branches: He that abideth in me, and I in him, the same bringeth forth much fruit: for without me ye can do nothing.

John 15:5

Being filled with the fruits of righteousness, which are by Jesus Christ, unto the glory and praise of God.

Philippians 1:11

12

Not rendering evil for evil, or railing for railing: but contrariwise blessing; knowing that ye are thereunto called, that ye should inherit a blessing. For he that will love life, and see good days, let him refrain his tongue from evil, and his lips that they speak no guile: Let him eschew evil, and do good; let him seek peace, and ensue it. For the eyes of the Lord *are* over the righteous, and his ears *are open* unto their prayers: but the face of the Lord *is* against them that do evil.

1 Peter 3:9–12

But I say unto you which hear, Love your enemies, do good to them which hate you, Bless them that curse you, and pray for them which despitefully use you.

Luke 6:27–28

Saying, Surely blessing I will bless thee, and multiplying I will multiply thee. And so, after he had patiently endured, he obtained the promise.

Hebrews 6:14–15 14

Bless them which persecute you: bless, and curse not ... Recompense to no man evil for evil. Provide things honest in the sight of all men ... Dearly beloved, avenge not yourselves, but *rather* give place unto wrath: for it is written, Vengeance *is* mine; I will repay, saith the Lord. Therefore if thine enemy hunger, feed him; if he thirst, give him drink: for in so doing thou shalt heap coals of fire on his head. Be not overcome of evil, but overcome evil with good.

Romans 12:14, 17, 19–21

If thine enemy be hungry, give him bread to eat; and if he be thirsty, give him water to drink: For thou shalt heap coals of fire upon his head, and the LORD shall reward thee.

Proverbs 25:21–22

Say not thou, I will recompense evil; *but* wait on the LORD, and he shall save thee.

Proverbs 20:22

Ye have heard that it hath been said, Thou shalt love thy neighbour, and hate thine enemy. But I say unto you, Love your enemies, bless them that curse you, do good to them that hate you, and pray for them which despitefully use you, and persecute you;

Matthew 5:43–44

13

But thou, O Daniel, shut up the words, and seal the book, even to the time of the end: many shall run to and fro, and knowledge shall be increased. Then I Daniel looked, and, behold, there stood other two, the one on this side of the bank of the river, and the other on that side of the bank of the river. And one said to the man clothed in linen, which was upon the waters of the river, How long shall it be to the end of these wonders? And I heard the man clothed in linen, which was upon the waters of the river, when he held up his right hand and his left hand unto heaven, and sware by him that liveth for ever that it shall be for a time, times, and an half; and when he shall have accomplished to scatter the power of the holy people, all these things shall be finished... But go thou thy way till the end be: for thou shalt rest, and stand in thy lot at the end of the days. *cf.* w/-Revelation 10:5–7

Daniel 12:4–7, 13

14

For the Lord himself shall descend from heaven with a shout, with the voice of the archangel, and *with the trump of God*: and *the dead in Christ shall rise first*: Then we which are alive and remain shall be caught up together with them in the clouds, to meet the Lord in the air: and so shall we ever be with the Lord.

1 Thessalonians 4:16–17, emphasis aded

Behold, I shew you a mystery; We shall not all sleep, but we shall all be changed, In a moment, in the twinkling of an eye, *at the last trump*: for the trumpet shall sound, and *the dead shall be raised* incorruptible, and *we shall be changed.*

1 Corinthians 15:51–52, emphasis added

If a man die, shall he live again? all the days of my appointed time will I wait, *till my change come.* Thou shalt call, and I will answer thee: thou wilt have a desire to the work of thine hands.

Job 14:14–15, emphasis added

For our conversation is in heaven; from whence also we look for the Saviour, the Lord Jesus Christ: Who shall change our *vile body*, that it may be *fashioned like unto his glorious body*, according to the working whereby he is able even to subdue all things unto himself.

Philippians 3:20–21, emphasis added

As for me, I will behold thy face in righteousness: I shall be satisfied, *when I awake, with thy likeness.*

Psalm 17:15, emphasis added

Then shall *the righteous shine* forth as the sun in the kingdom of their Father. Who hath ears to hear, let him hear.

Matthew 13:43, emphasis added

And at that time shall Michael stand up, the great prince which standeth for the children of thy people: and there shall be a time of trouble, such as never was since there was a nation even to that same time: and at that time thy people shall be delivered, every one that shall be found written in the book. And many of them that sleep in the dust of the earth shall awake, some to everlasting life, and some to shame and everlasting contempt. And *they that be wise shall shine* as the brightness of the firmament; and they that turn many to righteousness as the stars for ever and ever.

Daniel 12:1–3, emphasis added

## Peter, the Rock

1    Mark 4:2, 10–13; Mark 4:33–34; Matthew 13:34; Luke 12:1, 41; John 16:25; Luke 8:4; Luke 14:7; Mark 12:12; Luke 20:19; Matthew 16:6–12

2

The LORD is my shepherd; I shall not want ... Thou preparest a table before me in the presence of mine enemies: thou anointest my head with oil; my cup runneth over. Surely goodness and mercy shall follow me all the days of my life: and I will dwell in the house of the LORD for ever.

Psalm 23:1, 5–6

Who shall ascend into the hill of the LORD? or who shall stand in his holy place? He that hath clean hands, and a pure heart {cf. "God purifies our hearts by faith" Acts 15:8–9}; who hath not lifted up his soul unto vanity, nor sworn deceitfully. He shall receive the blessing from the LORD {cf. Gal. 3:7 ,14), and righteousness from the God of his salvation {cf. Phi1.3:9}. This is the generation of them that seek him, that seek thy face, O Jacob. Selah {cf. Matt. 6:33}. Lift up your heads, O ye gates; and be ye lift up, ye everlasting doors; and the King of glory shall come in. Who is this King of glory? The LORD strong and mighty, the LORD mighty in battle {cf. Eph. 6:10–12; Psm. 110:1–3}. Lift up your heads, O ye gates; even lift them up, ye everlasting doors; and the King of glory shall come in. Who is this King of glory? The LORD of hosts, he is the King of glory. Selah.

Psalm 24:3–10

To whom God would make known what is the riches of the glory of this mystery among the Gentiles; which is Christ in you, the hope of glory.

Colossians 1:27

3

And because ye are sons, God hath sent forth the Spirit of his Son into your hearts, crying, Abba, Father.

Galatians 4:6

And hope maketh not ashamed; because the love of God is shed abroad in our hearts by the Holy Ghost which is given unto us.

Romans 5:5

## Peter's Brethren

1   The gospel of the uncircumcision was especially committed to Paul, and the gospel of the circumcision especially to Peter; however, they both preached the gospel to all races and nations. [Peter:-Acts 10:44–47; Acts 11:1–18; Acts 15:7–9.... Paul:-Acts 9:13–*15*; Acts 13:16–26–42–48; Acts 14:19–27; Acts 18:5–6; Acts 21:18–19].

2   Peter said these things as a result of the vision given to him by God (Acts 10:11–16). The same words and phrases are used in Hosea 2:18 which is prophetic of the New Covenant. Hosea 2:23, 1 Peter 2:10 & Romans 9:23–26 are also correlative.

Now when he was in Jerusalem at the passover, in the feast day, many believed in his name, when they saw the miracles which he did. But Jesus did not commit himself unto them, because he knew all men, And needed not that any should testify of man: for he knew what was in man.

John 2:23–25

For we know that the law is spiritual: but I am carnal, sold under sin. For that which I do I allow not: for what I would, that do I not; but what I hate, that do I. If then I do that which I would not, I consent unto the law that it is good. Now then it is no more I that do it, but sin that dwelleth in me. For I know that in me (that is, in my flesh,) dwelleth no good thing: for to will is present with me; but how to perform that which is good I find not. For the good that I would I do not: but the evil which I would not, that I do. Now if I do that I would not, it is no more I that do it, but sin that dwelleth in me.

Romans 7:14–20

## Peter, Son of Jonas

1    James and John, the sons of Zebedee:

Matthew 4:21; Matthew 10:2; Matthew 20:20; Matthew 26:37; Matthew 27:56; Mark 1:19; Mark 1:20; Mark 3:17; Mark 10:35; Luke 5:10; John 21:2

2    SEA OF GALILEE
*SMITH'S BIBLE DICTIONARY:*-{in part}
Sea of Galilee - so called from the province of Galilee, which bordered on its western side. Matt. 4:18. It was also called "Sea of Tiberias,," from the celebrated city of that name. John 6:1. At its northwestern angle was a beautiful and fertile plain called "Gennesaret," and from that it derived the name of "Lake of Gennesaret." Luke 5:1.... The water of the lake is sweet, cool and transparent; and as the beach is everywhere pebbly it has a beautiful sparkling look. It

abounds in fish now as in ancient times. There were large fisheries on the lake, and much commerce was carried on upon it.

3    Matthew 16:18; Luke 22:32

4    "Stretch forth thy hands":

John 21:18; Matthew 26:51; Luke 22:53; Mark 1:41; Matthew 12:49; Luke 5:13; Hosea 7:5; Psalm 68:31;Psalm 44:20; Exodus 9:29; 1 Kings 8:22; Job 11:13; Psalm 143:6; Psalm 88:9

## The Church
1

*I am the good shepherd*, and know my sheep, and am known of mine. As the Father knoweth me, even so know I the Father: and *I lay down my life for the sheep*.
                                                    John 10:14–15, emphasis added

*My sheep* hear my voice, and I know them, and they follow me: And *I give unto them eternal life*; and they shall never perish, neither shall any man pluck them out of my hand. My Father, which gave them me, is greater than all; and no man is able to pluck them out of my Father's hand.
                                                    John 10:27–29, emphasis added

Then saith Jesus unto them, All ye shall be offended because of me this night: for it is written, *I will smite the shepherd*, and the sheep of the flock shall be scattered abroad.
                                                    Matthew 26:31, emphasis added

For thus saith the Lord GOD; Behold, I, even I, will both search my sheep, and seek them out.
                                                    Ezekiel 34:11, emphasis added

And David my servant shall be king over them; and they all shall have *one shepherd*: they shall also walk in my judgments, and observe my statutes, and do them. And

294

they shall dwell in the land that I have given unto Jacob my servant, wherein your fathers have dwelt; and they shall dwell therein, even they, and their children, and their children's children for ever: and my servant David shall be their prince *for ever*. Moreover I will make a covenant of peace with them; it shall be an *everlasting* covenant with them: and I will place them, and multiply them, and will set my sanctuary in the midst of them for *evermore*.

Ezekiel 37:24–26, emphasis added

2   Christ's Church is built upon *faith in the words of* the apostles and prophets.

Then he said unto them, O fools, and slow of heart to believe all that the prophets have spoken: Ought not Christ to have suffered these things, and to enter into his glory? And beginning at Moses and all the prophets, he expounded unto them in all the scriptures the things concerning himself.

Luke 24:25–27

Paul, a servant of Jesus Christ, called to be an apostle, separated unto the gospel of God, Which he had promised afore by his prophets in the holy scriptures,) Concerning his Son Jesus Christ our Lord, which was made of the seed of David according to the flesh; And declared to be the Son of God with power, according to the spirit of holiness, by the resurrection from the dead: By whom we have received grace and apostleship, for obedience to the faith among all nations [*universally*], for his name:

Romans 1:1–5, emphasis added

Now to him that is of power to stablish you according to my gospel, and the preaching of Jesus Christ, according to the revelation of the mystery, which was kept secret since the world began, But now is made manifest, and by the scriptures of the prophets, according to the commandment of the everlasting God, made known to all nations [*universally*] for the obedience of faith:

Romans 16:25–26, emphasis added

And that from a child thou hast known the holy scriptures, which are able to make thee wise unto salvation through faith which is in Christ Jesus. All scripture is given by inspiration of God, and is profitable for doctrine, for reproof, for correction, for instruction in righteousness

2 Timothy 3:15–16

But we are bound to give thanks always to God for you, brethren beloved of the Lord, because God hath from the beginning chosen you to salvation through sanctification of the Spirit and belief of the truth: Whereunto he called you by our gospel, to the obtaining of the glory of our Lord Jesus Christ.

2 Thessalonians 2:13–14

But those things, which God before had shewed by the mouth of all his prophets, that Christ should suffer, he hath so fulfilled.

Acts 3:18

Moreover, brethren, I declare unto you the gospel which I preached unto you, which also ye have received, and wherein ye stand; By which also ye are saved, if ye keep in memory what I preached unto you, unless ye have believed in vain. For I delivered unto you first of all that which I also received, how that Christ died for our sins according to the scriptures; And that he was buried, and that he rose again the third day according to the scriptures:

1 Corinthians 15:1–4

Him God raised up the third day, and shewed him openly; Not to all the people, but unto witnesses chosen before of God, even to us, who did eat and drink with him after he rose from the dead. And he commanded us to preach unto the people, and to testify that it is he which was ordained of God to be the Judge of quick and dead. To him give all the prophets witness, that through his name whosoever believeth in him shall receive remission of sins.

Acts 10:40–43

But this I confess unto thee, that after the way which they call heresy, so worship I the God of my fathers, believing all things which are written in the law and in the prophets: And have hope toward God, which they themselves also allow, that there shall be a resurrection of the dead, both of the just and unjust.

Acts 24:14–15

Having therefore obtained help of God, I continue unto this day, witnessing both to small and great, saying none other things than those which the prophets and Moses did say should come: That Christ should suffer, and that he should be the first that should rise from the dead, and should shew light unto the people, and to the Gentiles.

Acts 26:22–23

o King Agrippa, believest thou the prophets? I know that thou believest. Then Agrippa said unto Paul, Almost thou persuadest me to be a Christian.

Acts 26:27–28

Of which salvation the prophets have enquired and searched diligently, who prophesied of the grace that should come unto you: Searching what, or what manner of time the Spirit of Christ which was in them did signify, when it testified beforehand the sufferings of Christ, and the glory that should follow. Unto whom it was revealed, that not unto themselves, but unto us they did minister the things, which are now reported unto you by them that have preached the gospel unto you with the Holy Ghost sent down from heaven; which things the angels desire to look into.

1 Peter 1:10–12

3    The foundation upon which the Church is built is faith in the preaching of the crucifixion of Christ who is the Corner Stone of the foundation.

For after that in the wisdom of God the world by wisdom knew not God, it pleased God by the foolishness of preaching to save them that believe… But we preach Christ crucified, unto the Jews a stumblingblock, and unto the Greeks foolishness;

1 Corinthians 1:21, 23

And I, brethren, when I came to you, came not with excellency of speech or of wisdom, declaring unto you the testimony of God. For I determined not to know any thing among you, save Jesus Christ, and him crucified.

1 Corinthians 2:1–2

According to the grace of God which is given unto me, as a wise masterbuilder, I have laid the foundation,… For other foundation can no man lay than that is laid, which is Jesus Christ

1 Corinthians 3:10–11

4

But Jesus called them to him, and saith unto them, Ye know that they which are accounted to rule over the Gentiles exercise lordship over them; and their great ones exercise authority upon them. But so shall it not be among you: but whosoever will be great among you, shall be your minister: And whosoever of you will be the chiefest, shall be servant of all.

Mark 10:42–44

But Jesus called them unto him, and said, Ye know that the princes of the Gentiles exercise dominion over them, and they that are great exercise authority upon them. But it shall not be so among you: but whosoever will be great among you, let him be your minister; And whosoever will be chief among you, let him be your servant:

Matthew 20:25–27

Not for that we have dominion over your faith, but are helpers of your joy: for by faith ye stand.

2 Corinthians 1:24

Feed the flock of God which is among you, taking the oversight thereof, not by constraint, but willingly; not for filthy lucre, but of a ready mind; Neither as being lords over God's heritage, but being ensamples to the flock.

1 Peter 5:2–3

5    The promise the Apostle Paul referred to in Hebrews 11:39 is the promise of the Holy Spirit of life, which is received through faith in the word of truth, the gospel.

And these all, having obtained a good report *through faith*, received not *the promise:* God having provided some better thing for us, that they without us should not be *made perfect.* <5048>
(Hebrews 11:39–40 cf. Hebrews 10:1,2), emphasis added

For by one offering he hath *perfected* <5048> *for ever* them that are sanctified.

Hebrews 10:14, emphasis added

This only would I learn of you, Received ye *the Spirit* by the works of the law, or by the hearing of *faith?* Are ye so foolish? having begun in the Spirit, are ye now *made perfect* by the flesh?

Galatians 3:2–3, emphasis added

That the blessing of Abraham might come on the Gentiles through Jesus Christ; that we might receive *the promise of the Spirit through faith.*

Galatians 3:14, emphasis added

Is the law then against *the promises of God?* God forbid: for if there had been a law given which could have given *life,* verily righteousness should have been by the law.

Galatians 3:21, emphasis added

And *this is the promise* that he hath promised us, even eternal life.

1 John 2:25, emphasis added

And after three days and an half *the Spirit of life* from God entered into them …

Revelation 11:11, emphasis added

For the law of *the Spirit of life* in Christ Jesus hath made me free from the law of sin and death.

Romans 8:2, emphasis added

And if Christ be in you, the body is dead because of sin; but *the Spirit is life* because of righteousness.

Romans 8:10, emphasis added

For this cause was *the gospel preached* also to them that are dead, that they might be judged according to men in the flesh, but live according to God *in the spirit.*

1 Peter4:6 , emphasis added

In whom ye also trusted, after that ye heard the *word of truth, the gospel* of your salvation: in whom also after that ye believed, ye were sealed with that holy *Spirit of promise,*

Ephesians1:13, emphasis added

6    God's New Covenant promise of the 'gift' of the Holy Spirit of eternal life:

That the blessing of Abraham might come on the Gentiles through Jesus Christ; that we might receive the promise of the Spirit through faith … And this I say, that the covenant, that was confirmed before of God in Christ, the law, which was four hundred and thirty years after, cannot disannul, that it should make the promise of none effect … Is the law then against the promises of God? God forbid: for if there had been a law given which could have given life, verily righteousness should have been by the law. But the scripture hath concluded all under sin, that the promise by faith of Jesus Christ might be given to them that believe.

Galatians 3:14, 17, 21–22

For the wages of sin is death; but the gift of God is eternal life through Jesus Christ our Lord.

Romans 6:23

Then remembered I the word of the Lord, how that he said, John indeed baptized with water; but ye shall be baptized with the Holy Ghost. Forasmuch then as God gave them the like gift as he did unto us, who believed on the Lord Jesus Christ; what was I, that I could withstand God?

Acts 11:16–17

In whom ye also trusted, after that ye heard the word of truth, the gospel of your salvation: in whom also after that ye believed, ye were sealed with that holy Spirit of promise,

Ephesians 1:13

For the law of the Spirit of life in Christ Jesus hath made me free from the law of sin and death.

Romans 8:2

And if Christ be in you, the body is dead because of sin; but the Spirit is life because of righteousness.

Romans 8:10

{in part} - ... the spirit giveth life.

2 Corinthians 3:6

{in part} - ... he that soweth to the Spirit shall of the Spirit reap life everlasting.

Galatians 6:8

{in part} - And after three days and an half the Spirit of life from God entered into them, and they stood upon their feet....

Revelation 11:11

And grieve not the holy Spirit of God, whereby ye are sealed unto the day of redemption.

Ephesians 4:30

7

And now, brethren, I commend you to God, and to the word of his grace, which is able to build you up, and to give you an inheritance among all them which are sanctified.

Acts 20:32

Wherefore Jesus also, that he might sanctify the people with his own blood, suffered without the gate.

Hebrews 13:12

By the which will we are sanctified through the offering of the body of Jesus Christ once for all.

Hebrews 10:10

Of how much sorer punishment, suppose ye, shall he be thought worthy, who hath trodden under foot the Son of God, and hath counted the blood of the covenant, wherewith he was sanctified, an unholy thing, and hath done despite unto the Spirit of grace?

Hebrews 10:29

Jude, the servant of Jesus Christ, and brother of James, to them that are sanctified by God the Father, and preserved in Jesus Christ, and called:

Jude 1

For the LORD loveth judgment, and forsaketh not his saints; they are preserved for ever: but the seed of the wicked shall be cut off.

Psalm 37:28

For by one offering he *hath* perfected for ever them that are sanctified.

Hebrews 10:14

## Grace

1

Owe no man any thing, but to love one another: for he that loveth another hath fulfilled the law.

Romans 13:8

Love worketh no ill to his neighbour: therefore love is the fulfilling of the law.

Romans 13:10

I do not frustrate the grace of God: for if righteousness come by the law, then Christ is dead in vain.

Galatians 2:21

For as many as are of the works of the law are under the curse: for it is written, Cursed is every one that continueth not in all things which are written in the book of the law to do them.

Galatians 3:10

Christ is become of no effect unto you, whosoever of you are justified by the law; ye are fallen from grace.

Galatians 5:4

If ye fulfil the royal law according to the scripture, Thou shalt love thy neighbour as thyself, ye do well:

James 2:8

For when we were in the flesh, the motions of sins, which were by the law, did work in our members to bring forth fruit unto death. But now we are delivered from the law, that being dead wherein we were held; that we should serve in newness of spirit, and not in the oldness of the letter. What shall we say then? Is the law sin? God forbid. Nay, I had not known sin, but by the law: for I had not known lust, except the law had said, Thou shalt not covet. But sin, taking occasion by the commandment, wrought in me all manner of concupiscence. For without the law sin was dead. For I was alive without the law once: but when the commandment came, sin revived, and I died. And the commandment, which was ordained to life, I found to be unto death. For sin, taking occasion by the commandment, deceived me, and by it slew me. Wherefore the law is holy, and the commandment holy, and just, and good. Was then that which is good made death unto me? God forbid. But sin, that it might appear sin, working death in me by that which is good; that sin by the commandment might become exceeding sinful.

Romans 7:5–13

Is the law then against the promises of God? God forbid: for if there had been a law given which could have given life, verily righteousness should have been by the law. But the scripture hath concluded all under sin, that the promise by faith of Jesus Christ might be given to them that believe. But before faith came, we were kept under the law, shut up unto the faith which should afterwards be revealed. Wherefore the law was our schoolmaster to bring us unto Christ, that we might be justified by faith. But after that faith is come, we are no longer under a schoolmaster. For ye are all the children of God by faith in Christ Jesus.

Galatians 3:21–26

For sin shall not have dominion over you: for ye are not under the law, but under grace.

Romans 6:14

2 Among the many matters set forth in the legal, historical, sapiential and prophetical books of the Bible, there are only a few whose sense has been defined by the authority of the Church, and that there are equally few concerning which the opinion of the Holy Fathers is unanimous.
*Knights Of Columbus* (vol. #48, p.48): (Imprimatur: Most Reverend John F. Whealon, Archbishop of Hartford)

## Transubstantiation

1
But we all, with open face beholding as in a glass the glory of the Lord, are changed into the same image from glory to glory, even as by the Spirit of the Lord.

2 Corinthians 3:18

2 (http://www.goldenessays.com/free_essays/2/english/T/tess-of-d-urbervilles-key-points.shtml).

3 Jesus not only spoke to the multitudes in parables, He also spoke to his disciples in symbolic terms when He was alone with them.

And when his disciples were come to the other side, they had forgotten to take bread. Then Jesus said unto them, Take heed and beware of the leaven of the Pharisees and of the Sadducees. And they reasoned among themselves, saying, It is because we have taken no bread. Which when

Jesus perceived, he said unto them, O ye of little faith, why reason ye among yourselves, because ye have brought no bread? Do ye not yet understand, neither remember the five loaves of the five thousand, and how many baskets ye took up? Neither the seven loaves of the four thousand, and how many baskets ye took up? How is it that ye do not understand that I spake it not to you concerning bread, that ye should beware of the leaven of the Pharisees and of the Sadducees? Then understood they how that he bade them not beware of the leaven of bread, but of the doctrine of the Pharisees and of the Sadducees.

Matthew 16:5–12


These things have I spoken unto you [his disciples] *in proverbs*: but the time cometh, when I shall no more speak unto you *in proverbs*, but I shall shew you plainly of the Father.

John 16:25


4    Through faith in Christ's sacrifice for the remission of our sins we are given the promise of the Holy Spirit, the Spirit of eternal life, the Spirit of Christ, who dwells in us 'forever.'

I am crucified with Christ: nevertheless I live; yet not I, but Christ liveth in me: and the life which I now live in the flesh I live by the faith of the Son of God, who loved me, and gave himself for me.

Galatians 2:20
[ Also: 2 Corinthians 13:5; Galatians 4:6; etc. etc. ]


But ye are not in the flesh, but in the Spirit, if so be that the Spirit of God dwell in you. Now if any man have not the Spirit of Christ, he is none of his. And if Christ be in you, the body is dead because of sin; but the Spirit is life because of righteousness.

Romans 8:9–10


BECAUSE OF RIGHTEOUSNESS:

And be found in him, not having mine own righteousness, which is of the law, but that which is through the faith of Christ, the righteousness which is of God by faith:

Philippians 3:9

But now the righteousness of God without the law is manifested, being witnessed by the law and the prophets; Even the righteousness of God which is by faith of Jesus Christ unto all and upon all them that believe: for there is no difference.

Romans 3:21–22

Brethren, my heart's desire and prayer to God for Israel is, that they might be saved. For I bear them record that they have a zeal of God, but not according to knowledge. For they being ignorant of God's righteousness, and going about to establish their own righteousness, have not submitted themselves unto the righteousness of God.

Romans 10:1–3

5

... the bread that I will give is my flesh, which I will give for the life of the world.

John 6:51

I am the good shepherd: the good shepherd giveth his life for the sheep ... I lay down my life for the sheep ... I lay down my life ... No man taketh it from me, but I lay it down of myself ... And I give unto them eternal life.

John 10:11–28

Greater love hath no man than this, that a man lay down his life for his friends.

John 15:13

He was taken from prison and from judgment: and who shall declare his generation? for he was cut off out of the land of the living: for the transgression of my people was he stricken.

Isaiah 53:8

6

Which was a figure for the time then present, in which were offered both gifts and sacrifices, that could not make him that did the service perfect, as pertaining to the conscience;

Hebrews 9:9

The like figure whereunto even baptism doth also now save us (not the putting away of the filth of the flesh, but the answer of a good conscience toward God,) by the resurrection of Jesus Christ:

1 Peter 3:21

Now the end of the commandment is charity out of a pure heart, and of a good conscience, and of faith unfeigned: From which some having swerved have turned aside unto vain jangling;

1 Timothy 1:5–6

Not giving heed to Jewish fables, and commandments of men, that turn from the truth. Unto the pure all things are pure: but unto them that are defiled and unbelieving is nothing pure; but even their mind and conscience is defiled. They profess that they know God; but in works they deny him, being abominable, and disobedient, and unto every good work reprobate.

Titus 1:14–16

Holding the mystery of the faith in a pure conscience.

1 Timothy 3:9

And without controversy great is the mystery of godliness: God was manifest in the flesh, justified in the Spirit, seen of angels, preached unto the Gentiles, believed on in the world, received up into glory.

1 Timothy 3:16

7   VERILY: #281
AMEN: #281
{am-ane'}; of Heb. or. (543); prop. firm, i.e. (fig.) trustworthy; adv. surely (often as interj. so be it):- amen, verily. (Used 126 times in the New Testament)

... Verily, verily, I say unto you, He that entereth not by *the door into the sheepfold*, but climbeth up some other way, the same is a thief and a robber.

John 10:1

Then said Jesus unto them again, Verily, verily, I say unto you, *I am the door of the sheep.*

John 10:7

Little children, keep yourselves from idols. Amen.

1 John 5:21

The God of peace be with you all. Amen.

Romans 15:33

How shall he that occupieth the room of the unlearned say Amen at the giving of thanks, seeing he understandeth not what thou sayest?

1 Corithians 14:16

OATH: #3727
{kapporeth -kap-po'-reth}- a limit, i.e. (sacred) restraint (spec. oath): -oath.
(Used 10 times in the New Testament)
ACTS 2:30 -God swore with an oath
MAT. 26:72 -Peter denied Jesus with an oath
HEB. 6:16,17 -God confirmed the promise to Abraham by an oath.

(also: Matt. 5:33; Matt. 14:7; Matt 14:9; Mk. 6:26; Lk.1:73; Jas. 5:12)

OATH: *#3728* -

*{kaphash -kaw-fash'}* from a comp. of 3727 and a der of 3660; asseveration on oath: oath.

(Used 4 times in the New Testament)

And inasmuch as not without an oath he was made priest:

Hebrews 7:20

For those priests were made without an oath; but this with an oath by him that said unto him, The Lord sware and will not repent, *Thou art a priest for ever after the order of Melchisedec*

Hebrews 7:21

For the law maketh men high priests which have infirmity; but the word of the oath, which was since the law, maketh the Son, who is consecrated for evermore.

Hebrews 7:28

8

Whosoever hateth his brother is a murderer: and ye know that no murderer hath eternal life abiding in him. Hereby perceive we the love of God, because he laid down his life for us: and we ought to lay down our lives for the brethren.

1 John 3:15–16

9

But he that glorieth, let him glory in the Lord. For not he that commendeth himself is approved, but whom the Lord commendeth.

2 Corinthians 10:17–18